in company 3.0

INTERMEDIATE Teacher's Book

B1+

MACMILLAN

Macmillan Education Limited
4 Crinan Street
London N1 9XW

Companies and representatives throughout the world

ISBN 978-0-230-45526-9

Text, design and illustration © Macmillan Education Limited 2014
Written by Helena Gomm

The author has asserted her rights to be identified as the author of this work in accordance with the Copyright, Designs and Patents Act 1988.

This edition published 2014
First edition published 2002

All rights reserved; no part of this publication may be reproduced, stored in a retrieval system, transmitted in any form, or by any means, electronic, mechanical, photocopying, recording, or otherwise, without the prior written permission of the publishers.

Design by emc design Limited
Page make-up by MPS Limited
Cover design by emc design Limited

The publishers would like to thank the following people, schools and institutions for their help in developing this third edition: Pat Pledger, Pledger Business English Training, Hamburg; Louise Bulloch, Intercom Language Services, Hamburg; Elbie Picker and David Virta, Hamburg; William Fern, KERN AG IKL Business Language Training & Co. KG, Frankfurt; Belén del Valle, ELOQUIA, Frankfurt; Katrin Wolf, Carl Duisberg Centren, Cologne; Andrina Rout, Fokus Sprachen und Seminare, Stuttgart; Gerdi Serrer, ILIC, Paris; Sylvia Renaudon, Transfer, Paris; John Fayssoux; Kathryn Booth-Aïdah Araxi Formations Langues, Paris; Fiona Delaney and Allison Dupuis, Formalangues, Paris; Francesca Pallot and Susan Stevenson, Anglesey Language Services, Chatou, France; Paul Bellchambers, Business and Technical Languages (BTL), Paris; Louise Raven, marcus evans Linguarama, Stratford-upon-Avon.

Many thanks also to all the teachers around the world who took the time to complete our *In Company* online questionnaire and who have contributed to the development of the *In Company* series.

The author and publisher would like to thank the following for permission to reproduce the following material.

Material from the 'Financial Times Guide to Business Travel' by Bruce Tulgan © Bruce Tulgan. Reprinted with permission. Material from 'E-writing' by Dianna Booher, copyright © Dianna Booher 2001. Reprinted by permission of Booher consultants. www.booher.com. Material from the website www.firstdirect.com, copyright © HSBC Bank plc 2016. All Rights Reserved. Reprinted by permission of First Direct. Material from 'Cultures and Organizations, Software of the Mind, Third Edition' (McGraw Hill, 2010) by G. Hofstede, G. J. Hoftstede and M. Minkov, copyright © Geert Hofstede B.V. Reprinted with permission. Material from 'Make Meaning in Your Company' by Guy Kawasaki, dated 20.10.04, copyright © Guy Kawasaki 2004. Reprinted with permission. Material from 'The NY-LON Life' by Michelle Jana Chan, dated 13.11.00, copyright © Michelle Jana Chan 2000. Reprinted with permission. Material from 'Riding the Waves of Culture' by Fons Trompenaars & Charles Hampden-Turner, copyright © Fons Trompenaars & Charles Hampden-Turner. Reprinted by permission of Nicholas Brealey Publishing and The McGraw-Hill Companies Inc. Material from 'The Complete Idiot's Guide to Winning Through Negotiation' by John Ilich, copyright © John Ilich 1999. Published by Alpha Books, and reprinted by permission of the publisher. Extract from 'Getting Past No: Negotiating with Difficult People' by William Ury (Random House Business Books, 1991), copyright © William Ury 1991. Reprinted by permission of Penguin Random House UK & The Sagalyn Literary Agency.

These materials may contain links for third party websites. We have no control over, and are not responsible for, the contents of such third party websites. Please use care when accessing them.

Printed and bound in the UK by CLOC Ltd
2021 2020
15 14

Contents

Contents	**3**
Student's Book contents	**4**
Introduction	**6**

Teacher's notes with answers

01	Making contacts	12
02	Making calls	18
03	Keeping track	23
04	People skills: Listening	27
	Management scenario A: The networking event	31
05	Business travel	34
06	Handling calls	40
07	Making decisions	44
08	People skills: Influence	49
	Management scenario B: Meetings on the go	51
09	Small talk	54
10	Email	57
11	Presenting	61
12	People skills: Impact	65
	Management scenario C: Morale problems	68
13	Being heard	70
14	Snail mail	74
15	Solving problems	77
16	People skills: Collaboration	82
	Management scenario D: Tricky conversations	84
17	Eating out	86
18	Telecommunications	90
19	Negotiating	94
20	People skills: Assertiveness	99
	Management scenario E: The difficult customer	102

Student's Book contents

Unit	Business communication skills	Reading and listening	Language links
01 Making contacts p6	Describing people Discussing appropriate conversation topics Keeping the conversation going **Fluency** Networking with colleagues and business contacts	**Reading** A blog about conference attendance **Listening** An extract from a business travel programme on conference venues People gossiping at a conference People socializing at a conference	**Vocabulary** Conferences **Grammar** Present Simple and Present Continuous **Phrase bank** Networking
02 Making calls p13	Receiving calls Leaving voicemails **Roleplay** Exchanging information on the telephone	**Listening** Planning a telephone call Voicemail messages Telephone conversations	**Vocabulary** Telephone expressions **Grammar** Past Simple, time adverbs *ago, before, during, for, in, over* **Phrase bank** Telephoning
03 Keeping track p20	Checking and clarifying facts and figures **Fluency** Querying information Clearing up misunderstandings In company interviews Units 1–3	**Reading** Articles: two sportswear companies **Listening** Extracts from meetings A briefing meeting	**Vocabulary** Business phrasal verbs **Grammar** Comparatives and superlatives **Phrase bank** Checking understanding
04 People skills: Listening p26	Effective listening techniques **Fluency** Active listening	Reading Article about effective listening Listening Problematic and constructive conversations	
Management scenario A: The networking event p28	Identifying networker types Rules for successful networking **Fluency** A networking event	**Reading** Making the most of business networking events **In company in action** A1: The networking event A2: A useful contact	
05 Business travel p30	Expressing likes and dislikes about travelling on business Making polite requests and enquiries **Fluency** Dealing with travel situations Identifying signs as British or American English **Roleplay** Greeting visitors	**Reading** Article from *Newsweek* about people who live in two cities Article: travel tips **Listening** Business travel conversations Short exchanges in British and American English Conversations at the airport	**Vocabulary** Business trips **Grammar** Polite question forms **Phrase bank** Business travel
06 Handling calls p37	Discussing your attitude to using the telephone Making polite telephone requests using *if* and *Could you ...?* Making telephone expressions with *I'll* **Roleplay** Dealing with incoming calls	**Reading** Mini-texts: telephone statistics **Listening** Telephone conversations	**Vocabulary** Office life **Grammar** *will* **Phrase bank** Polite requests, Offering assistance, Ending a call
07 Making decisions p43	Doing a questionnaire on making decisions Using fixed expressions in meetings **Fluency** Using the language of making decisions In company interviews Units 5–7	**Reading** Article about James Bond films Actor profiles: James Bond contenders **Listening** Extracts from a documentary An extract from a meeting Interviews with James Bond contenders	**Vocabulary** Money and markets **Grammar** Conditionals (future reference) **Phrase bank** Decision-making
08 People skills: Influence p50	Influencing peers and subordinates **Roleplay** Using influencing techniques	Reading Managing up, down and sideways Listening Influencing tactics	
Management scenario B: Meetings on the go p52	Asking for favours Handling meetings on the go **Roleplay** Constructive meetings on the go	**Reading** How to handle meetings on the go **In company in action** B1: Meetings on the go B2: A constructive meeting B3: A failed request	
09 Small talk p54	Completing a questionnaire on cultural awareness Talking about experiences **Roleplay** Engaging in small talk	**Listening** Pre-meeting conversations	**Vocabulary** Exaggeration and understatement **Grammar** Past Simple or Present Perfect **Phrase bank** Engaging in small talk
10 Email p60	Discussing email likes and dislikes Guidelines for writing email Simplifying a lengthy email **Writing** Exchanging emails	**Reading** Emails **Listening** Voicemail messages	**Vocabulary** Computers **Grammar** Future forms **Phrase bank** Email

STUDENT'S BOOK CONTENTS

Unit	Business communication skills	Reading and listening	Language links
11 Presenting p67	Discussing qualities of a good presentation Pausing, pacing and sentence stress Delivering a presentation Structuring a presentation Using visuals **Fluency** Giving a short presentation In company interviews Units 9–11	**Reading** An extract from First Direct website **Listening** People conversing and giving a presentation An extract from a talk by Guy Kawasaki A presentation about a technical problem	**Vocabulary** Presentations **Grammar** Past Continuous, Past Perfect, Past Simple vs Past Continuous vs Past Perfect **Phrase bank** The language of presentations
12 People skills: Impact p74	Giving presentations with impact **Fluency** A product presentation	**Reading** The four Cs of presenting with impact **Listening** Extracts from presentations A pitch for a mobile app	
Management scenario C: Morale problems p76	Improving morale problems Motivating a team **Fluency** Delivering a motivation session	**Reading** Motivating your team **In company in action** C1: Poor motivation C2: Improving morale	
13 Being heard p78	Discussing attitudes to meetings Completing a questionnaire on assertiveness in meetings **Roleplay** Interrupting a speaker Discussing meeting styles in different countries	**Listening** People talking about their attitudes to meetings Meetings in different countries **Reading** Meeting styles in four countries	**Vocabulary** Meetings **Grammar** Modal verbs **Phrase bank** Interrupting and preventing interruption
14 Snail mail p85	Discussing different types of communication Correcting a formal letter **Writing** Letters following up a sales meeting or business contact	**Reading** A business letter **Listening** Someone correcting a colleague's business letter	**Vocabulary** Prepositions, Prepositional phrases, Preposition + noun + preposition **Grammar** Multi-verb expressions **Phrase bank** Letter-writing expressions
15 Solving problems p91	Discussing solutions to problems Expressions for making suggestions **Fluency** Conducting problem-solving meetings In company interviews Units 13–15	**Reading** Articles: advice on solving problems **Listening** Case studies: three problems solved Problem-solving meetings	**Vocabulary** People and products **Grammar** Conditionals (past reference) **Phrase bank** Problem-solving, Brainstorming
16 People skills: Collaboration p98	Working in a team **Fluency** Problem-solving team meetings	**Reading** Creating team spirit **Listening** A project problem	
Management scenario D: Tricky conversations p100	Handling tricky conversations **Roleplay** Difficult conversations	**Reading** Handling difficult conversations in the workplace **In company in action** D1: Failed conversations D2: Constructive conversations	
17 Eating out p102	Describing restaurants Doing a quiz on table manners and etiquette Describing typical dishes from your country **Roleplay** Doing business over lunch	**Listening** A conversation in a restaurant Conversations over lunch	**Vocabulary** Food and drink **Grammar** The passive **Phrase bank** Eating out
18 Telecommunications p108	Discussing teleconferencing Holding a short teleconference **Fluency** Dealing with emails and voicemail messages	**Listening** A teleconference **Reading** An email exchange	**Vocabulary** Managing a project **Grammar** Reporting **Phrase bank** Teleconferencing
19 Negotiating p115	Sounding more diplomatic Expressions for negotiating Completing notes while listening to two negotiations **Roleplay** Negotiating a contract In company interviews Units 17–19	**Reading** Extract from *Getting Past No* Joke from *Complete Idiot's Guide to Winning Through Negotiation* Article about football **Listening** People's views on negotiating Description of football players' transfer deals	**Vocabulary** Negotiations **Grammar** Language of diplomacy **Phrase bank** Negotiating
20 People skills: Assertiveness p122	Dos and don'ts of being assertive **Roleplay** Being assertive	**Reading** Hofstede's power distance **Listening** Asserting yourself	
Management scenario E: The difficult customer p124	Handling difficult customers Understanding interest-based negotiations **Roleplay** Dealing with difficult demands	**Reading** Uncovering interests in negotiations **In company in action** E1: A failed negotiation E2: A successful negotiation	

Additional material p126   **Listening scripts** p142

Introduction

A Business English classroom

Madrid. 3pm. At 37° the city is starting to simmer. The teacher, Liz, arrives a couple of minutes early for her class with the bank on the 13th floor. The training room is tastefully ergonomic, if a little soulless. Liz takes out her MP3 player, prepares the track, flips through her handouts, decides there isn't time now for a quick coffee and waits.

There are normally five people in her group: three quiet types from the legal department, Pablo, a talkative mergers and acquisitions specialist, and Lourdes, a young trainee with rather better English than the others (which is sometimes a problem). They all get on well. But only three will turn up today – unfortunately, not exactly the same three who turned up last time, so there'll be some catching up to do. A chunk of the unit in the course book will probably have to be missed out and Liz will have to think of something else to do instead. The message is that Pablo may join them later if he gets out of his lunch meeting in time. But that's unlikely. He misses three lessons out of five. Busy guy.

Three months ago, when Liz's employer discussed the English course with the banks' training department, a formal needs analysis prioritized work on the language of meetings, telephoning and email. Liz's students agreed that's what they need. But as the course went on, she noticed that they often didn't use the so-called useful expressions she was teaching them and they only really came to life when either talking about themselves or taking part in a light-hearted activity she'd originally planned as a filler. She's doing more of that kind of thing now, though, and it seems to be working.

This afternoon the students' heads are full of talk of the forthcoming merger. They're still arguing about it as they come in to the class. Gradually, animated Spanish dissolves into more hesitant English and the lesson begins. Today they're supposed to be doing 'fixing and changing appointments on the phone'. Present continuous. Here we go again. Grim prospect. But maybe Liz has a better idea …

in company 3.0

in company 3.0 is Macmillan's skills-based Business English series, aimed at professional, adult learners seeking to realize their full potential as speakers of English at work – both in and out of the office – and in social settings. This third edition builds on the success of the previous editions and has been enhanced and updated to reflect the realities of the 21st century professional. Business English learners now face a challenging, fast-paced, technologically-advanced workplace and the process of English language acquisition with **in company 3.0** has been adapted to match this. In addition to a comprehensive Student's Book that offers quick and tangible results, the series now provides students with a wealth of new material online. This allows learners to extend their studies, not only within the classroom, but also outside of the traditional learning environment, on-the-move and in their own time.

Ten key observations regarding teaching English to professional learners underpin the **in company** series:

1 Professionals like to be regularly reminded why they are studying and what's in it for them.
2 They are used to goal-setting and time constraints, and tend to welcome a fairly fast pace.
3 They are motivated by topics which directly relate to their own personal experiences.
4 They expect to see an immediate, practical payoff of some kind at the end of each lesson.
5 It is English, not business, they have come to you for help with (but see 7).
6 They want to be able to actually do business with their English, rather than just talk about it.
7 They appreciate texts and tasks which reflect what they have to do in their job.
8 They also appreciate texts and tasks which allow them to escape what they have to do in their job.
9 They don't regard having fun as incompatible with 'serious learning' (but see 1 and 4).
10 They like to see an overall plan and method behind the classes they attend.

Skills-based approach

in **company** 3.0 Intermediate is a practical course in how to do business in English. With target language selectively introduced on a need-to-know basis, each unit is a fast track to competence in a particular business skill. Recognizing that people need more than just phrase lists and useful language boxes to operate effectively in real-life business situations, each unit provides a substantial amount of guided skills work to give students the chance to fully assimilate the target language and 'make it their own', before going on to tackle fluency activities.

Target skills developed at this level include:

- keeping track in cross-cultural meetings
- creating a favourable impression in emails
- handling unexpected phone calls
- getting people to do things for you
- opening, closing and fuelling conversation
- querying and clarifying points under discussion
- making and reporting decisions
- applying and resisting pressure in negotiations
- exploiting the power of your voice in talks.

Student's Book

in **company** 3.0 Intermediate takes students through 20 progressively more challenging units ranging from basic networking, information-sharing and small talk to higher order skills such as problem-solving, presenting and negotiating. The course reflects the need for students at this level to consolidate their grammatical awareness, increase their lexical range and, above all, boost their communicative power in both professional and social situations.

Structure for the third edition

in **company** 3.0 Intermediate is organized into five sections. Each section consists of three 'Business communication' units, a 'People skills' unit and a 'Management scenario'.

Business communication units

These units deal with vital communication skills such as emailing, telephoning and networking at a conference. These units all contain grammar and lexis elements, and are followed by *Language links* which offer extra vocabulary practice, and grammar consolidation and extra practice.

Every third Business communication unit concludes with a video: *In company interviews*. These interviews showcase real business professionals discussing the preceding unit topics, and give a context for students' own discussion and additional worksheet activities.

People skills

Acquiring communication strategies for a variety of work-related and social contexts and developing interpersonal skills is the main emphasis of these units.

The functional language required for interaction with others is presented and practised through dialogues and extensive listening practice. This is then consolidated through a comprehensive roleplay, where students put into practice the skills they have explored in the unit.

Management scenarios

A new feature of the third edition of in **company** are the five Management scenarios which provide learners with additional extended communication practice through a simulation of a real-life business situation. More importantly, these business situations are illustrated through video, providing students with a visual support to the Student's Book activities which allows them to develop a range of different skills, including perception of body language, comprehension of various accents and an understanding of the importance of interpersonal skills.

Each Management scenario uses video as a prompt for discussion and then as a model for the students' own free roleplay. This fluency activity simulates a similar situation to the one the students have encountered in the video, but allows them the freedom to play their own characters. A self-evaluation form for every roleplay gives students the chance to assess not only their peers' performance, but also their own.

Language input

At an intermediate level, students have typically met much more grammar than they have mastered, and recognize far more vocabulary than they are, as yet, able to produce. A certain amount of recycling is, therefore, essential, but the worst thing we, as teachers, can do is simply to go over old ground again. A better idea is to try to help students apply and begin to integrate their existing knowledge – 'noticing' grammatical patterns in lexis, lexical patterns in grammar and the underlying function in a business context of both.

For instance, in teaching the expression *I'll get on to our suppliers right away*, students' attention could usefully be drawn to any or all of the following:

- the phrasal verb *get on to* (*contact*) and its complement in a business context *get back to*
- the time expression *right away* and other time expressions (*later today, sometime this afternoon, when I've got a minute*) that could fill the same slot in the sentence
- the collocation *get on to our suppliers* and some collocates for *suppliers* (*negotiate with, check with, change*)
- the grammar of *will* as a modal verb and its use in the first person singular to respond to urgent requests (*I'll find out for you, I'll see what I can do, I'll get back to you on that*)
- the use of *get* as a generative verb in the context of communication (*get through on the phone, get your ideas across in a meeting*).

INTRODUCTION 7

Vocabulary syllabus

in company 3.0 Intermediate devotes a lot of attention to vocabulary, showing students how to build words, many of which they may already know, into larger, multi-word items they do not know. For example:

- compounds – *search engine, help menu*
- collocations – *sharp rise, go out of production*
- noun phrases – *cost of living, rate of exchange*
- phrasal verbs – *sell out, buy up, cut back*
- discourse markers – *above all, by the way, to sum up*
- fixed expressions – *Leave it with me, I'll do my best, I'm afraid we'll have to break off here*
- partial frameworks or scripts – *two months ago we were having difficulties with ..., which was also affecting ... and ..., not to mention ... . So, what was going wrong? Well, the problem we were facing was not ... but ... Have a look at this ...*

Pre-constructed vocabulary chunks, like those above, are a crucial part of native-speaker interaction and, if judiciously selected, can significantly speed up the language processing time of non-native speakers too, allowing them to sound more fluent and confident in situations they can predict they are likely to encounter.

Vocabulary, therefore, is given a prominent place in the units. In addition, each of the 15 Business communication units is followed by extra vocabulary practice in the corresponding *Language links* that follow the unit. These exercises effectively double the lexical input in each unit and can either be set for homework or made the basis of vocabulary-building lessons.

Phrase banks

The *Language links* also include *Phrase banks*. These appear as exercises which, once completed, act as a reference bank for useful phrases.

Grammar syllabus

Of course, lexical chunks are only useful in so far as our students are able to produce them in real time, as and when they need them. When, for whatever reason, they are unable to do so, they will fall back on the generative power of grammar and the simplest words in their vocabulary to get the job done.

The approach in in company 3.0 Intermediate is to highlight target grammar as it naturally emerges in the activities, but there are no long detours in the units themselves into structural matters. The reasoning behind this is that, though some formal errors persist, when it comes to the basic grammar of English, intermediate students tend to have more problems with use than form – and such problems require more than a short exercise or two to put right. This is where the grammar sections of the *Language links* come in. Fifteen grammar sections in the *Language links*, cross-linked to the 15 Business communication units, systematically address the usual questions of time, tense, aspect, voice, modality and conditionality as well as broader areas such as reporting and diplomacy, where grammar becomes as much a matter of choice as of rules.

In this grammar section, students are encouraged to explore grammatical use and, to some extent, fathom out the rules for themselves. Tenses are usually presented contrastively. Practice exercises are more commonly text- or dialogue-based (rather than simply sentence-based) to give a feel for the discoursal role of different structures.

In Company Online

The addition of a blended learning element to the course gives in company 3.0 a neat and compact learning solution for both students and teachers. For students, this means the opportunity to practise their language online, via the Online Workbook, as well as on-the-move by downloading the class audio and video. For teachers, this online product means the ability to track students' progress through automatic gradebooks, the opportunity to download the audio and video content, as well as gain access to additional photocopiable material, tests and worksheets.

Online Workbook

The in company 3.0 Online Workbook provides extra skills, grammar and vocabulary practice for every unit of the Student's Book. It contains interactive activities, audio for listening practice and automatic marking – making it perfect for self-study. Your students can instantly check answers and try again, as many times as they want. The Workbook is also linked to an online gradebook, which means you can see your students' marks for each activity as well as the progress they are making. Students will also be able to chart their own progress.

The Online Workbook contains 20 units to match the Student's Book. Students can read and listen to texts on topics similar to those featured in the Student's Book unit, and develop the reading, listening and writing skills that each Student's Book unit introduces. Each Workbook unit also contains lots of extra grammar and vocabulary practice, and there is a grammar reference section for students to consult if they encounter any difficulties.

Resource Centres

In addition to the Online Workbook, students and teachers have access to the Student's and Teacher's Resource Centres. These contain a wealth of additional resource material for use both in and out of the classroom.

Class audio

This includes all audio tracks from the Student's Book class audio CD, along with full listening scripts. Students and teachers can download all the material to a mobile device for listening on-the-move.

Video

In company in action videos accompany each Management scenario in the Student's Book. In the Teacher's Resource Centre, each of these videos has an additional classroom-based worksheet to fully exploit the audiovisual material, including teaching notes and answer keys.

In company interview videos showcase business professionals around the world discussing key business skills and topics. Each interview is supported by a self-study worksheet for students to complete at home.

All video material can be viewed online or downloaded to a mobile device for watching on-the-move.

Tests

Progress and placement tests allow teachers to assess their students' work throughout the course. The automatic gradebook on the Online Workbook also provides the teacher with instant feedback on their students' progress.

Additional student support

Students have access to the following resources to support their learning:

- Unit-by-unit glossary
- Student's Book answer key
- Student's Book phrase banks

Additional teacher support

In addition to the above, teachers have access to an additional 35 photocopiable worksheets which extend and/or revise elements of the Student's Book. The worksheets are written by ten practising Business English teachers, they provide approximately 25 extra hours of material to supplement the Student's Book.

Fast-track map

An invaluable resource for the busy teacher is the new 'fast-track map' that accompanies every level of in company 3.0. This detailed map provides teachers with a fast-track route through the Student's Book, which is ideal for those students who have 30–60 hours of English lessons.

The fast-track map gives the teacher the option of following one of three routes (taster, language practice and language input), selecting the most relevant and useful activities to do in class. Each route also provides a comprehensive self-study plan, for students to enhance their learning outside the classroom.

Class audio CDs

Throughout the course, substantial use is made of audio recordings to input business expressions and grammatical structures. Indeed, very little of the language work is not either presented or recycled in a recording.

The recordings feature both native and non-native speaker accents, providing the students with extensive exposure to real spoken English. There is frequently an element of humour in the recordings which, besides entertaining the students, motivates them to listen again for things they may have missed the first time round.

There are full listening scripts at the back of the Student's Book. All Student's Book class audio material is also available online, accessible to both students and teachers through the resource centres. These audio tracks can be downloaded as MP3 files and played on various devices, from CD players to smartphones and tablets. This allows students to listen again to all audio material in their own time, even when on-the-move, giving them the flexibility to listen and re-listen to the class audio as much as they want.

In addition, the Listening section of the Online Workbook provides further listening practice with new recordings that students will not yet have heard in class.

How can I exploit the dialogues further?

Play some of the dialogues a second time and:

- pause the CD after questions for students to recall or predict the response (if they write these down as they go, you can ask them to recall the questions as well at the end)
- pause the CD after responses to questions and ask students to think of other possible responses
- pause the CD in the middle of lexical chunks (collocations, fixed expressions) for students to complete them either orally or by writing them down
- ask students to speculate about the personalities of the speakers in the dialogue
- ask students if they have ever met / done business with anyone like the speakers
- ask students if they would have reacted differently to the speakers in the dialogue.

Reading texts

The reading texts in in company 3.0 Intermediate have been chosen to involve, entertain and provoke students into lively discussion, as well as to contextualize key target vocabulary. Squeezing a text completely dry of all useful language usually demotivates a class, but many of the longer texts in in company 3.0 Intermediate are information- and lexically-rich and can usefully be revisited.

The reading section of the Online Workbook uses new reading texts to provide further reading practice in a different context.

How can I exploit the texts further?
Try some of the following:
- students set each other questions on a text
- students set you questions on a text, and vice versa
- give students several figures from a text and ask them to recall the context in which they were mentioned
- read the text aloud but slur certain words/phrases and have students ask for repetition/clarification
- students read/listen to a text and complete sentences to reflect their own reaction to it, e.g. *I thought the point about … was interesting; I'm surprised that …; I'm not sure I agree with what it says about …; I'm not convinced that …; I completely disagree with the idea that …*
- give students the first half of 8–16 collocations and a time limit in which to search for the collocates
- give students a set of miscollocates and ask them to correct them by referring to the text
- students find expressions which mean the same as, e.g. *incidentally = by the way; moreover = in addition; generally = by and large* or the opposite of, e.g. *in practice / in theory; in general / in particular*
- give students a set of prepositions and ask them to scan the text for noun phrases / phrasal verbs / idioms which include those prepositions
- read out the text, pausing in the middle of collocations / fixed expressions / idioms for students to predict the completions either by shouting out or writing down the answer.

Fluency work

Each unit culminates in at least one fluency activity which draws on both the specific language presented in the unit and the wider linguistic resources of the students. Activity types comprise:

1. skills workouts, where students practise a specific micro-skill (such as effective interruption or voice projection) in a semi-guided way
2. roleplays and simulations, where students are given a scenario and perhaps some kind of 'personal agenda'
3. case studies, where students are confronted with an authentic business problem and then compare their solution with that of the actual company concerned
4. 'framework' activities, where the students decide on the content for a presentation, email or phone call and the Student's Book provides them with a linguistic framework to help deliver that information

Preparation is essential for types 2–4 and it may sometimes be advisable to carry out the actual fluency activity in a subsequent lesson, allowing plenty of time for feedback.

Working with video

Here are some suggestions of different ways of working with video.

Video dictogloss

This gives the students practice in grammar and vocabulary, with emphasis on sentence building. Use a short part of a video. Tell the students to watch and listen carefully as you play the extract. Play it once and ask them to write down in any order any words they can remember from the conversation. Then, ask them to work first in pairs and then in small groups, and to use the words they have written to recreate as much of the dialogue as possible. This activity works better with practice!

Questions for answers

This activity gives the students practice in prediction skills and practises question formation. Find five or six examples of questions and answers in the video script. Write the answers on the board or on a sheet of paper. Ask the students to work in pairs and guess what the questions for these answers are. Listen to their ideas, but don't correct them. Play the video so they can check if their predictions were correct.

Multi-listening tasks

This activity practises taking notes while viewing. Divide students into three or four groups and give each group a different listening task. At the end of the viewing, groups exchange papers with someone else from the same group. Show the video again. Have them check their partner's answers and add more information. Finally, students form groups of three: with one person from A, B and C, and discuss what they learned.

Subtitles off / Subtitles on

This activity practises listening for detail. Write sentences from a section of the video, preferably a continuous conversation. Photocopy the sheet (one copy for every three students) and cut up the slips of paper. Put students into groups of three. Hand out a set of slips to each group, in the wrong order. As students listen to the video (subtitles off), they put the slips into order. Play the video again (subtitles on), so students can check their order. Finally, have them practise the dialogue in their groups.

Stop and predict

This activity motivates students and develops classroom discussion. Press 'Pause' at an appropriate moment and ask students to guess what is going to happen next. Alternatively, ask students what the speaker is going to say next. Elicit ideas from your class. Then watch the next part of the video and find out the answer. Who guessed correctly? This activity only works when students watch the video for the first time.

Shadow reading

This activity gives students practice in rhythm and intonation. After students have watched the video, give them a copy of a short section of the script, preferably a dialogue. Give them a few minutes to read it through silently. Get them to practise reading the text aloud in small groups. Then play the video again and ask students to read the script aloud in time with the video. This can be difficult for students at first but, with practice, it can really help with stress, weak forms and rhythm. Start by doing this with short sections and gradually increase their length.

Fast-forward viewing

This activity helps students to understand the main ideas. Write a few basic questions on the board relating to the video clip students are going to watch. Play the entire clip on fast-forward (no sound). Encourage students to guess the answers from the quick viewing. Elicit other details they learnt.

Teacher's Book

In this book, you'll find comprehensive teaching notes which give an overview of each unit, detailed procedural instructions for all the exercises, and full listening scripts and answer keys.

A recurring feature of the previous edition is the inclusion of **1:1** teaching tips found following every group-based or roleplay activity throughout the procedural notes. These have been updated and their number increased for this third edition. The aim of these notes is to offer tips on adapting the material to suit one-to-one classes, which are so common in in-company teaching. This allows the teacher to make better use of the material, in all teaching contexts.

The procedural notes also contain *Language link* highlights, which are reminders of exercises in the *Language links* pages where students can find grammar explanations or further practice in a particular grammar or vocabulary area. This allows the teacher to focus students' attention on particular areas of difficulty or interest.

We hope you enjoy working with **in company** 3.0.

Mark Powell

September 2013

01 Making contacts

Learning objectives

Most business people attend a conference at some point in their careers, and this unit is about making business contacts and socializing at conferences.

Students begin by talking about their attitudes to conferences and discussing conference venues. They learn language for engaging in small talk and keeping the conversation going, and they listen to people chatting at a conference. They will also practise networking at a conference.

The grammatical focus is on the Present Simple and Present Continuous tenses, and the lexical focus is on collocations relating to conferences.

Digital resources: Unit 1

Online Workbook; Placement test; Extension worksheets; Glossary; Phrase bank; Student's Book answer key; Student's Book listening script; Fast-track map

---

This first section is about attitudes to conferences. It gives students an opportunity to talk about their own experiences and opinions.

Warm-up

Read the quotation by Fred Allen to the class and ask for reactions. Find out how often your students attend or take part in conferences. If they have been to one recently, ask them to say where it was and whether they enjoyed it.

1 Find out which, if any, of the cities the students have already visited. Invite them to share their experiences and impressions with the class. Then ask everyone to make their choice of city.

2 As students discuss the cities with a partner, go around listening to their conversations and make a note of any interesting points. At the end, ask for any interesting information to be reported back to the whole class. If students are hesitant to talk to the whole class about their discussions, use the notes you have taken to prompt them.

> **1:1** If you have been to any of the cities listed, you should be able to discuss with your student what you would do on your extra day. If not, make sure you do some research in advance so that you have information and ideas to share.

3 Go through the blog with the class. Then ask students to work individually to think up tips for the business traveller.

4 Ask students to work with a partner to share and discuss their tips. Then have a class feedback session and ask the students to vote for the best three tips.

5 Ask students to work with a partner and decide who will be Speaker A and Speaker B. Ask them to turn to their respective pages and read the replies. The two replies give conflicting advice on a number of issues. Make sure the students compare the two opinions. They should then decide which advice they think sounds the best. Find out what the general consensus is in a class feedback session.

> **1:1** Take one of the roles yourself and work with your student to compare the advice. Ask the student to decide which advice sounds best.

Conference venues

In this section, students meet some common collocations associated with conference venues. Recorded extracts from a business travel programme are used to show these collocations in action and also to train students to listen for detail, in this case picking out numbers and saying what they refer to.

1 1.01 Focus attention on the three photos and ask them to say which of the conference venues they would be most interested in going to.

As you play the recording, students match the extracts to the venues.

ANSWERS

Venue A (Disneyland® Paris) = 2; Venue B (Hilton Hotel in Cancún, Mexico) = 1; Venue C (Burj Al Arab Hotel in Dubai) = 3

1.01

Extract 1

Two thousand years ago, it was the home of the ancient Mayan civilization. Today, Cancún is the most popular resort in Mexico; its unspoilt coastline a water sports paradise. With its 426 rooms overlooking the Caribbean, 24-hour room service, express checkout, outdoor pools, residents-only health club and 200 metres of exclusive private beach, the Hilton Cancún is rated among the three best hotels in Latin America. Whether swimming with the dolphins or playing roulette in its own offshore casino, you can be sure of an experience to remember. Or why not take advantage of the Hilton's car rental service and explore the nearby ruins of Chichen Itza? Whatever your company's needs, send them your requirements and they will plan the logistics for you. What's more, if you book on special value dates, you'll get a generous 10 to 30% discount. This year, why not let your annual conference be part of Cancún's 2,000-year-old tradition?

12   01 MAKING CONTACTS

BUSINESS COMMUNICATION

Extract 2

Half an hour from the world's most romantic city and rated by conference organizers the 'hottest' venue in Europe, Disneyland® Paris's corporate clients include American Express, Unilever and MCI. If you think business and *The Lion King* don't mix, the Disney® magic will soon change your mind. With its unique atmosphere and superb fully equipped convention centre for 2,300 people, its 95 meeting rooms and 3,000 square metres of exhibition space, Disney's theme park is sure to be a huge success with both you and your family. As well as fabulous banqueting facilities for over a thousand people, Disney is able to arrange special private events, such as the amazing 'Journey through Time' and the 'Cape Caribbean' adventure or, if you prefer, golf tournaments and team-building activities. Walt Disney's aim was always 'to make people happy' and that aim now extends to corporate hospitality in the cultural heart of Europe.

Extract 3

At 321 metres high, higher than the Eiffel Tower and only 60 metres shorter than the Empire State Building, the magnificent Burj Al Arab is one of the world's tallest and most luxurious hotels. Diamond white by day and a rainbow of colours at night, occupying a central location in Dubai with flight connections to all the major cities of the world, the Burj Al Arab combines the latest technology with the finest traditions of the past. Spacious deluxe suites from 170 to 780 square metres, in-room laptops with Internet access, full conference facilities on the 27th floor, a VIP helipad on the 28th, a golden-domed ballroom and a world-class restaurant with spectacular views across the Arabian Gulf all make this the ultimate business venue. As they say in the Emirates, 'Welcome, honoured guest.'

2 1.01 Before playing the recording again, read all the figures aloud, or ask students to read them, ensuring that everyone is clear on how each is pronounced.

You may need to play the recording several times and pause it between extracts for students to match the figures to the venue and note down what the figures refer to.

ANSWERS

a Venue C (height of the building in metres)
b Venue B (number of rooms)
c Venue C (floor with conference facilities)
d Venue A (number of people the convention centre can house)
e Venue B (discount available on special value dates)
f Venue A (size of exhibition space in square metres)
g Venue C (size of deluxe suites in square metres)
h Venue A (number of meeting rooms)
i Venue B (length of private beach in metres)

3 See if students can match the collocations from memory. If necessary, play the recording again for them to check.

To make the exercise more interactive, you could divide the class into two teams, numbering the members of the team. In turn, one member of each team calls out the first word in a collocation and the corresponding member of the other team replies with the second word.

ANSWERS

Venue A: a 2 b 3 c 1 d 6 e 4 f 5
Venue B: a 3 b 1 c 2 d 5 e 6 f 4
Venue C: a 2 b 3 c 1 d 6 e 4 f 5

4 Students can discuss the question with a partner or in groups and report back to the class.

Who's who?

In this section, students are introduced to the kinds of things they will need to say at conferences, beginning by identifying specific people by appearance, manner, location, etc and saying something about them.

1 This exercise equips students to identify people they want to talk about. When students have completed the questions and answers individually, ask them, with a partner, to act out a conversation with one student choosing a question and the other giving an appropriate response. Do not let this go on for too long as they will be doing a similar thing in the next exercise, but with a freer choice of words.

ANSWERS

a by b with c in d at e to f in g for h at i on

2 Students work with a partner to make new sentences following the structures practised in 1. Make sure students can pronounce some of the trickier items such as *pharmaceuticals*, *buffet* and *moustache* before they start. Invite some pairs to perform short conversations for the class.

Language links

Direct students to the **Language links** section on pages 11–12 for further explanation of the construction and use of the Present Simple and Present Continuous, and exercises to practise these tenses.

3 1.02–1.05 Focus attention on the photo and ask students to use some of the language they have been practising to identify the people.

For fun, you might like to invite students to see who can put together the longest description of one of the people in the photo. For example, *the woman in the black dress, pink scarf and short dark hair, talking to the man in the dark suit drinking an orange juice*.

Before playing the recordings, establish the meaning of *gossip* and perhaps ask the students to suggest some potential gossip about the people in the photo. Play the recordings and ask students first to decide which of the people in the photo the speakers are discussing.

Play the recordings again for students to complete the information. You may need to play them several times and pause to give students time to write their answers.

01 MAKING CONTACTS 13

BUSINESS COMMUNICATION

ANSWERS

1 Siemens; director of R&D; Munich; Hilton; data security; headhunted from Philips at double his previous salary
2 Sony®; head of research; UK; Sheraton; New Generation Gaming Systems; may lose his job if Sony move R&D to Frankfurt and appoint a German instead of him
3 Warsaw University of Technology; professor; Warsaw; Marriott; innovation strategies; quite influential and things can go badly for you if you get on the wrong side of her
4 Cisco; head of technical department; the Netherlands; Hyatt; new server technology; was the boss of one of the speakers, she fired him when they disagreed about the management of a project

1.02
Conversation 1

A: Oh, hi, David. How are things? We were just talking about the guy over there.
B: Who?
A: The big, tall guy in the green tie behind those women. The guy standing at the bar.
B: Oh, yeah.
A: You know him?
B: Yes, that's Karl Schelling.
A: Karl who?
B: Schelling. He's the new director of R&D at Siemens.
A: In Munich?
B: Yeah, that's right. Nice guy. I was talking to him last night in the bar.
A: Oh, he's at the Hilton?
B: Yeah. He was telling me about how he got the job.
A: Really?
B: Yeah, apparently he was headhunted from Philips. They made him an offer he couldn't refuse. Doubled his salary.
A: Headhunted? Don't expect Philips are too happy, then. All that sensitive information.
B: Well, no, quite.
A: He's presenting, isn't he?
B: Yeah, he's on this afternoon. He's talking about data security.
A: You're joking.
B: No, here he is on the programme: Data Security in the Connected Economy.

1.03
Conversation 2

C: Chris, who's that man over there in the light suit?
D: You mean the grey suit?
C: No, not him! Over there, standing by the entrance. Talking to that woman in black.
D: Oh, yes, that's, er, what's-his-name? William Hill. Hall. William Hall, that's it. He's at the Sheraton where I'm staying, actually. He's head of research at Sony® UK. Yes, he's giving a talk on … where's my programme? … Ah, yes, here it is. Erm, … yes, on New Generation Gaming Systems. Ten o'clock on Saturday. I think I'm going to that.
C: Mm, sounds interesting. He doesn't look very happy, though, does he?
D: Well, no. Neither would you in his position.
C: How do you mean?
D: Well, this is just a rumour, mind you, but, erm, I've heard they may be moving R&D to Frankfurt.
C: Really? Are you sure?
D: Well, no, but that's what I heard.
C: And he doesn't want to make that move?
D: Well, the thing is: I'm not sure they're keeping him on. I think they want a German to lead the team.
C: Oh, I see. Well, no wonder he's unhappy …

1.04
Conversation 3

E: Anne, you know nearly everybody here. Who's that woman in the brown jacket with the long red hair? She's talking to that other woman, the one with the blonde hair.
F: Oh, you mean, Irena, Irena Stefanowitz?
E: Yes, who is she? I saw her coming out of the Marriott last night with a whole group of people. Going to some dinner party, by the look of it. Sounded like they were speaking Polish.
F: Yes, she's a professor at the Warsaw University of Technology. And I think she does quite a lot of consultancy work as well. Amazing speaker. You should go to her talk.
E: Really? What's she talking about?
F: I think she's doing a session this year on innovation strategies.
E: Interesting. You know, I'm going to be working on a project in Krakow next year.
F: Krakow? Oh, you'll love it there. Very nice city.
E: Yes, if all goes well, there might be a lot more work in Poland.
F: Oh, well, in that case, perhaps you should meet Irena. I'm sure she'd be interested in talking to you.
E: Yes, perhaps you're right.
F: I should warn you, though …
E: What?
F: Well, she's quite influential in Warsaw.
E: Oh, yes?
F: Yes. Let's just say it doesn't pay to get on the wrong side of her. A friend of mine knew her well. They had a bit of a disagreement and his latest project proposal was rejected by the authorities.
E: Hmm. Okay, I'll remember that.
F: But you must meet her. In fact, why don't I introduce you now?
E: Erm, well, okay then …

BUSINESS COMMUNICATION

🔘 **1.05**

Conversation 4

G: ... So, anyway, that's how it ended up costing me 75 euros just to get from the airport to the hotel!

H: Oh, dear. Well, I did warn you about some of those mini-cab drivers.

G: Yes, yes, I know. I'll wait in the queue with the rest of you next time ... Anyway, let's change the subject ... Who's that blonde woman over there?

H: Hmm?

G: The one in the black dress. Over there, talking to those two guys.

H: Which two guys?

G: Those two. The woman with her back to us!

H: Oh, her! That's Margo Timmerman.

G: Ah, so that's Margo Timmerman. I thought so. She still works for Cisco, right?

H: Yeah. Heads up their technical department in the Netherlands.

G: Isn't she giving the keynote presentation tomorrow morning?

H: Yes, she's talking about new server technology or something. Why?

G: Hmm, I'd quite like to talk to her if I get the chance. Is she staying at the Marriott, do you know? I might leave her a message.

H: Erm, no, she's probably over at the Hyatt. That's where most of the Cisco people are staying.

G: Ah, right ... Listen, you seem to know her. You couldn't introduce us, could you?

H: Er, well, to tell you the truth, I'm really not the best person to ask.

G: Oh?

H: No. She, er, used to be my boss. You know, years ago. We, er ... Well, let's just say we had very different ideas about how to manage a project. And she, er, let me go.

G: You mean she fired you!

H: Yes, well, all right. Keep your voice down! I wasn't exactly fired ...

Language links

Direct students to the *Language links* section on page 11 for more practice of language for 'talking shop'.

Taboo or not taboo?

In this section, students discuss the issue of what is and is not a suitable topic for conversation with people you meet at a conference for the first time.

1 Establish the meaning of *taboo*. Ask students whether taboo topics in their culture differ according to how well you know the people you are talking to and the circumstances of the conversation. Invite them to suggest topics which they think would be taboo when meeting someone at a conference for the first time and other topics which would be safe.

Point out other categories given in this exercise: *conversation killers* and *a bit risky*. Ask for examples, e.g. subjects that are not exactly taboo but wouldn't encourage people to continue a conversation, and subjects that are risky because they may cause offence.

Ask students to share with the class any amusing or embarrassing moments they've actually experienced in conversation. If your students are from different cultures, ask them to work individually at first to group the items in the box under the headings. They can then compare their answers with a partner or in small groups. If students share a culture, encourage them to discuss and do the grouping with a partner. As a follow-up activity, you could ask the class to make a list of topics which they think would be completely safe in most cultures.

2 🔘 **1.06–1.10** Students may be able to decide whether the speakers get on or not before they identify the specific details of the topics of conversation. Ask only for this the first time you play the recordings to encourage students to realize that it isn't always necessary to understand every word of a recording in order to pick up the gist of what is said or the attitude of the speakers.

Play the recordings again for them to note down the topics of conversation that they hear and allow them to compare answers with a partner before checking with the class.

ANSWERS

	Topics of conversation	Do the speakers get on?
a	Russia, work, drink	yes
b	food, astrology	no
c	speaker's talk, conference, weather	yes
d	work (the merger), rail strikes	no
e	watch, hotel, Mexico, food	yes

🔘 **1.06**

Conversation a

A: Is this your first visit to Russia?

B: Er, yes it is, actually. Fascinating place.

A: Yes, isn't it? I come here quite a lot. What do you do, by the way? I see you work for Glaxo.

B: How did you know? ... Oh, yeah, my badge. Yeah, I'm in R&D. Molecular modelling, to be precise.

A: Really? We should talk. Can I get you a drink?

B: Er, no thanks. I'm fine.

A: Sure?

B: Well, just a coffee, then. Thanks. So, what line of business are you in?

🔘 **1.07**

Conversation b

C: Hi, Fiona Hunt. Sun Microsystems. Mind if I join you?

D: Erm, no. Er, Michael Steele.

C: Pleased to meet you, Mike. Try one of these – they're delicious.

01 MAKING CONTACTS 15

BUSINESS COMMUNICATION

D: Er, thanks, but I'm allergic to seafood.
C: Oh, then try the cheese dips instead. They're really good! Have we met somewhere before? Oslo, perhaps?
D: I don't think so.
C: Mm. I was sure I recognized you … You're an Aquarius, aren't you? I can tell.
D: Well, I don't know. I'm not really into horoscopes, I'm afraid.
C: When's your birthday?
D: Oh, er, February the 2nd.
C: I knew it! A typical Aquarius.
D: Er, yes. Geez, is that the time? If you'll excuse me, I have to make a phone call. It's been nice talking to you.

1.08
Conversation c
E: I really enjoyed your talk this morning.
F: Oh, thanks. Yeah, it went quite well, I think.
E: You had some very interesting things to say. I'm Amy Cooper, by the way. Yes, I'd like to talk to you about some of your ideas. My company may be interested in your product. Where are you staying?
F: At the Regency.
E: I'm at the Hyatt. Why don't we fix up a time to chat over a drink? Here's my card.
F: Oh, thanks. I've got mine here … somewhere.
E: Don't worry. I know who you are. So, how are you enjoying the conference?
F: Well, it's been good so far. More people than ever this year. But, er, isn't this weather awful? Half a metre of snow this morning, I heard.
E: Yeah, it gets pretty cold here in Moscow, that's for sure.
F: Erm, would you excuse me a moment? I'll be right back.

1.09
Conversation d
G: So, how's business?
H: Fine. This merger's meant quite a lot of work for us, but, fine.
G: Hmm. Well, mergers are often difficult. So, er, what do you think about the strikes in Europe?
H: I'm sorry?
G: The rail strikes in France. It was in the news again this morning.
H: Er, well, I, er …
G: I mean, it must affect a company like yours – you being in logistics.
H: Er, no, I think you've made a mistake. I'm not in logistics. I work for Audi.
G: Audi? Oh, sorry. Thought you were someone else.
H: That's okay. Er, if you'll excuse me, I must just go and say hello to someone.

1.10
Conversation e
I: I like your watch. An Omega, isn't it?
J: Er, well, to be honest, don't tell anyone, but it's a fake.
J: No! Well, it looks real to me. Where did you get it?
J: Turkey. It cost me 25 dollars.
I: Amazing! So, do you know many people here?
J: No, not really. It's the first time I've been to one of these conferences.
I: Me too. So, what's your hotel like?
J: Hmm, pretty comfortable. Nothing special, but it's okay, I suppose.
I: Yeah, you're at the Sheraton, aren't you? Last year they held this thing in Mexico. The Hilton Cancún. Fabulous hotel, they say.
J: Cancún! A bit warmer than here, then!
I: Oh, yeah. I went there on holiday once. Beautiful place. Can I get you anything from the buffet?
J: Oh, that's all right. I'll come with you. I'd like some more of that Beluga caviar before it all goes!

Keeping the conversation going

This section gives students some of the tools for keeping a conversation going once it has started.

1 1.06–1.10 Ask students to work individually to complete the expressions. Then allow them to compare with a partner before playing the recordings for them to check their answers. Write the expressions on the board and ask the students to close their books. Wipe off some of the words and see if the students can remember the expressions. Gradually wipe off more words so that fewer and fewer remain, each time checking if the students can still remember.

> **ANSWERS**
> a Is this your   b What do you   c Can I get   d What line of
> e Try one of   f Have we met   g If you'll excuse   h It's been nice
> i I really enjoyed   j How are you   k Isn't this weather
> l Would you excuse   m I must just   n Do you know   o Can I get

2 Ask students to discuss the questions with a partner or in small groups. Explain that some expressions can be used more than once. Then have a class discussion on what they would do in their own language(s) to open, continue or end a conversation.

> **ANSWERS**
> a a, c, e, f, i, j, k, n, o
> b b, c, d, e, j, k, n, o
> c g, h, l, m

BUSINESS COMMUNICATION

At a conference party

In this section, students practice what they have learned about starting and maintaining a conversation at a conference by roleplaying a conference party. Students work together as a class to do this, and they are given plenty of support by preparing questions and answers in advance.

1 Students could use their real names and nationalities, but some may find it less embarrassing to assume a fictitious identity. The fantasy role approach may also work better with in-company groups and those who already know each other well; it certainly allows more room for gossip.

2 Ask students to write the questions first and check the answers with the class before getting them to fill in the answers. Students work individually to devise answers for their character, and you will need to go around offering help and advice where needed.

ANSWERS

So, who do you work for?
Is this your first time in Paris?
And what do you do there?
How are you enjoying the conference?
Where are you based?
Are you giving a presentation?
How's business?
Do you know many people here?
Can I get you a drink?
So, where are you staying?
Where are you from originally?
Can I get you anything from the buffet?

Language links

Direct students to the *Phrase bank* in the *Language links* section on page 12 for a further exercise on making questions and answers to use when networking.

3 If you have the time and the facilities to do so, you might like to add to the reality of this roleplay by having some refreshments available and by encouraging students to bring to class business cards (real or imaginary) and name badges.

Focus attention on the fact that they are not limited to the questions and answers they have just prepared. They have already practised other techniques in this unit for talking about other people in the room and keeping the conversation going. They could even engage in a little (fictitious) gossip about the other people they have met at the conference.

Have a class feedback session at the end in which students report back to the class on the people they met, the gossip they heard and the appointments they have made.

1:1 Ask your student to invent one persona to play at the drinks party, but prepare several for yourself. Each time you have a conversation, assume a different persona and steer the conversation in a different direction.

Language links

ANSWERS
Vocabulary
Conferences
a up; plant   b in; distributor   c off; workers   d out; product
e of; job   f to; office   g under; takeover   h with; supplier
i for; contract   j down; factory

Grammar
Present Simple
1 a **A** *Does he work* for the BBC?
     B No, he *doesn't* work for them anymore. He *works* for CNN.
  b **A** Where *do you work*?
     B I *work* for a design company in Frankfurt.
  c At our firm, we *don't* work on Friday afternoons.
  d On Mondays our CEO usually *flies* to Oslo.
2 1 b, f   2 c, h   3 e, g   4 a, d

Present Continuous
3 1 a, e   2 d   3 b, c

Present Simple or Continuous?
4 a do you do   b I'm   c Do you know
  d are you enjoying   e I guess   f Are you giving
  g I only come   h are you staying   i I usually stay
  j you aren't doing

Phrase bank: Networking
a 9   b 6   c 4   d 2   e 10   f 5
g 11   h 7   i 1   j 8   k 3

01 MAKING CONTACTS 17

02 Making calls

Learning objectives
Making and receiving telephone calls in English is perhaps one of the most difficult skills which business students need to acquire, and certainly one which can cause a lot of stress.

This unit provides strategies to make telephoning in English less stressful and gives some useful formulaic expressions which will facilitate dealing with calls. Students practise listening to and dealing with voicemail messages and returning calls. Finally, students do a guided roleplay, initiating a phone call in order to find out certain information.

The grammatical focus is on the Past Simple and time adverbs, and the lexical focus is on telephone expressions.

Digital resources: Unit 2
Online Workbook; Extension worksheets; Glossary; Phrase bank; Student's Book answer key; Student's Book listening script; Fast-track map

---

This first section provides an opportunity for students to explore their attitudes and worries about speaking English on the phone. Students will listen to different versions of phone calls, and analyze what went wrong and why the revised version was more successful. They will also learn some common telephone expressions. The aim here is to demonstrate that many people have difficulty with telephone calls and it is nothing to be ashamed of. Several techniques will be given in this unit which should help.

1:1 Having only one student is a positive advantage when it comes to teaching and practising telephone skills, as it is possible to make real phone calls to demonstrate and practise the language. Use every opportunity to call your student on the phone or ask them to call you to practise the language and skills taught in this unit.

Warm-up
Read the quotation to the class and ask for reactions. How do the students feel when they encounter a telephone answering system that requires them to make endless choices by pressing different keys on their phone and never getting to speak to a real person?

Ask how often students have to use the telephone at work and how often they make or receive phone calls in English. Ask them to talk about any problems they have experienced.

1 Check that students have completed the questions in the questionnaire correctly before giving them time to think about and discuss their answers to them. Encourage students to give details of the incident when their answer is *yes*. Ask them to report back to the class on any interesting anecdotes they shared.

Remind students that planning calls in a foreign language is vitally important. If you prepare what you are going to say when you make a call, the conversation is likely to progress much more smoothly and with less chance of misunderstanding. If you are aware of what you should say when you receive a call, then you will sound more confident, and you are less likely to cause offence by not using the established formulae which the caller will expect.

ANSWERS
A misunderstood B sounded C had D kept E shouted
F lost G wished H tried I wanted

2 **1.11** Play the recording and elicit answers to the question around the class. Encourage students to suggest the kinds of things the person answering the phone could have said instead of his abrupt one-word responses (*Hello. Yes. Yes.*) and which would have been more helpful.

ANSWERS
The caller gets angry because the person who answers the call is abrupt and doesn't give full answers, which gives the impression of rudeness or lack of interest in the caller's reason for calling.

1.11
A: Hello?
B: Hello.
A: Hello. Is that Dutch Hydro?
B: That's right.
A: Can I have the accounts department, please?
B: Yes.
A: Sorry?
B: This is the accounts department.
A: Oh, right. Erm, I'd like to speak to Marius Pot, please.
B: Yes.
A: Sorry?
B: That's me.
A: Well, why didn't you say so?
B: Can I help you?
A: I hope so! I'm calling about an invoice I received.

3 **1.12** Play the recording for students to listen and complete the phrases. When you have checked the answers, ask them to say what would be an appropriate way of answering the phone in their own situations.

ANSWERS
Hello, accounts department. Marius Pot speaking.

1.12
B: Hello, accounts department. Marius Pot speaking.
A: Ah, Mr Pot. Just the person I wanted to speak to. I'm calling about an invoice I received.

18 02 MAKING CALLS

BUSINESS COMMUNICATION

4 🔘 **1.13** Play the recording and elicit answers to the question. Again, you could ask students to say how the caller's utterances could be improved before you play the better version.

ANSWER

He hesitates a lot and has not prepared what to say.

🔘 **1.13**
A: Good morning, Cheney and Broome. Can I help you?
B: Yes, please ... er, ... Just a moment ...
A: Hello? Are you still there?
B: Yes, sorry ... erm ...
A: How can I help you?
B: Oh, yes, can I speak to, er, to, er ... just a minute ... yes, to, er, Catherine Mellor, please?
A: Certainly. Who's calling, please?
B: Sorry?
A: Can I have your name, please?
B: Oh, yes, it's Ramón Berenguer ... from Genex Ace Pharmaceuticals.
A: Thank you. Can I ask the purpose of your call, Mr Berenguer?
B: Oh, yes. It's about, er ... an invoice.
A: Thank you, Mr Berenguer. Putting you through now.

5 🔘 **1.14** Play the recording for students to listen and complete the phrases.

Students can then work with a partner to briefly roleplay the first part of a telephone call, with one answering the phone properly and the other saying who they are, where they are calling from, who they want to speak to and what the call is about. They can then swap roles.

ANSWERS

This is Ramon Berenguer *from* Genex Ace Pharmaceuticals. *Can I speak* to Catherine Mellor, *please? It's about* an invoice.

🔘 **1.14**
A: Good morning, Cheney and Broome. Can I help you?
B: Er, yes. This is Ramón Berenguer from Genex Ace Pharmaceuticals. Can I speak to Catherine Mellor, please?
A: Certainly, Mr Berenguer. Can I ask the purpose of your call?
B: It's about an invoice.
A: Putting you through now.

6 Students will find the expressions given here useful in a wide variety of phone calls. When they have found as many expressions as possible, divide the class into two teams. Each team takes a turn to call out the first part of an expression (the first three columns) and the other team has to complete it (from the last two columns).

Point out to students that the key to successful telephoning in English is confidence. If they have a range of expressions at their fingertips to cope with all the practical aspects and eventualities of telephoning (the person being out, on another line, offering to take a message, etc), then they will sound more confident and will have more time to concentrate on the more important parts of the call (imparting information, finding something out, etc).

7 In this exercise, students predict what the person at the other end of the phone must have said to cause the responses given. Give students time to write the questions individually. Tell them that there may be more than one correct answer.

SUGGESTED ANSWERS

a Can I help you?
b Can I ask who's calling? / Can I have your name, please?
c Can/Could you spell that, please?
d Can I give her a message?
e Can you tell him I called?
f Can you read that back to me?
g Can you speak up, please?
h Can you tell me when she'll be back?
i Can you get back to me within the hour?
j Can you ask him/her to call me back?
k Can I get back to you on that?
l Can I leave a message?

Language links

Direct students to the *Language links* section on page 18 for more practice of useful telephone expressions for dealing with difficulties and distractions.

8 🔘 **1.15** Play the recording for students to check their answers against the ones given.

For a more interactive way of checking answers, select a pair of students and ask one of them to read out the question they have written. If the question is correct, the other student should give the response from the book. If the question is not correct, he/she should either say nothing or give a response which is appropriate to the question that has actually been asked. Establish what the correct question should be before moving on. Do this for all the questions, selecting a different pair of students each time.

🔘 **1.15**
a Can I help you?
b Can I ask who's calling?
c Can you spell that, please?
d Can I give her a message?
e Can you tell him I called?
f Can you read that back to me?
g Can you speak up, please?
h Can you tell me when she'll be back?
i Can you get back to me within the hour?
j Can you ask her to call me back?
k Can I get back to you on that?
l Can I leave a message?

02 MAKING CALLS 19

BUSINESS COMMUNICATION

Voicemail

In this section, students practise listening to voicemail messages and identifying the important information in them. The messages are then used for grammar work on the Past Simple and pronunciation of Past Simple regular verb endings. The students end by recreating voicemail messages from written messages.

1 1.16 Encourage students to take meaningful notes when they listen to the messages. Elicit that these notes should contain the important information from the messages, which is likely to include the name of the caller, what the message is about and any action that the receiver of the call is required to take.

ANSWERS
a 4   b 1   c 2   d 6   e 3   f 5

1.16
Message 1
Hello. This is Cheryl. I phoned you about five times yesterday, but you weren't in. Anyway, I corrected those figures you faxed me. Okay, speak to you later.

Message 2
Hi, Peter. Anne here. I wanted to talk to you about the project meeting tomorrow, but you're obviously not there. The good news is we finished phase one on time. As I explained, I may be a little late for the meeting. So just go ahead and start without me. I'll join you at about ten.

Message 3
Er, this is Zoltán. Just to let you know, I started the report this morning and just emailed you the first part. Oh, I included the quarterly accounts in the report, too. Let me know what you think.

Message 4
Mr Carter. It's Philip Heath. I talked to our stock control manager about the Venezuelan consignment and he says we despatched the goods a week ago. The shipping agent says they delivered them this morning. So, problem solved!

Message 5
Hello, Mr Carter. This is Ryan Hope from SilverStar. I called you a couple of weeks ago about an estimate for a contract in Malaysia. Erm, we discussed my client's requirements and, well, I expected to hear from you last week. Could you give me a call on 01865 555959 as soon as possible, please?

Message 6
Pete. It's me. Sorry, mate, I tried everything, but head office say we can't have any more time. They say they waited six months for the preliminary report, another six months for the feasibility study and now they want to see some results. Anyway, I booked the conference room for three tomorrow. Give me a call when you get in. We need to talk.

2 1.16 Make sure students have read the questions before you play the recording again so that they know exactly what information they are listening for.

ANSWERS
Message 1   About five
Message 2   It was finished on time.
Message 3   The quarterly accounts
Message 4   This morning
Message 5   Last week
Message 6   Students' own ideas

3 1.16 You could ask the students to try to put the words into the correct columns before you play the recording again, and just use the recording for them to check their answers. Elicit that the verbs in the /ɪd/ column all have infinitives ending in the /t/ or /d/ sound.

When students have to categorize things by pronunciation, always encourage them to say the words aloud to see what sounds right. Developing an instinct for what sounds right will help them throughout their language learning careers.

ANSWERS
/d/: phoned, explained, emailed, delivered, called, tried
/t/: faxed, finished, talked, despatched, discussed, booked
/ɪd/: corrected, wanted, started, included, expected, waited

Language links
Direct students to the *Language links* section on pages 18–19 for further explanation of the construction and use of the Past Simple, and exercises to practise this tense.

4 Go through the example with the class and point out how the prompts in the message have been turned into a spoken message. Students work with a partner to do the same with the remaining messages. Go around, offering help and encouragement. When checking answers, point out that there may be several correct answers.

SUGGESTED ANSWERS
See Listening script 1.17.

5 1.17 Play the recording for the students to compare their answers with the original voicemails. Emphasize that these are not the 'correct' answers. What the students have written may be just as valid.

1.17
Message A
Hi, it's Seiji. Listen, the negotiations here in Nagoya are going pretty well, but we seem to be deadlocked on price. Can you authorize me to offer them a 14% discount on 50,000 units? I think that should do it.

Message B
Hi, it's Jim. Listen, I'm in a bit of a panic. I'm at the Expo in Dublin and, you won't believe this, but I've lost the memory stick with my entire presentation on it! Could you email over my PowerPoint slides as attachments as soon as possible? Thanks!

Message C
Hi. Tony here. I'm still stuck in a meeting at head office. Are you making progress with the conference arrangements? Please make sure you contact the speakers to confirm their attendance. Cheers.

Message D
Hi, Kate here. I'm with the people from InfoTag in Seattle and they're querying our invoice for the third quarter. Can you ask someone in accounts to check the figures and reinvoice them if necessary? Thanks.

Message E
Hello, this is Alicia. This is urgent. I really need a copy of the Turin report from you by tomorrow afternoon at the latest. Call me straight back if you're having problems.

Message F
Hi there, this is Mike. Listen, I've got an appointment over at your offices on Friday. Do you want to meet up? Maybe go for a coffee or something? Oh, by the way, Ian sends his regards. Catch you later. Bye.

Returning a call

In this section, the students work on responding to a voicemail message.

1 1.18–1.19 Play Call 1 and do the questions relating to it before you play Call 2.

Make sure students have read the questions before they listen to the recording of Call 1 so that they know exactly what information they are listening for. Check answers before moving on to Call 2.

Again, make sure students have read the questions for Call 2 before they listen so that they concentrate on listening only for the information they need. Encourage discussion with a partner or in small groups for question f.

ANSWERS

Call 1
a Sylvia Wright's
b To know how the meeting with the people from Temco Supermarkets went.
c 1 Hello. This is Patterson Meats,
  2 Sylvia Wright's office. Thank you
  3 for calling. I'm afraid
  4 I'm not able to take
  5 your call right now,
  6 but if you'd like to leave
  7 a message
  8 please do so
  9 after the tone and I'll get back
  10 to you as soon as I can.

Call 2
a 2 b 1 c 2 d Sorry *about that*. I just *had to sign for something*. Where *were we?* e UK customers accepting kangaroo meat

1.18
Call 1

A: Hello. This is Patterson Meats, Sylvia Wright's office. Thank you for calling. I'm afraid I'm not able to take your call right now, but if you'd like to leave a message, please do so after the tone and I'll get back to you as soon as I can.

B: Hello, Sylvia. It's Tim Curtis from the Sydney office. I just wanted to know how the meeting with the people from Temco Supermarkets went. This is a really good chance for us to start exporting to Britain. I hope their visit was a success. Er, give me a ring when you get in, would you? Bye now.

1.19
Call 2

A: Hello. Tim Curtis.
B: Hi, Tim. It's Sylvia here. I got your message.
A: Sylvia, hi. So, how did it go?
B: It went pretty well, I think. They sent three people in the end.
A: Three? Well, that's a good sign.
B: Yeah, there was Bill Andrews, head of meat purchasing. I think you met him when you went to the UK last month.
A: That's right. He seemed pretty interested when I spoke to him then.
B: Yeah, he asked me a lot of questions about our quality control.
A: Uh huh. I thought he might. I hope you told him he's got no worries there.
B: I certainly did.
A: Good. So who else came? Er, did Stephanie Hughes come?
B: Er, they sent Jonathan Powell from their marketing department instead and Melanie Burns, who's in charge of imported produce.
A: Oh, right. I didn't meet them in London. So, did you show them the processing plant?
B: I did. There wasn't time to do a tour of the factory, but I showed them the packing department and the freezer units. Then we gave the presentation – Ian and I – and took them out to dinner afterwards.
A: Great. Did they say when they'd let us know? I mean, do you think they'll place an order or not?
B: Well, it's too early to say. But I think they were quite impressed.
A: Hmm.
B: They said they'd be in touch in the next couple of days or so. They were a bit worried at first about British customers accepting our product. Although they do sell other exotic meats already. Ostrich, for example, and that's quite popular.
A: Erm, excuse me for a moment, Sylvia … Sorry about that. I just had to sign for something. Where were we? Oh, yeah, they were worried about UK customers accepting our product, you say?
B: Well, I don't think it's a problem. Er, you know what the Brits are like – animal lovers and all that. They weren't sure if people would accept kangaroo meat as an alternative to beef.

BUSINESS COMMUNICATION

> **A:** Kangaroos are too cute and lovable to eat, huh?
> **B:** Well, something like that. But I told them they're not exactly endangered. There are twice as many kangaroos in Australia as there are Australians. Kangaroo's been on the menu here for years. They agreed it tastes good and, as I said to them, it's a really healthy option – ten times less fat than a beef steak and no chance of getting mad cow disease!

2 Students should not have much difficulty in putting these verbs into the Past Simple, so the time limit has been introduced to encourage them to work quickly and to give an element of fun. You could structure the activity as a race, with the winner being the first student to write all 14 verbs in the Past Simple and raise their hand.

ANSWERS
was/were, came, did, got, gave, went, had, met, said, sent, spoke, took, told, thought

3 Students should be able to identify fairly readily which extract is incorrect and why.

ANSWERS
Extract a is incorrect because the word order is wrong in both questions.

Language links
Direct students to the *Phrase bank* in the *Language links* section on page 19 for more on language for telephoning.

Finding out

In this final section, the focus is on getting students to put into practice all the skills they have learned in the unit so far. They have a choice of subjects on which to base their roleplay, and there is plenty of preparation work and guidance before they embark on their calls.

Make sure students don't just ask a series of questions when it is their turn to initiate the call. They have a lot of information to find out, but they must listen and react to their partner's answers to one question before they proceed to the next. It might also be useful to go over some of the language they could use to introduce each new question so that the impression of a list is reduced.
For example:

By the way, which … Oh, and I've been meaning to ask, what … And I was wondering how long …

Focus attention on the useful phrases for showing interest in the box at the top of the page. If necessary, practise a few of these around the class by telling individual students some information and getting them to react appropriately.
For example:

You: *I've just won a lot of money.*
Student 1: *Great!*
You: *I've just bought a new car.*
Student 2: *Really?*

You: *Someone I haven't seen for 20 years is coming to dinner on Sunday.*
Student 3: *Oh, that's interesting.*

Ask the students first to decide what the subject of their phone calls will be and then to look at the relevant sections of notes and decide not only how to ask the different questions, but also how they will answer the questions their partner is likely to ask. They can then roleplay their calls. Roleplayed phone calls often work better when students are seated back to back and cannot see each other.

When students have done their roleplays, encourage some of them to perform them for the rest of the class.

1:1 Agree with your student which situations to roleplay, and give the student a chance to be both the person asking for information and the person supplying it. Remember to set a good example by reacting to what your students says, using some of the useful phrases in the box at the top of the page.

Language links

ANSWERS

Vocabulary

Telephone expressions
a 7 b 5 c 1 d 4 e 2 f 8 g 9 h 3 i 6

Grammar

Past Simple
1 A *Did* Enrique *phone* about those figures?
  B No. I *waited* all morning, but he *didn't phone*.
  A Typical! And I suppose he didn't *do* the report either.
  B No. Did he *go* to the meeting yesterday?
  A No, but I *didn't expect* him to.
2 hurried, occupied, referred, conferred, dropped, flopped, committed, transmitted, played, enjoyed, offered, suffered, developed, visited
Verbs that change the *y* to an *i* to form the Past Simple tend to be multi-syllable verbs with the stress on the first syllable. *Play* is a one-syllable verb and *enjoy* has the stress on the second syllable. Single syllable verbs with short vowel sounds before a consonant and multi-syllable verbs with the stress on the final syllable double the consonant. *Offer*, *suffer* and *visit* have the stress on the first syllable, and *develop* has the stress on the middle syllable.

Time adverbs
3 a ago b before c For d over e During f In
4 a wanted b were c decided d asked e was
  f lit g thought h said i had j took k pressed
  l showed m worked n stated o could p proved
  q turned r put s got t went u closed v came
  w sat x leaned y whispered
5 a 1 b Stefan told him. c 3
  d Who did *you* tell? *Who* told you?
6 a Who *said* so?; So where *did he say* we're moving to?
  b What *happened*?; What *did I say*?
  c And what *did she think*?; So who else *came* to the meeting?

Phrase bank: Telephoning
1 a C b C c C d R e R f B g C
  h R i B j B k B l R m C n C o C
2 It is more polite because it is more formal and less direct.

22 02 MAKING CALLS

03 Keeping track

Learning objectives

Meetings in a foreign language pose a problem for many business students. Loss of concentration in meetings is one issue, and inability to obtain clarification on points that have been missed or misunderstood can be an obstacle to business success.

This unit provides some simple techniques which students can use to keep themselves abreast of what is being said. Then they learn some formulae for asking for clarification, checking what people have said and asking them to repeat or slow down. These can go a long way towards making students more adept at dealing with meetings in English.

The grammatical focus is on comparatives and superlatives, and the lexical focus is on phrasal verbs.

Digital resources: Unit 3

Online Workbook; 📹 In company interviews Units 1–3 and worksheet; Extension worksheets; Glossary; Phrase bank; Student's Book answer key; Student's Book listening script; Fast-track map

---

In this first section, students examine the problem of conducting meetings in a foreign language.

Warm-up

Read the quotation from Mike Murphy to the class and ask for reactions. How often have they attended meetings which they felt were a complete waste of time? How do they ensure that the meetings they attend are productive?

1 The aim is for students to identify what kind of speaker they find the hardest to understand in meetings. Have a class discussion on this question. If anyone has an interesting story about a time they misunderstood something in a meeting, encourage them to tell the class about it.

2 Ask students to work individually to complete the sentences with the missing pairs of words.

ANSWERS

a missed; say   b catch; slow   c understand; explain   d 'm; go
e follow; run   f see; be

3 Once students have identified which expressions you can use when you didn't hear and when you didn't understand, give students practice in using these expressions by saying something to them in a way that will make it very hard for them to understand, for example, mumbling, speaking too fast or too softly, being too general, etc. Select individual students and elicit an appropriate response from them.

ANSWERS

1 a, b   2 c, d, e, f

4 When the students have matched the verbs to their meanings, encourage them to produce example sentences using them.

ANSWERS

a 2   b 3   c 1

Language links

Direct students to the *Language links* section on page 24 for some common business phrasal verbs.

5 Bring to the class enough dice for pairs to have one each. This game helps students to remember the key expressions in 2 by giving them only a few prompt words to use to reproduce them. They throw the dice and recreate the sentence for that number.

Sorry?

In this section, students practise clarifying information that they have not understood.

1, 2 🔊 1.20 Once students have completed the sentences and have checked the answers by listening to the recording, you could give them more practice by devising some more prompt sentences to feed to individual students who then have to come up with appropriate clarification questions. Respond to their questions and encourage them to end the exchange with one of the expressions used in the exercise.

Here are some extra prompts you might use:
Our main difficulty is the timing of the project.
We have to deliver these units by February 25th.
New equipment will cost us at least $25,000.

Alternatively, ask the students to prepare some suitable prompts themselves and have conversations with a partner.

ANSWERS

a what   b when   c how much   d who   e where   f how long

🔊 **1.20**

Extract a
A: The problem is money.
B: Sorry, what did you say?
A: The problem is money.
B: Oh, as usual.

Extract b
A: We have to reach a decision by next week.
B: Sorry, when did you say?
A: Next week.
B: Oh, I see.

03 KEEPING TRACK 23

BUSINESS COMMUNICATION

Extract c
A: An upgrade will cost $3,000.
B: Sorry, how much did you say?
A: Three thousand dollars, at least.
B: Oh, as much as that?

Extract d
A: Ildikó Dudás spoke to me about it yesterday.
B: Sorry, who did you say?
A: Ildikó Dudás – from the Budapest office.
B: Oh, yes, of course.

Extract e
A: The company is based in Taipei.
B: Sorry, where did you say?
A: In Taipei.
B: Oh, really?

Extract f
A: The whole project might take 18 months.
B: Sorry, how long did you say?
A: Eighteen months.
B: Oh, as long as that?

3 Students decide who will be Speaker A and Speaker B. They then turn to their respective pages to read their parts of the article about Adidas and Puma aloud, with their partner asking for clarification where necessary. Make sure that as they do this they are genuinely making the words in bold difficult to hear or understand and that their clarification questions are appropriate.

4 Elicit some examples of comparatives and superlatives. Ask students to underline those they find in the article. Students can work together to find them and this will give them a chance to read their partner's part of the text

ANSWERS
(Part 1) the second and third biggest sportswear manufacturers, two of the most profitable and globally recognized brands, by far the greatest athlete of his day, steadily grew worse and worse, a great deal more than just professional rivalry; (Part 2) over four times bigger than Puma, the world's leading soccer brand, the fastest man ever, not quite as prominent in soccer as Adidas, considerably greater presence, the number one producer, best-selling shoes, few family business break up as dramatically as the Dasslers did, even half as successful, twice as many local job opportunities

5 Students work with a partner to complete the quiz. Encourage stronger students to work out the answers without looking back at the article or their answers to 4.

ANSWERS
A second biggest   B third most profitable   C least   D by far
E worse; worse   F lot; great deal   G Twice as   H Half as
I Four times   J most; ever   K best-selling; leading

Language links
Direct students to the *Language links* section on pages 24–25 for further explanation of the construction and use of comparatives and superlatives, and exercises to practise them.

Didn't I say that?

In this section, students practise techniques for dealing politely and appropriately with situations where they disagree about facts in meetings.

Warm-up
Ask students if they have had any experience of having to correct inaccuracies in what someone has said. Encourage them to tell the class of any incidents they can remember and what strategies they used for correcting the person without causing offence.

1 Read the explanation with the class and then ask them to look at the examples in the side panel. Point out that in each case B is politely correcting a factual mistake that B thinks A has made and that B is sure that his or her information is correct. By doing this indirectly, asking a question rather than simply stating what is wrong, the correction is softened. Intonation is also important here. A tone of mild puzzlement is polite in these situations; intonation suggesting astonishment would be impolite. Read one of B's lines first with intonation suggesting astonishment and then with intonation suggesting slight puzzlement so that students can hear the difference. Then ask students to practise the conversations with a partner.

2 Students take turns to read and respond to the statements. Go around making sure that their intonation is appropriate. Encourage students also to use *Isn't it …?* and *Shouldn't that be …?* where appropriate.

SUGGESTED ANSWERS
a Belgium? Don't you mean the Netherlands?
b Japanese? Don't you mean Korean?
c 1998? Wasn't it 1997?
d Hardware? Shouldn't that be software?
e Ford™? Don't you mean Tata Motors?
f America? Shouldn't that be Finland?
g News? Don't you mean music?
h Yahoo®? Isn't that Google?
i The Taipei 101? Shouldn't that be the Burj Khalifa?

1:1 Having only one student gives you the opportunity to do plenty of work on getting the intonation right. Don't forget to demonstrate the effect that the wrong intonation can have on the person who is being corrected by having your student give some information and then correcting it with intonation that suggests astonishment. However, you will probably want to let your student do all the correcting, with you reading out the false information in 2 in order to give them the maximum amount of practice.

3 Students work individually to invent their own false statements for the rest of the class to correct. This could be done in the form of a team game with teams writing a series of false statements. The opposing team has to come up with an appropriate correction in order to win a point.

BUSINESS COMMUNICATION

1:1 Make sure you have prepared a number of false business facts in advance which you are sure your student will be able to correct. The point is not to catch them out on their business knowledge, but to provide opportunities for them to practise the language of polite correction, so don't choose obscure information.

4 🔊 **1.21** Give students a few minutes to read the sentences before you play the recording so they can identify exactly what information they are listening for. Check the answers before moving on to 5.

ANSWERS
Sentences a, c and d are correct.

🔊 **1.21**

A: Okay, so, just to give you a summary of the sales figures for last month.
B: Last month? Don't you mean this month?
A: No, I mean last month. This month's figures aren't ready yet, are they?
B: Oh, no, of course not. Sorry.
A: So, overall, sales for last month are up again – by 2.6%, in fact, which is pretty good.
C: Er, 2.6%? Shouldn't that be 6.2?
A: Yeah, up by 6.2%. Didn't I say that?
C: No, you said 2.6.
A: Oh, ... right. Well, you know what I mean. So, anyway, the thing is, we're getting the best results in Denmark and Norway – 30,000 units.
C: Thirty thousand? That doesn't sound right to me. Thirteen thousand, surely?
A: No, the figures are here – Denmark and Norway: 30,000 units.
B: Denmark and Norway? Are you sure? That can't be right. Sales have never been good in Scandinavia.
A: That's just the point. Sales in Scandinavia are usually terrible, but they were excellent in June.
C: June? Isn't it July we're talking about?
A: July! Yes, of course, July! If you'd just let me finish! What I want to know is if we could sell our product in Scandinavia in June, ...
C: July.
A: ... in July, then why can't we sell it there every month?
B: Good point. Have you spoken to John about it?
A: John? You mean Jim.
B: Jim, yes. Whoever's in charge of Northern Europe these days.
A: Jim Munroe. I couldn't. He had to fly to Scotland. His mother's ill apparently.
C: There must be some mistake.
A: Hmm?
C: Well, I saw Jim this morning as I was coming in – on his way to play golf, by the look of it.
A: What? Are you sure? Wait till I see him!

5 🔊 **1.21** Play the recording again, and then ask individual students to correct sentences b, e, f and g.

ANSWERS
b Overall, sales are up by 6.2%.
e Last month was July.
f Jim Monroe is head of Northern Europe.
g Munroe is not in Scotland. He is playing golf.

6 The expressions given here are useful when something does not sound quite right, but you are less sure about what is wrong. Students should be able to complete the expressions without listening to the recording again, but be prepared to play it if necessary. Note that these expressions don't represent the total response to a mistake. The person using them is likely to go on to say what they think the real facts are, as in the examples in the box at the top of the page: *Isn't it ...? Don't you mean ...? Shouldn't that be ...?*

You could invite students to make up some more false statements and practise using the expressions to respond to each other's statements. Make sure they use follow-up questions to establish what they think the facts are.

ANSWERS
a sure   b mistake   c right   d sound

7 It doesn't matter how many of these the students actually get right, as disagreement over the facts will lead to more language practice. Students can find the correct answers on page 126 of their books.

8 Ask a pair of students to demonstrate the example conversation. Then the rest of the class work with a partner, and decide who will be Speaker A and Speaker B. They should then turn to their respective pages and follow the instructions there. The discrepancies are fairly obvious, but you might like to check in a feedback session that everyone has understood them. You could ask students to explain the discrepancies for homework.

ANSWERS

Speaker A
a Dublin is in Ireland, not Scotland.
b Citroën is a French car, not a German car.
c Ulrike can't be one of the speaker's closest friends if he or she only met her today.
d Someone who eats as many as ten chocolates a day cannot be said to have nearly given up chocolates.
e If the woman is the speaker's wife, he cannot introduce someone to her husband as that is himself.

Speaker B
a One of each means one of each gender. There are only two genders, male and female, so if the speaker has three children, they can't be one of each gender. Two of them must be the same gender.
b Lisbon is the capital of Portugal, so the French negotiating team would not have their headquarters there.
c Dutch is the language of the Netherlands, not Denmark.
d If the managing director is 70, then his grandfather is unlikely still to be alive, let alone running the company.
e A company called Network Software is more likely to make computer software than domestic appliances.

03 KEEPING TRACK 25

BUSINESS COMMUNICATION

The briefing meeting

1.22 Go through the instructions carefully and allow students time to read the notes so they know exactly what information they are listening for.

When you have checked the answers, ask the students if they have ever experienced a situation where they were expecting to do one job and suddenly found that they had to do something completely different.

ANSWERS
a Daniel Cash   b VP for corporate finance   c Hall
d in charge of corporate loan department   e White
f mergers and acquisitions specialist   g Sellers   h interpreter
i Empire House   j leading the negotiations
k two o'clock tomorrow   l 13th

1.22

A: So, welcome to Tokyo, Matt. It's good to have you on the team.
B: Thanks, Sally. It's good to be here.
A: I think you're going to enjoy your three months here, Matt. Now, this is Sharon Hall. She's the person you'll mostly be working with on the project.
C: Hi, Matt.
B: Hi … Sorry, I didn't catch your name.
C: Sharon. Sharon Hall.
B: Hi, Sharon.
A: Sharon's in charge of our corporate loan department. She's sorting out an office for you at the moment You'll probably be working over at Empire House.
B: Sorry, where did you say?
C: Empire House. It's our office building on the other side of town.
B: Oh, okay.
A: Don't worry, I'll take you over there later. Now, you and Sharon will be reporting directly to Daniel Cash, our VP for corporate finance.
B: Sorry, who?
C: Daniel Cash.
B: Oh, right. And he's the vice-president for …?
A: Corporate finance. I thought you two had met? Anyway, Daniel's had to rush off to a meeting, but he told me to say he'd meet you both at two tomorrow.
B: Sorry, I don't understand. I thought the whole team was meeting tomorrow at nine?
A: We were. But, er, something came up. Anyway, Sharon can fill you in on most of it. Sharon?
C: Yes, you'll have two assistants working with you, Matt. Janet White and Robin Sellers.
B: Okay, Janet White and Robin …?
C: Sellers. Janet's our top mergers and acquisitions specialist. I think you two will get on well. She'll be helping you with your research. And Robin's your interpreter. He's very familiar with business procedures here – as well as being fluent in Japanese, of course.
B: Sorry, I'm not with you. Interpreter? What do I need an interpreter for? I thought I was just here as an advisor.

A: Erm … The situation's changed a little since we last spoke, Matt. We'd now like you to lead the negotiations with the Sapporo Bank. In fact, that will be your main responsibility.
B: I don't quite see what you mean, Sally. Erm, I'm no negotiator, especially not for a takeover as big as this. I'm the guy with the pocket calculator. I just make sure the figures add up.
C: Oh, come on, Matt. You're too modest. We know your track record. Janet can take care of the figures. We want you to lead the first round of negotiations on the 13th.
B: You mean the 30th, right? The 13th is next week.
A: That's right. We've scheduled the first meeting for next Wednesday. Janet will be able to brief you before then. This is your big chance. I'm counting on you, Matt. I know you won't let me down.

In company interviews Units 1–3
Encourage students to watch the interview and complete the worksheet.

Language links

ANSWERS
Vocabulary
Business phrasal verbs
a on
   continue = move on; accept = take on; rely = count on; wait = hold on
b out
   say = point out; discover = find out; do = carry out; solve = sort out
c off
   fire = lay off; end = break off; cancel = call off; postpone = put off
d up
   rise = go up; raise = put up; arrange = fix up; develop = build up
e down
   reduce = cut down; relax = calm down; reject = turn down; decrease = go down

Grammar
Comparatives and superlatives
1 clever 1, hot 3, dirty 4, helpful 5, hard 1, heavy 4, high 1, global 5, bad 6, wealthy 4, easy 4, rich 1, sad 3, thin 3, fat 3, late 2, effective 5, reliable 5
One- and two-syllable adjectives tend to take the -er and -est endings, sometimes with changes of spelling. Three-syllable adjectives use more and most to form the comparative and superlative.
3 a world's highest   b much better   c a lot more
   d little safer   e even worse   f by far the lowest
   g compared with   h 10% longer   i twice as likely
   j significantly happier   k as famous as   l a little more

Phrase bank: Checking understanding
a … didn't hear?
b … didn't understand?
c … understood differently?
The effect of using the words in brackets is to make the expressions less direct and therefore more polite.

04 Listening

Learning objectives

This unit is about the skill of listening. Students read a text about effective listening and the importance of being a good listener in a business context. They listen to conversations and identify the main problem in each one, before learning about some techniques for becoming a good listener. In further conversations, they identify the main topic of conversation and which of the listening techniques the listener is using. Some useful language is presented for putting the skills they have been learning about into practice and they then have the opportunity to practise active listening skills with a partner.

Digital resources: Unit 4

Online Workbook; Extension worksheets; Glossary; Student's Book answer key; Student's Book listening script; Fast-track map

1:1 Make sure that your own active listening skills are good so that you can demonstrate the techniques and advice presented in this unit when you are listening to your student!

Warm-up

Ask the students to brainstorm ideas for what makes someone a good listener. Make sure they understand that this doesn't mean someone with good hearing, but someone who has skills that make them easy to talk to; the sort of person that people go to when they want someone to listen to their problems or their concerns. Put the students' ideas on the board and leave them there as you may want to refer back to these ideas later when they discuss effective listening skills later in the lesson.

1 Focus attention on the cartoon, and elicit or explain that the CEO is not a good listener because he talks too much and listens only to himself, not to other people. Have a class discussion of the two questions, but don't push the point if discussion of real people known to the students is a sensitive cultural issue. Put any useful vocabulary which emerges on the board for students to use later.

2 Ask students to work individually to complete the sentences and then to discuss their sentences with a partner. Have a class feedback session to find out how much consensus there is about what is irritating and rude, and what kind of behaviour is acceptable.

3 Give students plenty of time to read the article, and then go back and find where the statistics are mentioned. Discuss as a class whether any of them are surprising.

ANSWERS

80%: according to research by Roffey Park, 80% of managers do not listen well
4–5: people think four to five times faster than they can speak
700wpm: 700 words per minute is the speed at which people think
¾: according to Nichols and Stevens, three-quarters of the average employee's working day is spent in conversation
½: approximately half of that time they are required to listen
25%: most employees are only 25% effective as listeners
$50,000 and $14,000: Nichols and Stevens estimate that an employee earning $50,000 a year is paid $14,000 of that not to listen
2:1: the number of ears we have relative to our one mouth!

4 🔊 **1.23** Play each extract in turn, pausing the recording and asking the class to discuss what is going wrong. You may need to play it more than once to allow them to do this. Finally, ask them to summarize the main problem in each conversation.

SUGGESTED ANSWERS

Extract a James is a particularly inattentive listener, whose mind seems to be on something else throughout the conversation. Perhaps he believes in multitasking, but it sounds like he's not very good at it! Perhaps Ingrid should have realized sooner that it would be better to come back later when James is not so distracted.
Extract b Tim and Nicole both seem to want to talk at the same time! There's far too much interruption throughout their conversation. Of course, as Tim points out, this is a conversation they've had many times before, but the fact that they're having it again suggests that they finally need to listen to each other.
Extract c Mr Hepburn has the unfortunate and irritating habit of finishing other people's sentences for them. Occasionally, this can show that you're paying attention and listening closely to what the other person is saying. But, more often, it makes the other speaker feel like they're an unnecessary part of the conversation. And, of course, the danger is that you assume you know what the other person is going to say when you don't – as Mr Hepburn finds out to his cost!

🔊 **1.23**
Extract a
A: James, do you have a minute? ... James?
B: Oh, hi, Ingrid ... Err, sorry, what was that?
A: Well, it's just that I need to have a word with you about the quarterlies. But if you're busy, I can come back later.
B: Yeah, okay ... I mean no, no, that's fine ... Sorry, what was it you wanted to talk to me about?
A: The quarterlies, James. Only the meeting's on Friday, and I still haven't received figures from Hugh and Alison ... James?
B: Yes, yes, I'm listening! Erm, so Alison still hasn't sent you her figures?
A: No, she hasn't, but I'm dealing with that. It's Hugh I'm having problems with.
B: Hugh? I thought we were talking about Alison.

04 LISTENING 27

PEOPLE SKILLS

A: And Hugh, James! This is the third time now he's been late with his quarterlies. I keep sending him reminders and he keeps ignoring them! I thought you might talk to him.

B: Hmm, would you like me to talk to him?

A: That's what I just ... Look, James, you're obviously in the middle of something else. I think I'd better talk to you later when you can give me your undivided attention!

B: Sorry, Ingrid, sorry! ... Okay, where were we?

Extract b

C: Tim, we really need to talk about your team's expense claims. Frankly, they're getting out of control. I don't how to put this, but some of these restaurant bills are just ridic ...

D: Nicole, we've discussed this before and, as I've told you ...

C: Tim, could I just finish what I was saying?

D: There's no need, Nicole. We have this same conversation just about every month, don't we?

C: But your team's total expenses are now almost twice as much as everyone else's! You know we have a set budget for ...

D: Nicole, let me stop you right there. My team has far more client contact than anyone else's! So it's hardly surprising we're spending more on meals and entertaining, now is it? And I might remind you that we are also bringing in a lot more business than any other team.

C: If you'd just let me finish ...

D: No, let me finish, Nicole! I have repeatedly asked for expense budgets to be performance-related and you have repeatedly blocked that idea because ...

C: Whoa, now wait a minute! I haven't blocked anything. As a matter of fact, ...

Extract c

E: Now, then, Mr Hepburn. There are obviously one or two details we still need to sort out, but, in principle, I think, er ...

F: ... we've got a deal?

E: Well, yes, I think so.

F: Splendid! So if you'll just sign here.

E: Erm, yes, of course, in just a moment. Now, as you know, reliability ...

F: ... is a major concern for you. Yes, I know that. And, let me assure you, you have no worries there. You'll be one of our priority customers! I'll see you get the very best service.

E: Er, yes, well, that's good to know. It has been quite a few years since we last did business with you. Must be at least ...

F: ... six years, as a matter of fact. I checked in our computer records.

E: Six years? Is it really that long? Well, anyway, you'll understand I just want to make sure ...

F: ... you don't end up with the wrong consignment like you did last time!`

E: I'm sorry?

F: The wrong consignment. We sent you the wrong consignment. And then it took us weeks to get the right one to you because of an administrative error. Rest assured, Ms de Vries, that won't happen again. We've got a completely new order system now. One hundred per cent efficient!

E: Erm, well, actually, I'd forgotten all about that consignment ... I was going to say we need to make sure you're able to shorten your delivery times whenever our stocks run low.

F: Ah.

E: But now you mention it, that delay we had six years ago did cause us all kinds of problems ... In fact, now I think of it, it was something of a nightmare. Erm, maybe I need to have another look at your proposal, Mr Hepburn, and get back to you on it in a couple of weeks.

F: Oh ...

5 Students work with a partner to match the guidelines to what you need to do. When you have checked answers, get the students to say whether they agree with the advice.

ANSWERS

a 4   b 1   c 5   d 3   e 6   f 2

6 1.24–1.27 Elicit or explain that the 'constructive' conversations they are about to hear are more successful ones, where the participants are good listeners. Ask students to listen and identify both the main topic of conversation and which of the listening skills in 5 the listener is using. You may need to pause the recording between extracts and play some of them again to allow the students time to do this. Perhaps pause after each one, and have a class discussion to identify the topic and the skill.

ANSWERS

Extract 1 Topic: Making training and development more efficient; Skill: Test understanding
Extract 2 Topic: Using digital business cards at an Expo event; Skill: Encourage
Extract 3 Topic: Replacing a project team member; Skill: Inquire
Extract 4 Topic: Implementing change; Skill: Summarize

1.24

Extract 1

A: Ian, I think it's time we had a chat about training.

B: Sure, Sally. What's on your mind?

A: Well, I've been looking at our annual spend on T&D and, frankly, it's pretty high.

B: Hmm, are you saying we've run over budget on that?

A: Well, no, we're still within budget – just. Don't worry. We keep a tight control on that. But when you look at the percentage of employees receiving training each year, it's only about 20% of them. For what we're spending, that doesn't seem very cost effective.

B: Do you mean we should be shopping around for cheaper training?

A: Well, that's certainly one thing we could do to save money. But I think it's more a question of efficiency.
B: What do you mean by 'efficiency'?
A: Well, look at this. Last year, we ran three separate time-management courses for three separate units in Italy. Couldn't we have put all those people on just one course?
B: Sorry, I'm not quite with you. Aren't there limits on the number of participants to get the maximum benefit?
A: Well, yes, of course, but most of these courses weren't even fully attended.
B: Oh, right.
A: So why don't we centralize training?
B: Centralize? How do you mean exactly? Don't we use freelancers for training?
A: Yes, but if we offered all training from the most central office in each country we operate in, we could combine courses, save money and actually train more people.
B: Mm, I see what you're saying …

1.25
Extract 2
A: Amund! Come on in. How's it going?
B: Oh, fine, Louise, fine. I'm pretty busy at the moment with the Expo arrangements. But it's all going well.
A: Oh, the Expo. Yes, of course. It's going well, you say?
B: Well, yes, I think so.
A: Great, great! Well now, you said you had an idea you wanted to run past me.
B: Er, yes. Well, you know how normally we give out hundreds of business cards at these events?
A: Uh huh.
B: And then people just lose them, throw them away or forget who it was that gave them to them in the first place!
A: Uh huh, go on.
B: Well, I found this company that produces fairly inexpensive digital business cards that look just like an ordinary business card, but you can put them into the CD drive of your computer and they contain all this multimedia content.
A: Really? Multimedia business cards, you say?
B: Yeah. I mean, you can put slideshows, animations, audio, video, everything on them – a full company presentation, client testimonials, commercials, show-reels, the lot.
A: Oh, that's interesting. Video and slideshows would be great.
B: Exactly. I mean, we are a media company, after all. Shouldn't our business cards be a little more high-tech than a piece of cardboard?
A: Right, I'm with you. Good point. So how much are these cards?
B: Well, if we order a thousand, it works out at less than a euro per card. I mean, that would be a fortune for a normal business card, I know. But this is the sort of thing people will make sure they don't throw away

because they'll want to see what's on it. What do you think?
A: Hmm, nice idea. I like it. Of course, we'd have to put the content together.
B: No problem. Leave that to me.
A: Okay, then, let's give them a try. Order a thousand and we'll see what the response is …

1.26
Extract 3
A: Maria, are you busy? I need to talk to you about Jeanne.
B: Problem?
A: Well, you remember how she blew up at last week's kick-off meeting?
B: How will I ever forget? Have you spoken to her about that?
A: I have, but I'm afraid it didn't do much good. Seems like there's just a lot of bad chemistry between her and the rest of the team.
B: Hmm.
A: Anyway, I've given the situation some thought. And I've decided to pull her off the project altogether.
B: Oh, really? Do you think that's wise? I mean, how is that going to affect our timeline? Jeanne's the most experienced person we've got working on this.
A: I know, but I'm thinking of bringing Martin in to take over her role.
B: Martin? Yes, he's good. But wouldn't that mean taking him off the Minerva project?
A: It would, but, to be honest, I think he's rather wasted on that.
B: Oh, why do you say that?
A: Well, Minerva's not really a priority right now, is it? And I think we could use Martin better on this. Besides, Martin thinks the whole project should be targeted much more towards the Latin American market. And, frankly, I agree with him.
B: Latin America? Are you sure? Do you have figures for that?
A: I do, as a matter of fact. I'll email them over to you.
B: Okay, fine. Just one question: what are you going to do about Jeanne?
A: Oh, don't worry about that. Leave Jeanne to me.

1.27
Extract 4
A: So, Grant, how are people in your unit reacting to these new structural changes to the company?
B: Well, we've had a lot of mixed reactions, to be honest. It's not been easy.
A: So what you're saying is you're getting some push-back from your people.
B: Well, some resistance certainly. But, I mean, that's normal when you're implementing change on a scale like this. It's really a question of keeping people informed, managing their expectations, you know …

04 LISTENING 29

PEOPLE SKILLS

A: Hmm, it sounds like you think we should be having more information-sharing meetings.

B: Yes, that's right. I think it's important to be open and honest about what's happening and how it will affect people at all levels of the company.

A: In other words, show people that we have nothing to hide, that we're not doing anything behind their backs. We want to involve them.

B: Right.

A: Okay, so the way you see it is we need more openness, more transparency. I think I'd go along with that. Does anyone else have any views on this? Yeah, Alicia.

C: Well, I agree with a lot of what Grant says, but I also think we need to deal better with people's fears. We need to be preventing rumours flying around; showing people that, in many ways, it's business as usual.

A: So, for you, it's a question of restoring some stability. Yes, that's a good point. Okay, well, thanks for your input, everybody. I think it's good to be discussing these issues at this stage …

7 1.24–1.27 Encourage students to try to do the exercise without listening to the recordings again, but play it if they need to hear it to find the answers. Then play it again for them to check.

ANSWERS
a 4   b 1   c 2   d 3

8 Go through the instructions with the class and make sure everyone understands what they have to do. Students work with a partner and choose one of the extracts to read out. Each student must follow the instructions in brackets in their partner's text and then respond to their partner's comments on their own text, so they should look through their partner's text to work out what they are going to say at each point and at their own text to prepare answers for what their partner is likely to say. Allow plenty of time for them to prepare and remind them of the useful expressions in 7. When they are ready, ask them to take turns reading out their texts and responding to what their partner is saying in the way indicated. Go around monitoring, assisting and taking note of any particularly good examples which could be repeated for the class.

1:1 It may be tempting to get your student to take the role of listener for both texts as you read them out, as this would give them extra practice in being a good listener. However, this would deny them the opportunity to practise responding to a good listener. So take the role of listener for one of the texts and get your student to read it out.

9 Ask students to work with a partner. Tell them to turn to page 127 and follow the instructions. There is quite a lot to do in this exercise, so you could ask students to choose their topics in class but do the preparation work at home so that they are ready to do the speaking part in the next lesson. Remind them that they will need to listen to each other carefully so that they can do the summarizing part of the activity.

1:1 Prepare two of the topics yourself so that your student can practise being a good listener and summarizing what you say.

MANAGEMENT SCENARIO A

The networking event

Learning objectives

This scenario is based on the issue of effective networking. Students begin by discussing their own experience of attending a network event and then read descriptions of types of people they are likely to meet at such an event. They then watch a video in which the sales manager of an IT company attends a small business networking event and meets a variety of people. They assess how well he deals with them and discuss how he might improve his networking skills. After reading an article giving advice on getting the most out of networking, they watch another video and compare the sales manager's performance this time around. Finally, they practise their own networking skills with a partner and evaluate their own performance.

Digital resources: Management Scenario A

In company in action A1–A2 and worksheet; Extension worksheets; Glossary; Student's Book answer key; Student's Book listening script; Fast-track map

Warm-up

Focus attention on the photo and ask students to say where they think the people are and what they are doing.

1 Go through the instructions and give students time to read the web page and find the answers to the questions.

ANSWERS

a In the OXO2 Events Space at the OXO Tower Wharf in London on 27 June.
b CIO = Chief Information Officer (sometimes referred to as CTO, Chief Technology Officer), MIS = Management Information System.
c There's going to be a short talk by Adrian Moore, CIO for Radcliffe Hotels, followed by a mix-and-mingle session with a gourmet breakfast.
d It's to help delegates to keep in touch and develop business relationships with the contacts they make (and the ones they didn't get the opportunity to speak to) after the event.

2 Have a class discussion of the questions and encourage students to tell each other about their own experiences of networking events. If no one has ever attended one, ask them to say how useful they think they would be, and what sorts of people they would hope and expect to meet at one.

3 Give students time to read the descriptions, then ask them to match them to the four networker types. Check answers before asking students to say if they have ever met anyone who matches any of these types. If so, ask them to say how they dealt with the person and how they felt about it. You could also ask if anyone will admit to having acted in these ways themselves.

ANSWERS

a 1   b 3   c 4   d 2

1:1 Ask your student to talk about his/her experience of networking and the kinds of people encountered. Be prepared to describe experiences of your own to help the conversation along.

4 A1 Go through the instructions with students before playing the video and asking them to assess how well Anton deals with the different people he meets. As preparation for this exercise, you might like to play the video with the sound off first and ask students to try to identify which person he meets is which type of networker by looking at such things as their body language and Anton's reaction to them. Have a class discussion of how well Anton deals with them and be prepared to play sections of the video again if there is any disagreement.

ANSWERS

The autobiographer   2 ☹ (Anton is unable to get a word in!)
The time waster   4 ☺ (Anton successfully manages to get an appointment, but his contact does not yet seem ready to buy.)
The escape artist   3 ☹ (Anton is left with someone he didn't plan to speak to while his contact goes and talks to someone else.)
The hard seller   1 ☺ (Anton successfully makes his escape.)

A1

Randall: Mr Vega?
Anton: Er, yes?
Randall: Of FIS?
Anton: That's right, yes.
Randall: I thought so! Randall Holmes. Superway Routers and Switches. Perhaps you've heard of us?
Anton: Um, pleased to meet you, Mr Holmes. Superway? No, I don't think I have …
Randall: We're based in San Diego, but I'm from the Zurich office. And I have been trying to speak to you all morning. I'm fairly sure we're more competitively priced than the suppliers that you're currently using and I'd like to fix a meeting to run some figures by you. Who are your current suppliers, by the way, if you don't mind my asking?
Anton: Um, well, actually, we use a number of suppliers. The thing is, Mr Holmes …
Randall: Please call me Randall.
Anton: Right, Randell. The thing is, I've arranged to meet someone at, er, ten …
Randall: Here's my card.

A THE NETWORKING EVENT   31

MANAGEMENT SCENARIO

Anton: Oh, right, thank you. Oh, right, yes, here's mine. Er, yeah, the thing is, I've arranged to meet someone at ten, so perhaps we could continue this conversation later. Or better still, email me some quotes and I'll, er, give you a call if we're interested, okay? Great to meet you. Bye now.

Estela: So, as I was saying, Beauclerc has been in business now for over 120 years and we have always been at the forefront of pharmaceutical research.
Anton: Yes, and I would imagine that you require very sophisticated IT systems to manage the different areas of your research?
Estela: In fact, I don't know if you know this, but we played a major part in the development of the first tuberculosis vaccine.
Anton: Really?
Estela: In my day, it was all about molecular modelling. But today, of course, gene therapy is the thing, biotechnology. It has completely changed the pharmaceutical industry, I can tell you.
Anton: Yes, it must have. So what sort of IT arrangement do you have at the moment?
Estela: And quantum chemistry, now there's something you've probably never even heard about.
Anton: No, I must confess, I haven't …
Estela: Ah, yes! Let me tell you, it's very exciting, you should come and see all the research …

Anton: So, you see, with a supply chain management system like this, you don't ever need to waste money upgrading for new features you don't require.
Jennifer: Oh, really?
Anton: Well, no, you just add on what you want, er, through a series of apps. In a way, it works just like a smartphone.
Jennifer: Ah, Lucy! This is who you really need to be speaking to about this, Anton. Lucy Tan. CIO for Northern Star Transport. Lucy, this is Anton Vega, sales manager for FIS.
Anton: Pleased to meet you.
Lucy: Nice to meet you.
Jennifer: They design management information systems like yours. Didn't you say you were in the market for a new SCM system?
Lucy: Um, well, we might be.
Jennifer: Perfect, I'll leave you two together to talk business. I must go and say hello to Adrian. Poor man. No one's said a word to him since he finished his talk.
Anton: So, you say you're thinking of replacing your SCM system?
Lucy: Well, it's not a priority right now, but yes we are looking at upgrading the system …
Anton: Well, it's fortunate I'm here because …

Anton: So that's the whole system. Are there any other questions you'd like to ask me?
Lucy: No, I don't think so. I think I've got a pretty good idea now of how this might improve efficiency for us.
Anton: Great. So shall we fix a time to meet and look at some figures?
Lucy: Um, well, as I said, it's not really a priority for us right now.
Anton: Ah.
Lucy: I mean, this is all very interesting, but I'd have to have my tech team take a look at it first. For something so specialized I need their input before proceeding any further.
Anton: So, why don't I let you do that and give you a call in, say, a week?
Lucy: Um …
Anton: How about Wednesday? Or would Thursday suit you better?
Lucy: Um … Well, Thursday would be better than Wednesday. It would have to be in the morning, though …
Anton: Okay, shall we say eleven?
Lucy: Er, yes, all right, eleven's fine.
Anton: Great, I'll speak to you again then. Nice to meet you.
Lucy: Yes, likewise.

5 Students work with a partner to discuss the questions. Ask them to report back to the class on the advice they would give Anton to improve his networking skills.

SUGGESTED ANSWER

b Anton clearly needs to be better at politely bringing unproductive conversations to a close. He also needs to be more assertive with people who dominate conversations. With people who don't give him their full attention, he should offer to talk to them at another time.

6 Give students plenty of time to read the article, or set it for homework. Answer any questions on difficult vocabulary and ask them to complete the comments on the right. They should compare answers with a partner before you have a class feedback session to see how much consensus there is. The comment about attitudes to small talk in particular may produce some interesting answers if you have a multinational class.

7 A2 Go through the instructions with the class and establish that in the second video clip, students will see Anton having more success at the networking event. Ask them to watch and identify which advice from the article in 6 he has taken.

SUGGESTED ANSWER

Anton starts the conversation by referring to a talk he saw Fischer give at a conference the year before and paying him a compliment about it. (Rule number one: Start with small talk.) He listens well and uses what Fischer tells him about failing to reach a deal with FIS on a previous occasion as the basis for setting up another possible meeting. He reinforces this by offering to introduce Fischer to an ex-colleague from business school. (Rule number three: Find out what you can do for others.) He closes by agreeing to meet in a few weeks if Fischer is still interested in FIS's new app store. (Rule number four: Keep it short and arrange to meet again.)

A THE NETWORKING EVENT

🎥 A2

Anton: Dr Fischer? Schmeiser Group?

Fischer: Yes, that's right.

Anton: I thought so. I saw you speak at the Networx-IT Conference in Frankfurt last year. Very interesting talk.

Fischer: Ah. Well, thank you, Mr Vega. Oh, you're with FIS, I see. I spoke to someone from your sales team a short while ago. A Mr Zuckermann.

Anton: Sugarman. Alan Sugarman. Yes, he's one of our team.

Fischer: Yes, in fact, we nearly signed a deal with you for an MIS for our Hamburg office, but I'm afraid there were one or two difficulties.

Anton: Oh?

Fischer: Yes, in fact, the system your man Sugarman sent me was almost exactly what we wanted, but we were looking for something with a bit more flexibility.

Anton: Well, it's interesting you say that, because we now have our new app store for supply chain management software, which gives you almost total flexibility.

Fischer: Oh, really?

Anton: Yes, you can download what you want and delete what you don't as you go. You've got complete control.

Fischer: Well, that's interesting. Could you send me some information about that?

Anton: Of course.

Fischer: Let me give you my card.

Anton: And here's mine. Oh, I see you've moved to Cologne.

Fischer: Yes, that's right; we relocated there a couple of months ago.

Anton: As it happens, I'm going to be in Cologne in the next few weeks. If you like the look of our app store, why don't we fix up a time to meet?

Fischer: Yes, let's do that. Well, great to have met you, Mr Vega.

Anton: Likewise.

Fischer: Oh, look, there's Angela Pepperberg. I'd like to talk to her about a new project we're working on. Do you know Ms Pepperberg?

Anton: As a matter of fact, I do. We were in the same class at business school.

Fischer: Oh, really? At Wharton?

Anton: Yes. Why don't I introduce you?

Fischer: Would you?

Anton: No problem at all.

Fischer: Oh, that's very kind, thank you …

8 Ask students to turn to page 128 and follow the instructions there. They may need some time to prepare their profiles and business cards – this could be done for homework. Each student takes a turn to be Speaker A. Their partner can choose to be any one of the networking types listed. However, encourage them to play the more positive role of good networker at least once. It may be more fun to play the escape artist or the autobiographer, but these roles will not lead to as much language and skills practice. Point out that in 9 they will be required to evaluate their own performance so they will need to pay close attention to what happens in each of their conversations.

9 Focus attention on the feedback form on page 127 and ask students to complete it for themselves. Encourage them to show their form to the partner they worked with in 8 and see if their partner agrees with their evaluation.

05 Business travel

Learning objectives

Aspects of business travel covered in this unit include attitudes to travel, requests that business travellers might make and methods of coping with nightmare journeys involving a succession of problems. Students read about the modern phenomenon of living simultaneously in London and New York, and commuting between the two. This stimulates an exercise on differences between American and British English. The students then practise things people say when they meet business colleagues at the airport. The unit also has some travel tips from an experienced business traveller.

This unit teaches some useful expressions for talking about opinions on business travel, making requests, dealing with problems, greeting people at the airport and making polite conversation.

The grammar focus is on polite question forms and the lexical focus is on collocations relating to travel.

Digital resources: Unit 5

Online Workbook; Extension worksheets; Glossary Phrase bank; Student's Book answer key; Student's Book listening script; Fast-track map; Quick progress test 1

In this first section, students have an opportunity to explore their attitudes to business travel, and talk about what they like and dislike about it. They are introduced to ways of emphasizing opinions, and words other than *like* which they can use to make their conversations about likes and dislikes varied and interesting.

Warm-up

Focus attention on the quotation from Paul Theroux and ask students if they agree with it. Ask them to describe any 'remarkable' airplane journeys they have had.

1 Find out how often your students travel on business, where they generally go and whether they enjoy it. If they don't travel on business, ask them whether they would like to and what they imagine business travel entails.

2 To make this exercise more interactive, or to check the answers, you could get individual students to pick another student and then read out words from the first three sections for the other student to finish. That student then chooses another student and reads another set of words for completion by their chosen student, and so on. When checking answers, accept any combinations that make sense and are grammatically correct.

3 Go through the expressions for adding emphasis to opinions and then ask students to work in groups to practise using them. If students don't travel on business, remind them that they can talk about travelling in general. Encourage them from now on to use these expressions when they want to give a strong opinion.

Language links

Direct students to the *Language links* section on page 35 for more practice of language for business trips.

On the move

This section provides more useful structures relating to business travel. Students first listen to some conversations involving business travellers and identify where the speakers are. They then examine some of the language used, notably structures for making polite requests and enquiries. They then practise using them in new requests.

1 🔘 **1.28** Ask students to listen and identify where the speakers are, and write the correct numbers in the boxes. When you are checking the answers, you could ask students to tell you what clues they used to deduce where the people were.

ANSWERS
In the taxi: 7, 12, 16 On the plane: 5, 9, 15
At check-in: 2, 4, 10 At customs: 3, 11, 14
In departures: 8, 13, 18 At the hotel: 1, 6, 17

🔘 **1.28**

Conversation 1
A: Excuse me. Is there somewhere I could send a fax from?
B: Certainly, sir. There's a business centre on the third floor.

Conversation 2
A: Did you pack your bags yourself, sir?
B: Well, no, my wife ... Oh, er, I mean, yes. Yes, of course.

Conversation 3
A: Could I ask you to open your luggage, please, madam?
B: Oh ... all right. Will this take long? Only someone's meeting me.

Conversation 4
A: Window or aisle?
B: Er, window, please. But not near an emergency exit, if possible. You can't put the seats back.

Conversation 5
A: This is your captain speaking. We're now at our cruising altitude of 11,000 metres, making good time and just passing over the Costa Brava.
B: Oh, look. There it is. Full of British tourists.

BUSINESS COMMUNICATION

Conversation 6
A: Can you tell me what time you stop serving dinner?
B: Half past ten, madam. Are you a resident? I can reserve you a table if you like.

Conversation 7
A: Er, Heathrow airport, please. Terminal 1. I'm in a bit of a hurry.
B: Well, I'll do what I can, sir. But the traffic's terrible this morning. Some sort of accident it said on the radio. Might be quicker taking the Tube.

Conversation 8
A: British Airways regrets to announce the late departure of flight BA761 to Buenos Aires. This is due to the late arrival of the plane from Argentina. Estimated departure time is now 15.10.
B: Oh, here we go again!

Conversation 9
A: This is your captain speaking again. We're in for some turbulence, I'm afraid. So, for your own safety, would you please return to your seats and make sure your seatbelt is fastened while the 'fasten seatbelt' sign remains on. Thank you.
B: Erm, excuse me. You're sitting on my seatbelt. Thanks.

Conversation 10
A: I'm sorry, but this bag is too heavy to take on as hand luggage. You're only allowed six kilos. You'll have to check it in, I'm afraid, sir.
B: But I've got my computer and everything in there. And gifts for my family.

Conversation 11
A: I'm afraid I'll have to check your hand luggage too, madam. Could you open this side pocket? And, er, would you mind not smoking, please?
B: Oh, I'm sorry. I didn't realize.

Conversation 12
A: Have you got anything smaller, sir? Don't think I can change a twenty.
B: Uh? Oh, just a minute. I'll see.

Conversation 13
A: There has been a change to the schedule for flight BA761 to Buenos Aires. This flight will now depart from Gate 59. Would all passengers travelling to Buenos Aires please go to gate 59.
B: Gate 50-what?

Conversation 14
A: Right. That's fine, thank you, madam. You can go through now.
B: What! You've just unpacked everything in my suitcase! How am I supposed to go through like this?

Conversation 15
A: Could you switch off your laptop now, please, sir? We're about to land.
B: Uh? Oh, yes, of course.

Conversation 16
A: Here you are. Keep the change.
B: Oh, thank you very much, madam. Have a good flight.

Conversation 17
A: Excuse me. Erm, do you think I could have an alarm call at half past six tomorrow morning?
B: Certainly, madam. Could I have your room number, please?

Conversation 18
A: Good afternoon, ladies and gentlemen. Flight BA761 to Buenos Aires is now ready for boarding. Would you please have your passports and boarding cards ready for inspection.
B: And about time too!

2 Ask students to do this individually or with a partner, and then check answers. Help them to practise using the language by getting one student to read out the first part of a question and another student to finish it.

> **ANSWERS**
> a 2 b 3 c 4 d 1 e 6 f 5 g 8 h 7

> **Language links**

Direct students to the *Language links* section on pages 35–36 for further explanation of the construction of polite question forms and exercises to practise them.

3 Ask students to match the question beginnings in 2 with the new endings. Check answers by having one student ask a question and another give a response.

> **ANSWERS**
> borrow your mobile?: a
> buy some stamps?: a, b, e, h
> hurry or I'll miss my plane?: b, e
> which terminal I need?: d, f
> lending me some money until I find a cashpoint?: c
> to wait outside for five minutes?: f

Travel tips

In this section, students read and complete some travel tips from an experienced business traveller. They then discuss them and decide whether or not they agree.

1 Go through the instructions with the class and then ask students to work individually to complete the tips with the pairs of words. Allow them to compare answers with a partner before checking with the class.

> **ANSWERS**
> a business; pleasure b movies; view c travellers; lines
> d thing; problem e connections; flights f work; plane
> g evening; destination h children; passengers i water; bags
> j receipts; cards k magazines; newspapers

2 Students work with a partner to discuss the tips. Have a class feedback session to find out who agrees with them.

05 BUSINESS TRAVEL 35

BUSINESS COMMUNICATION

The nightmare journey

In this section, one student takes the role of a harassed business traveller, whilst the other takes a variety of roles representing the people the traveller encounters on the journey. They practise asking and responding to polite questions. Less confident students may need some time to prepare what they are going to say. Confident students could perform their nightmare journeys for the class, perhaps with mimed gestures and/or props. In a feedback session, encourage students to tell the class of any real nightmare journeys they have experienced.

> **1:1** The role of Speaker A involves the most language practice, so encourage your student to take this role.

Transatlantic crossing

The article in this section presents an unusual situation, but one which may become increasingly common: living in two countries simultaneously and commuting between the two. Students are invited to talk about whether they would prefer to relocate to Britain or the United States and to discuss questions on the text with a partner.

1 Ask students to give reasons for their answers and find out if any of them have spent a prolonged period of time in either Britain or the United States as part of their work.

2 Ask students to speculate on the title. Check that students understand that NY-Lon here refers to New York and London, but that nylon is a man-made fabric.

3 Students read the article and discuss the comprehension questions with a partner. Get feedback in particular on students' answers to question d, as the difference between the English spoken in New York and that in London will be the focus of the next section, and it will be useful to establish what students already know on the subject.

4 Guessing the meaning of new words from context is an important skill. Point out that sometimes there are clues in the surrounding words, for example, *drawn together* and *shared*, *trendy* and *modern*. Sometimes we can infer from the context: for example, a penthouse must be desirable because Joel Kissin dreamed of living in New York and a penthouse represented the fulfilment of his dream.

ANSWERS
wealthiest neighbourhood: richest residential area
on a first-name basis: sees them so often that they call each other by their first names as friends would
are drawn together by: are connected by
flows: moves
boom: a period of expansion and prosperity
real estate: buying and selling land and buildings
trendy: fashionable
penthouse: an expensive top-floor apartment/flat (usually the best in the building)

Where in the world?

In this section, students practise differentiating between American and British English. The exercises are fairly light-hearted as it really doesn't matter which form students choose to use. It will, however, be useful for them to be able to recognize and understand the differences.

1 You could do this exercise as a quiz with students working individually and scoring points for correct answers. It might be interesting to see if students can suggest what the equivalents in the opposite city might be for some of the words in the signs. Many of the signs themselves, such as *Walk / Don't walk*, don't have a direct verbal equivalent (crossings in Britain have a picture of a man which flashes green when it is safe to cross and red when it is unsafe), but there are many words which have UK or US equivalents. For example:

b US freeway = UK motorway
c US city center (also *downtown*) = UK city centre
d US rest rooms = UK toilets (sometimes *lavatories*)
e UK underground = US subway (in Britain a subway is a passage under a road for pedestrians)
f UK lift = US elevator
g US gas station = UK petrol station
i UK roundabout = US traffic circle
j US Monday thru (through) Friday = UK Monday to Friday
k US parking lot = UK car park
l UK taxi = US cab; UK queue = US line
n UK chemist's = US drugstore or pharmacy
o US truck = UK lorry
p UK colour = US color
r UK trolleys = US luggage carts

ANSWERS
a NY b NY c NY d NY e L f L g NY h L i L j NY
k NY l L m L n L o NY p L q NY r L

2 🔊 **1.29** Ask students to identify the locations as they listen and then say what clues helped them to decide.

ANSWERS
London: 2, 4, 5, 8 (clues: quid, pounds, Underground; day return, boot, taxi; bill, chemist's; petrol station, roundabout)
New York: 1, 3, 6, 7 (clues: rest room, elevators; shopping mall, drugstore, parking lot; blocks, cab, subway, bucks; round trip, cart, phone booths, quarters)

🔊 **1.29**

Conversation 1
A: Excuse me, could you tell me where the rest room is?
B: Certainly, sir. There's one just across the lobby, by the elevators.
A: Thank you.
B: You're welcome.

Conversation 2
A: That's five quid, please.
B: Erm, I've only got a ten, I'm afraid.

A: That's fine. So that's five pounds I owe you. Just a minute.
B: By the way, could you tell me which way's the nearest Underground?

Conversation 3

A: Excuse me, am I going the right way for the shopping mall?
B: Er, no. Erm, you need to go back the way you came till you come to a big drugstore.
A: Uh huh.
B: Turn left, then take a right at the parking lot and the mall's right in front of you.
A: Thanks.
B: Have a nice day!

Conversation 4

A: Day return, please.
B: To the city?
A: Yes, please ... Oh, no!
B: Is there a problem?
A: I've just realized I left my briefcase with my wallet in the boot of that taxi!

Conversation 5

A: Your bill, madam.
B: Oh, thank you. Er, who do I make the cheque out to?
A: Er, just Webster's will be fine. Did you enjoy your meal?
B: Er, yes ... Everything was ... fine. Er, is there a chemist's nearby, do you happen to know?

Conversation 6

A: Which way you headed, ma'am?
B: Er, Liberty Street.
A: That's quite a few blocks from here. Can I call you a cab?
B: Won't that be expensive? Maybe I should take the subway.
A: I wouldn't at this time of night. Cab'll probably only cost you five or six bucks.

Conversation 7

A: One way or round trip?
B: Er, one way, please. Is there a cart I could use for my baggage?
A: Sure. They're over by the phone booths. You'll need two quarters.
B: Oh, then could you change this for me?

Conversation 8

A: Erm, excuse me. I'm looking for a gas station.
B: Oh, right. A petrol station. I think there's one at the next roundabout.
A: Pardon me? ... Oh, you mean a traffic circle. Great. Thanks a lot.
B: No problem.

In arrivals

Meeting or being met by business colleagues at an airport is a common experience for business travellers. In this section, students practise greetings, offers and ways of making polite conversation in such situations. They begin by listening to some people being met at the airport and answering questions about them. They then go on to complete expressions used in the recordings and practise using them in an airport roleplay.

1 1.30–1.33 Play the recordings. You may need to pause between each conversation to give students time to make notes. Play the recordings again and check answers with the class.

ANSWERS

	Conversation 1	Conversation 2	Conversation 3	Conversation 4
Have the speakers met before?	no	yes	no	no
What topics do they discuss?	flight, weather	family, promotion	business, flight	business colleagues, tiredness
What plans do they make?	go to hotel; meet Mr Hill in a couple of hours	have lunch; go to office; Greg is staying with Caroline	meet team this afternoon; relax in evening	go to hotel; meet in 45 minutes

1.30
Conversation 1

A: Hello. You must be waiting for me.
B: Mr de Jong?
A: That's right.
B: How do you do, sir. Let me take those for you. Did you have a good flight?
A: Not bad, not bad. It's even colder here than Cape Town, though. And we're having our winter.
B: Oh, yes. It's rained all week, I'm afraid. Always does for Wimbledon.
A: Hmm? Oh, the tennis. Actually, I was expecting to meet Mr Hill.
B: Yes, sir. I'm afraid Mr Hill had to go to a meeting. He sends his apologies. He said to take you straight to your hotel, give you a chance to freshen up and he'll meet you in a couple of hours or so.
A: Oh, right. Fine.
B: You must be tired after your long flight.
A: Oh, not too bad. Luckily, I managed to get some sleep on the plane.

05 BUSINESS TRAVEL 37

BUSINESS COMMUNICATION

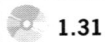

1.31
Conversation 2

C: Greg! I'm over here …

D: Caroline! Good to see you again! Wow, it's crowded here. I nearly missed you.

C: I know. Didn't you see me waving? So, how are things?

D: Fine, fine. Susan sends her love.

C: How is she?

D: Very well. Congratulations, by the way.

C: Hmm?

D: On your promotion.

C: Oh, that. Yeah, well, if you work for the same company long enough … Now, my car's just five minutes away. Let me help you with your bags.

D: Oh, that's all right. Well, maybe the really heavy one.

C: Now, I thought we could get some lunch first, and then go back to the office and do some work. Oh, you're staying with us, by the way. David's dying to meet you.

D: Sounds good to me. David, yes. A new job and a new husband. So, how's married life?

1.32
Conversation 3

E: Miss Sheridan?

F: Yes, you must be Alan Hayes.

E: That's right.

F: Hello. Thanks for coming to meet me.

E: Not at all. We thought it would be quicker. This way you can meet the whole team this afternoon. We thought you might just want to relax this evening.

F: Oh, yes. Probably.

E: So, how's business?

F: Couldn't be better. So we're all set for the meeting tomorrow?

E: We certainly are. Martin sends his regards, by the way.

F: How is he?

E: He's fine. So, how was your flight?

F: Oh, pretty good. I got upgraded.

E: Lucky you! That never seems to happen to me.

F: Mm. It certainly makes a difference. I could get used to it.

E: Well, now, we'll go straight to the office if that's okay with you. I'd like you to meet Graham Banks. He's the head of our legal department.

F: Yes, I think I spoke to him on the phone.

E: Oh, yes, of course. Now, let's see if we can get a taxi …

1.33
Conversation 4

G: Mr Okada?

H: Er, yes.

G: Hello. Welcome to London. I'm Sharon Miller.

H: Er, from Sabre Holdings?

G: That's right. I'm the head of the M&A department – Mergers and Acquisitions.

H: I see. I was expecting … Never mind. So, Miss Miller. Pleased to meet you.

G: Pleased to meet you, Mr Okada. Now, I've got a taxi waiting outside. So why don't we let the driver take those bags of yours?

H: Oh, thank you very much.

G: We'll drop your things off at the hotel. We booked you into the Savoy. I hope that's okay. I think you'll be comfortable there.

H: Yes, that will be fine.

G: Great. Then I thought we could meet up with my assistant Geri King and get some lunch.

H: Gerry King? I don't think I know him.

G: Her, actually. No, she's just joined us. She's got a lot of questions she'd like to ask you.

H: Yes, of course. I wonder … It was a very long flight … Do you think I could go to my hotel first?

G: Yeah, sure. We booked a table for 1.30, but that's okay.

H: I am a little tired and I need to freshen up.

G: Of course. We'll check you into your hotel and then meet in, say, three quarters of an hour?

2 Before looking at the table of expressions, ask students if they can remember any of the things that the speakers on the recording said when they greeted each other. It might be helpful to tell students to close their books and write anything they can remember on the board.

Students then complete the table with the missing words. Encourage them to use these useful expressions for greeting people when they do the roleplay in the next exercise. You could give students some practice in advance of the roleplay by doing some quick conversation exchanges with them using these expressions.

ANSWERS

a must   b Let   c booked   d how   e got   f okay   g sends
h get   i meet

Language links

Direct students to the **Phrase bank** in the **Language links** section on page 36 for a further exercise using language for speaking to people in arrivals, in the taxi and at the hotel.

3 Give students plenty of time to turn to their respective pages and read the situations outlined there. They should work individually, and will also need time to think about what they are going to say and decide on expressions from 2 that they can use. However, discourage them from writing anything down and then reading it out. Ask confident students to perform their roleplays for the class.

1:1 The role of Speaker A is the slightly more demanding one and offers more language practice, so you might wish to get your student to take this role. You can play Speaker B.

Language links

ANSWERS

Vocabulary

Business trips

a flight   b the airport   c check-in   d shopping   e lounge
f plane   g movie   h sleep   i destination   j control   k bags
l customs   m arrivals   n traffic   o hotel   p your things
q a meal   r night

Grammar

Polite question forms

1 a Could you make some coffee, please?
  b Would you please remember to use the spell check in future?
  c Could I have a word with you in private?
  d Is there somewhere where I could plug this mobile in?
  e Would you mind checking these figures again?
  f Could you tell me how this computer works, please?
  g Do you happen to know the dialling code for Greece?
  h Do you think I could ask you to work overtime this evening?
2 a Could I have a window seat, please?
  b Would you mind helping me with my bags, please?
  c Do you know where there is a cashpoint?
  d Would you mind changing this £20 note?
  e Could you drive a little slower, please? / Do you mind not driving so fast?
  f Would you mind lending me your mobile?
  g Is there somewhere where I could recharge my laptop?
  h Could you give me three separate receipts, please?
  i Could you tell me the time, please?
  j Do you happen to know how far it is to the airport?

Phrase bank: Business travel

a You must be   b How   c Let me   d We've booked
e Okay, I'll   f Can you   g Could I   h What time do
i Could you tell me

06 Handling calls

Learning objectives

In Unit 2, students learned some strategies for making and receiving telephone calls in English. This unit continues this topic, first by giving students the opportunity to discuss how important phone calls are in their work and how they handle calls when they are busy.

They then learn and practise useful expressions for making polite requests. The next section gives them strategies and language for dealing with unexpected phone calls.

They practise dealing with incoming phone calls in a roleplay and use some of the expressions they have learned to make excuses to end a call.

The grammar focus is on *will* and the lexical focus is on collocations relating to office life.

Digital resources: Unit 6

Online Workbook; Extension worksheets; Glossary; Phrase bank; Student's Book answer key; Student's Book listening script; Fast-track map

---

In this first section, students discuss the amount of time they spend on the phone and the importance of this. They discuss attitudes to answering the phone and look at some statistics which suggest that answering the phone may not be the best use of a business person's time.

Warm-up

Read the quotation to the class and ask for reactions. Ask students whether they prefer to make phone calls at work or send emails. Does this depend on the reason for their communication?

1 Students discuss the questions in groups and report back to the class. Expand the class discussion to include whether they use an answerphone or some other device to find out who is calling them before they answer the phone. Brainstorm other ways you can avoid receiving phone calls and on what occasions people are likely to try to avoid them.

2 Instead of just getting the students to read the texts, you could use them to revise some telephone techniques for asking for repetition or clarification, getting the speaker to slow down, etc. Ask students to close their books. Then, holding a mobile phone or other prop to your ear, read the first text but speak too quickly or too softly for the students to hear, or mispronounce some words. Encourage students to use the skills they have learned to ask you to repeat, slow down, spell out a word, etc. You could then ask two students to do the same with the other two texts, with the rest of the class interrupting and asking for clarification. You can then ask them what points each text is making about phone calls at work.

SUGGESTED ANSWERS

Business phone calls can reduce productivity because of the time they take up. Even a modest reduction in calls can increase productivity. Most business calls are not important enough to justify executives stopping what they are doing to answer them. Devices such as the Blackberry® can become so much a part of business people's lives that they think they are receiving calls even when they aren't. Overuse can also lead to medical problems. Addiction to mobile phones can intrude into your personal life. People are becoming incapable of ignoring ringing phones no matter what else they are doing at the time.

3 Students work individually to complete the sentences. Check answers with the class and then ask them to practise the expressions by using them in sentences of their own.

ANSWERS

a busy; ring   b disturbed; hold   c possible; answer
d expecting; pick up   e important; leave   f real; unplug
g out; divert

4 Students work individually to decide which of the sentences in 3 are true for them and then compare with a partner. If they disagree with any of the sentences, ask them to explain what they would do in a similar situation.

Asking politely

This next section gives students training in making polite requests. It also provides a lot of vocabulary which they will find useful when talking about office procedures or asking people to do things around the office.

1 Once students have completed the expressions, ask them to think of a suitable ending for each, e.g. *If possible, I'd prefer to meet on Friday. If you would send me confirmation, I'd be very grateful*, etc. When they have done this, ask them to read them out to the class and see how many alternatives students have come up with for each one.

ANSWERS

a if possible   b if you can/would   c if you would/can   d if you're not too busy   e if you've got time/a minute   f if you've got a minute/time   g if it's not too much trouble

40 06 HANDLING CALLS

2 Students will find all this vocabulary useful for talking about office life.

ANSWERS

Could you …?
email me my flight details
let me have a copy of the report
get on to our supplier
get back to me within the hour
take a quick look at the proposal
arrange for somebody to meet them at the station
set up a meeting with the heads of department
send their accounts department a reminder
fix me an appointment
book the conference room for three
fax the figures through to me
organize a tour of the plant for some visitors

Language links

Direct students to the *Language links* section on page 41 for a further exercise in the form of an amusing poem which practises vocabulary for office life.

3 Students work with a partner to roleplay making and answering polite telephone requests. It is often useful to have pairs of students sit back to back when they do phone call roleplays. This removes the visual clues that we tend to rely on when speaking face to face with someone, and which tell us when something we have said has not been understood. Without visual clues, students have to rely on voice alone and ask for repetition or clarification when they need it. Encourage students to use as much of the language from the previous exercises as they can. The phone calls do not have to be long and complicated. Once the request has been made and agreed or refused, pairs should start a new call.

1:1 To give your student more practice in both making and receiving phone calls, take turns to be Speaker A and Speaker B.

Unexpected phone calls

This section is all about dealing with unexpected phone calls. These are probably the most difficult to deal with, particularly when they are in a foreign language. The aim is to prepare students for these eventualities and give them some strategies to deal with surprise calls, so that they can appear confident and professional on the phone at all times.

1 1.34–1.37 Go through the descriptions with the class before you play the recordings so they know what they are listening for. Allow students to compare their answers with a partner before checking with the class.

ANSWERS

Call 1 d   Call 2 c   Call 3 a   Call 4 b

1.34
Call 1
A: Allo!
B: Oh, hello. Do you speak English?
A: Er, … yes, a little. Can I help you?
B: This is Anne Cook from *What Car?* magazine.
A: I'm sorry?
B: Anne Cook. *What Car?*
A: What car?
B: Yes, that's right.
A: You want a car?
B: No, no, sorry. I work for *What Car?* I'm a journalist. Er, can you put me through to Yves Dupont?
A: I'm afraid I don't understand. Can you speak more slowly, please?
B: Yes, I'd like to speak to Yves Dupont, if he's available.
A: Ah … One moment, please. I'll get someone who speaks better English.
B: Thank you!

1.35
Call 2
A: Hola …
B: Hello. Is that Joaquín Fuentes?
A: Er … Yes, speaking.
B: Joaquín. It's Geoff White.
A: Geoff White?
B: NetWorth Systems? We spoke last week.
A: Oh, yes. I'm sorry. Geoff, of course.
B: Er, yes. Anyway, I'm calling about those prices you wanted, …
A: Oh, yes … Listen, Geoff, I'm afraid I can't talk right now. I'm in a meeting.
B: Oh, I see.
A: Yeah. Can you call me back – say, in an hour?
B: Erm, yeah, sure … No problem.
A: Okay, I'll speak to you later … No, wait, could you just email me the figures instead?
B: Erm, yeah, yeah, sure.
A: Thanks a lot.
B: I'll do that right away.
A: Great. Thanks for calling.
B: Yeah, bye.
A: Bye.

1.36
Call 3
C: Jim, can you get that?
A: Uh? Oh, okay … Yeah?
B: Hello? Is that Western Securities?
A: Uh huh. What can I do for you?
B: This is Laura Como from Tricolor. I'd like to speak to Karl Lesonsky, please. It's about a pension fund.
A: Just a minute. Anybody seen Karl? … He's not here.
B: Do you know when he'll be back?

06 HANDLING CALLS 41

BUSINESS COMMUNICATION

A: No idea. He's usually in by now. Probably taken a long lunch.
B: Oh, I see. Well, perhaps you can help. Who am I speaking to?
A: Er, Jim Savage. But, er, ... Oh, just a minute ... Er, hello Ms Como?
B: Yes!
A: Look, I don't normally deal with pensions. I think you'd better wait till Karl gets back.
B: Well, when will that be?
A: I really don't know.
B: Well, that's helpful.
A: Okay. Look, give me ten minutes. I'll see if I can reach him on his cellphone.
B: No, don't bother. I'll call back later.

🔘 **1.37**
Call 4

A: José Senna.
B: Ah, Mr Senna. Hello. I'm sorry to bother you. Your secretary gave me your mobile number.
A: Er, that's okay ... Can I ask who's calling?
B: Oh, I'm sorry. This is Nigel Waters. We met at the Expo in São Paulo last year.
A: Oh, yes, Mr Waters. How are you?
B: Fine, fine. You said if I was ever in Rio you'd introduce me to your boss? Remember?
A: Oh, ... Yes. Um, so you're here in Rio?
B: That's right.
A: Erm, well, it's a bit difficult right now. I'm on my way to a meeting. But ... er, leave it with me. I'll see what I can do.
B: Right.
A: Can you give me a contact number?
B: Oh, yes, I'm staying ...
A: Just a minute, where's my organizer? ... Okay.
B: Yes, I'm staying at the Mirador in Copacabana. It's 548 8950, er, room 314.
A: 3-1-4 ... Okay. I'll try to make the arrangements. Don't worry, I'll sort something out.
B: Great.
A: And, er ... Oh, the traffic's moving. Look, I'll get back to you tomorrow. Okay?
B: I can't hear you very well.
A: No, the signal's breaking up. Speak to you tomorrow.
B: Okay, fine. I'll wait to hear from you then. Bye.

2 🔘 **1.34–1.37** If your students are confident, you might like to see how many of these questions they can answer before you play the recordings again. Even if they can't answer every one, going through the questions and thinking about the answers will be good preparation for the second listening.

Play the recordings again and check answers with the class. See how much agreement there is over question c for each call; these questions ask about the students' own experience and opinions.

ANSWERS
Call 1
a The receiver doesn't speak English well and thinks the caller wants a car, rather than that she works for *What Car?* magazine.
b He gets someone who speaks better English.
Call 2
a He says he is in a meeting and asks the caller to email the figures.
Call 3
a He is unprofessional, informal and casual.
b A pension fund.
Call 4
a At the Expo in São Paulo.
b An introduction to the boss.

3 When students have completed the expressions, checking the answers might be more fun if you ask individual students to read out at random the beginning of an expression for the rest of the class to finish.

ANSWERS
Call 1
a Can you put   b I'm afraid I   c Can you speak
Call 2
a I'm calling about   b I'm afraid I   c Can you call
Call 3
a What can I   b Do you know   c Who am I
Call 4
a I'm sorry to   b Can I ask   c Can you give

4 Once students have completed the expressions, read out the statements and ask individual students to give the correct response. Alternatively, ask students to practise the statements and responses with a partner.

ANSWERS
a Okay, I'll see what I can do.
b Okay, I'll see if I can reach him on his cellphone.
c Okay, I'll call back later.
d Okay, I'll do that right away.
e Okay, I'll speak to you later.
f Okay, I'll wait to hear from you then.
g Okay, I'll sort something out.
h Okay, I'll get someone who speaks better English.
i Okay, I'll get back to you tomorrow.

Language links

Direct students to the *Language links* section on pages 41–42 for further explanation of the use of *will* as a modal verb and exercises to practise this modal verb.

5 Sitting back to back will make these roleplays more realistic for the students. Give students time to read the instructions on their respective pages and to think about what they are going to say, but discourage them from writing down their lines and reading them out. As you go around the class listening to the roleplays, make a note of any particularly good or amusing ones, and ask those students to perform their roleplays for the class.

BUSINESS COMMUNICATION

6 This exercise leads up to another phone call roleplay, but the aim here is to personalize it so that students are dealing with calls from people that they know and about things which they actually have to deal with in their daily lives. In each conversation, the person making the call should pretend to be the person listed on the other student's diagram. Students can have great fun thinking up imaginative ways of putting an end to a call.

See if you can establish a class champion for getting people off the phone as quickly as possible (whilst still remaining polite). Ask a volunteer who believes they are good at this skill to take the role of the receiver. Using a stopwatch to time the calls, invite other students to challenge the receiver by attempting to keep him or her on the line as long as possible.

> **Language links**

Direct students to the **Phrase bank** in the *Language links* section on page 42 for more on polite requests, offering assistance and making excuses to end a call.

> **Language links**

ANSWERS

Vocabulary

Office life

1 do   2 fax   3 Check   4 get   5 circulate   6 delegate
7 Update   8 running   9 Hold   10 cleared   11 Print
12 Grab   13 Cancel   14 listen   15 put   16 Meet
17 Crash   18 Arrange   19 Pick   20 Give   21 Make
22 missed   23 Break   24 Contact   25 Fix   26 can
27 Get   28 postpone   29 Finish   30 phone   31 Leave
32 Hit   33 celebrate   34 blew   35 Screwed
36 Feeling   37 Draft   38 hand

Grammar

will

1 a Will you help me?
  b Stop making personal calls or I'll charge you for them.
  c I expect the company will do well.
  d I won't accept anything less than 2%.
  e Don't worry, he'll phone you back within the hour.
  f I'll take that call, if you like.
  g I'll send the figures right away.
2 1 c 2 g 3 f 4 a 5 e 6 d 7 b
3 1 A I really need that report today.
    B I'll finish it this morning.
    A Okay, I'll look forward to seeing it.
  2 A My plane gets in at seven.
    B I'll come and meet you at the airport.
    A Great. I'll see you there, then.
  3 A I'm just off to a meeting.
    B I'll phone you later, then.
    A Fine, I'll just give you my mobile number.
  4 A Eva's off sick today.
    B I'll have to speak to her, I'm afraid.
    A Okay, I'll see if I can reach her at home.
  5 A She wants to see you – now!
    B I'll be right there.
    A Good. I'll tell her you're on your way.
4 a busy, later   b give, right   c desk, look   d try, time
  e make, know   f wait, details   g leave, okay
  h nothing, away

Phrase bank: Polite requests
a P   b D   c D   d E   e P   f D   g E   h P   i D

Offering assistance
a see   b get   c see   d sort   e get   f call   g speak   h do
i get   j get

Ending a call
a have   b keep   c get; Speak   d got; Catch

07 Making decisions

Learning objectives

In this unit, students look at decision making, beginning by answering a quiz which reveals how good they are at making quick decisions. They then discuss the art of decision-making and listen to a podcast on the subject, taking notes and then comparing the views expressed with their own.

The next two sections look at the decision-making process and the language used at the different stages. Further work on the language of meetings is presented in the form of a crossword.

Students then practise taking part in a decision-making meeting to decide who should play James Bond in the next Bond film.

The grammar focus is on conditionals and the lexical focus is on collocations relating to the market place.

Digital resources: Unit 7

Online Workbook; In company interviews Units 5–7 and worksheet; Extension worksheets; Glossary; Phrase bank; Student's Book answer key; Student's Book listening script; Fast-track map

This first section is about making a quick decision. Students answer a quiz, decide who they think is the most decisive person in their class and then read an analysis to see if their decision matches the information given.

Warm-up

Write the word *decision* in a circle in the centre of the board and brainstorm all the words that the students know that are derived from it, e.g. *decide, decisive, indecisive, deciding (factor), indecision, undecided, decided(ly)*. Write these at the ends of spokes radiating out from the circle. Ask students to explain the meanings of the words or to use them in sentences.

Focus attention on the quote from Napoleon and ask the students if they would describe themselves as decisive.

1 Make sure students realize that they have only 90 seconds to answer the questions in the quiz. Then get them started, so that they don't have time to realize that any *yes* or *no* answers are irrelevant to the purpose of the quiz, which is to determine how many of the questions they would answer with *it depends*.

2 Before the students turn to page 128 to look at the analysis, ask them to decide who is the most decisive person in the class. This should be based on their knowledge of the person concerned, not on their replies to the quiz. Then let them look at the analysis and find out which category they fall into. Ask the person who was voted the most decisive to say which category they fall into.

The art of decision-making

This section begins with a discussion of statements about decision-making. Students then listen to a podcast on decision-making in business. They take notes and compare the views in the podcast to those in the statements in the first exercise.

1 Ask students to work with a partner. Give them time to read and discuss the statements. Encourage them to report back to the class on how far they agree with each one.

2 1.38 Tell students to take brief notes on the podcast. Play the recording more than once if the students need to hear it again in order to take their notes.

1.38

A: Welcome to the *In Company* Business Podcast. This week: the art of decision-making …

B: In business, is it better to make good decisions or better to make lots of decisions? Peter Kindersley, the founder of Dorling Kindersley Books, is in no doubt. 'It doesn't matter,' he says, 'if the decision you make is right or wrong. What matters is that you make it and don't waste your company's time. If you make the decision, you begin to distinguish the good from the bad.' But Michael Begeman, who runs the Meeting Network at 3M®, takes a different view. He claims that 'not all successful meetings end with a decision'. 'Decisions,' he says, 'are the Valium of meetings.' People think, 'Great, we've finally made a decision. Now we don't have to worry about that issue any more.' So who's right? Does decisiveness lead to good decision-making? Or is the best decision sometimes no decision?

The answer is partly cultural. In countries like the United States, for example, the ability to make speedy decisions is valued because decisions tend to lead to action. And, as America is an action-oriented culture, being seen to be actively doing something is an important part of a manager's job. In Japan, on the other hand, managers may prefer to gradually build up agreement among their colleagues until the right course of action simply emerges – without a conscious decision ever having been made. By contrast, in France the decision-making procedure is very different from both the American and Japanese approaches. For the French, a long process of logical debate generally precedes all important decisions – some of which, as Begeman recommended, may never be made!

How do you make your decisions – by logically analyzing all the available data or by trusting your gut instinct? Research done by Daniel Goleman, the originator of Emotional Intelligence, shows that highly successful decision-makers do both. But according to Dan Ariely, a psychology professor at

Duke University, much of our decision-making is actually highly irrational. For instance, it was noticed some time ago that culturally similar countries varied considerably in their willingness to donate their bodily organs after their death. In Austria, for example, organ donation is 100%, whereas in Germany it's only 12. In Sweden, it's 86%, but in Denmark only 4. How do we explain this dramatic difference? In fact, it turned out to be the result not of culture, but of the way the organ donation questionnaire was worded. In Germany and Denmark, people were asked to tick the box if they wanted to participate in the organ donation program. Most didn't tick it and so didn't participate. In Austria and Sweden, however, people were asked to tick the box if they didn't want to participate in the organ donation program. Again, most didn't tick it, but by deciding not to tick it, they ended up participating!

So it seems like, given the choice, most of us are more comfortable not doing than doing. Maybe that's why in 1999, George Bell – the former CEO of web portal Excite – turned down the opportunity to buy a start-up search engine company because the asking price of $750,000 just seemed too high. The search engine, of course, was Google, with a current market value of $250 billion – a 330,000-fold increase since Bell decided not to buy it!

3 Students work with a partner to compare their notes and discuss the extent to which the views in the podcast are similar or different to the points in 1.

The decision-making process

In this section, students put the stages of the decision-making process into the most likely order. They then match meeting agenda items to the things that were said.

1 The order given in the answers matches those in the meeting in 2, but students may argue that they would consider the options before collecting information.

SUGGESTED ANSWERS
a 3   b 1   c 2   d 6   e 5   f 4

2 When students have matched the agenda items to the statements, invite one or two of them to read out the things said at the meeting in the correct order.

ANSWERS
1 a, j   2 c, f   3 e, k   4 b, h   5 d, i   6 g, l

> **Language links**
>
> Direct students to the *Phrase bank* in the *Language links* section on page 49 for another exercise linking stages of the decision-making process to things that people might say.

The language of meetings

This section looks at the sorts of things people actually say in meetings. These are presented in a crossword, and then students listen to an extract from a meeting in which all but one of the expressions are used. They then examine the function of these expressions, before matching statement halves with *if*, *unless* and *provided/providing (that)*.

1 You could do this exercise as a race with the first student to complete all the clues and shout out the advice spelled out in the boxes winning.

ANSWERS
a business   b moment   c disagree   d clear   e think
f understand   g point   h saying   i on   j question   k later
l break   m suggestions   n here   o mean   p today   q afraid
The advice is: Stick to your agenda.

2 🔊 **1.39** Students tick the expressions as they listen and should, at the end, be able to identify expression p as the only one not used. With weaker classes, you may need to play the recording more than once.

ANSWER
p I think that's as far as we can go today.

🔊 **1.39**

A: Thanks for coming, everybody. Okay, let's get down to business. As you know, we're here to talk about the relocation to the UK and I'd like to hear what you have to say. Now, the plan is to make the final move in January, but that's a busy month for us. So, what do you think?

B: Can I just stop you there for a moment, Elke? This relocation idea – I mean, it's ridiculous. I don't think anyone here actually wants to go and live in Britain.

A: With respect, you don't quite seem to understand, Erich. The decision has already been taken.

B: Sorry, I don't quite see what you mean. I thought we were here to discuss this.

A: No, perhaps I didn't make myself clear. We are relocating to Cambridge in November. That's been decided ...

B: So why are we having this meeting?

A: If I could just finish what I was saying. What we are discussing today is how to implement the decision. This affects our Scandinavian office too, you know. There's a lot to talk about. Now ...

C: Can I just come in here?

A: Yes, what is it, Axel?

C: Well, I can see why we should have a branch in the UK instead of Scandinavia. We do most of our business there. But we're a German company. Head office should be here in Germany, surely.

A: I'm afraid that's completely out of the question. The decision to relocate makes good logistic and economic sense. We're still a fairly small business. Having branches in different countries is just not an option.

BUSINESS COMMUNICATION

B: I totally disagree. Our market is Northern Europe and Germany is at the heart of Northern Europe.

A: Yes, but 70% of our market is in the UK. Look, perhaps we can come back to this later. I can see some of you are not happy about it and I agree with you up to a point, but I am not in a position to change company policy. Okay, let's move on. How are we going to handle administration during the relocation? Does anyone have any suggestions? How about using the Stockholm office while we move from Bremen to Cambridge? Kjell?

D: Well, to be honest, Elke, we feel very much the same as our German colleagues here. We think the decision to close down the Bremen and Stockholm offices is a mistake.

A: I see …

C: Look, maybe we should take a short break, Elke. I think one or two of us would like to have a word with you – in private if that's okay.

A: Right. Well, sorry everybody. We'll have to break off here, I'm afraid. Axel, Kjell, Erich, I'll see you in my office …

3 Identifying the functions of the expressions should help students to make them their own and encourage them to use them in their own speaking practice.

ANSWERS

1 a   2 e   3 b, n   4 h   5 l   6 i   7 o   8 c   9 g   10 c, f
11 k   12 m   13 j   14 p, q

4 Students work with a partner to match the sentence beginnings to their endings before checking the answers with the class.

ANSWERS

a 4   b 8   c 6   d 7   e 3   f 2   g 5   h 1

Language links

Direct students to the *Language links* section on pages 48–49 for further explanation of the construction and use of conditionals with future reference, and exercises to practise these. You might like to point out that in the *if*-clause, both present and past tenses can be used to refer to the future. When we use a past tense to refer to the future, it makes the statement more tentative, hypothetical or off the record. For example:

If we laid off half the staff, we might just be able to save the company. (I know this is extreme, but it's an idea.)

If we didn't have a stand at the Fair, it would be a disaster. (We must have a stand!)

When we use a past tense to refer to the present, we are imagining a totally unreal situation. For example:

If we were already based in Europe, it would be a lot easier to sell in Italy. (But we aren't.)

You wouldn't say that if you had to deal with the marketing department. (But you don't.)

The decision-making meeting

This section gives students the opportunity to use the language and skills they have learned in this unit in a simulated decision-making meeting.

Warm-up

Explain to students that they are going to make a decision regarding the actor who will play James Bond in the next Bond film. Find out how many of them have seen a Bond film, whether they have a favourite one and which of the actors who have already played Bond (Sean Connery, George Lazenby, Roger Moore, Timothy Dalton, Pierce Brosnan, Daniel Craig) they liked best in the role.

1 Students work with a partner to make collocations. When they have finished, get one pair to read out the first part of a collocation and another pair to supply the second part. Then ask them to read the article.

Alternatively, once they have matched the collocations, ask the students to close their books and read the article aloud yourself, pausing every time you read the first part of each of the collocations for the students to call out the second part. Award points to students who complete the collocations correctly. Then ask them to open their books and read the article again to themselves.

This article could also be used for a homework exercise in which students write six comprehension questions. They bring these to class and exchange them with other students who have to answer the questions they are given.

ANSWERS

a current turnover   b profit margins   c best-selling brand
d combined earnings   e key factor   f brand awareness
g commercial success   h front-page news   i film series

2 Ask students to say whether or not they agree with the analysis in the article of the success of the Bond films.

ANSWERS

the 007 brand name, the actors playing Bond, the Bond character

3 1.40 Give the students plenty of time to list the qualities they think an ideal Bond actor should have. Help them prepare for the meeting by reminding them of useful language patterns to express their list of ideas such as *The role requires someone who … An actor who plays Bond should be able to …* and encourage them to use the expressions on pages 44 and 45. Point out to the students the meeting agenda and the actor profiles on page 47. When the students start their meetings, go around offering help and encouragement where necessary.

Encourage the students to evaluate how each candidate rates against their ideal qualities. For example:

If he can …, then he can …; He won't be suitable if he can't …; The disadvantage with X is that he …; X is the sort of person who could …; Even though X can … he can't …; Despite his lack of experience in acting, X can …

46   07 MAKING DECISIONS

For contrasts of the four candidates, encourage the use of patterns such as *Although X is ... Y is ...; X has ..., whereas Y has ...; X is not as good as Y in that ...* With weaker students, review the language for evaluation and contrast before they start their meetings. You might also want to go over some of the vocabulary in the profiles with them.

When they come to item 4 of the agenda and need to listen to the interview extracts, either take the CD player around to individual groups, or get all groups to listen together.

1.40
Interview 1

A: So, Peter, how do you see the Bond role?

B: Well, Richard, I think playing Bond is really about getting the balance right.

A: The balance?

B: Yes. I mean, on one level, Bond is a fairly predictable superhero. He travels the world, meets beautiful women, drives fast cars, has a joke for every dangerous situation he finds himself in, gets captured by the bad guy, but always wins through in the end. I mean, that's fine. That's an important part of the Bond formula. It's what people come to the cinema to see.

A: Right.

B: But for us to care about the character, I think he has to give us some surprises. We have to see behind his superhero mask from time to time. We have to see the man behind the legend – and struggling to live up to the legend. We have to see some small signs of weakness. I think we have to believe that this time Bond just might not make it.

Interview 2

A: Well, Sam, you're an American. Is that going to be a problem for you playing Bond?

C: No, I don't think so. And I've been working on my English accent. How's this? 'The name's Bond. James Bond.'

A: Not bad.

C: But actually, Richard, ... er ... I don't see why Bond has to be British. I mean, Bond's just whatever you want him to be. The music, the stunts, the bad guys, ... they're not what make the film. Humour is the important thing. Because if Bond isn't funny, then it's just a silly film with lots of explosions and car chases, and exotic women who get killed just after they meet Bond. Bond isn't Batman. He's not a psychologically damaged superhero. He's an old-fashioned adventurer like Indiana Jones. And he has to keep his sense of fun.

Interview 3

A: Now, Jon, how do you see yourself playing the part of Bond?

D: Well, firstly, Richard, I'd make sure Bond looks dangerous. Because that's what Bond is, first and foremost – a killer. He has a licence to kill. Everything else – the women, the cars, the gadgets – are just perks of the job.

A: You don't think that's a bit ... um, two-dimensional?

D: Come on, Richard, this is Bond we're talking about! I think people need to believe in the actor playing Bond, believe that he's really capable of violence, even does his own stunts. Of course, people expect the special effects, the exotic locations and the glamour, but that's no good unless Bond looks like he really means business. So I'd just play Bond as me, Richard. That's all I ever do anyway!

Interview 4

A: Charles, you've wanted the Bond part for a long time. How would you play him?

E: Well, Richard, we've seen a lot of different versions of the Bond character now, haven't we? The assassin, the chauvinist, the lover, the comedian, the mixed-up loner.

A: I guess so.

E: And each time a new actor takes over, the story gets updated – newer gadgets, more current issues.

A: Yes, that's right.

E: I actually think it might be time to stop those endless revisions and go back to the world of the original novels.

A: You mean set the movies in the 1960s again?

E: Yes, why not? I mean, that's where Bond really belongs. And I think by putting Bond back in the 60s, you avoid the problem of trying to reinvent him in every film.

A: Hmm.

E: Look, when you ask people who the best Bond actor was, who do they generally choose?

A: Well, different people have different preferences, but generally, I suppose most people would say the classic James Bond was Sean Connery.

E: Exactly. Now why is that? I'd say it's because his Bond was true to the time. And that's what I'd like to recreate.

1:1 Ask your student to read the profiles of the different actors before coming to class and to be prepared to argue for their choice. Make your own choice and argue in favour of the one you would like to see as the new Bond.

BUSINESS COMMUNICATION

4 **1.41** Students should try to reach a decision before they turn to Plan B on page 139, which offers a radical alternative – a female Bond.

1.41

A: Diane, this would be quite a professional challenge for you, taking over as Bond. Would people accept a woman in the part, do you think?

F: Well, frankly, no, I don't think they would, Richard. It'd be like having a woman play Superman. And what are you going to call her? Jane Bond? It would be ridiculous. But ... erm ... I don't really see myself becoming Bond ... so much as replacing him. I think you've got to begin again really. Maybe have James finally killed off in one of those spectacular opening sequences before you introduce the new female character. Now, Bond is a pretty hard act to follow after 50 years, so, obviously, my character has to be larger than life and twice as dangerous! The great thing would be you could do all the old sexist jokes in reverse and nobody would complain. But ... erm ... I think the secret of a female Bond is, she's got to have style and a wicked sense of humour or everyone will just hate her for getting James's job.

In company interview Units 5–7
Encourage students to watch the interview and complete the worksheet.

Language links

ANSWERS

Vocabulary

Money and markets

1 Verbs: a hike b raise c freeze d cut e slash
 Adjectives: f soaring g rising h stable i falling j plunging
2 a record b huge c modest d reasonable e crippling
 f heavy g moderate h slight
3 break into (the) market, be forced out of (the) market, competitive market, declining market, dominate (the) market, enter (the) market, flood (the) market, growing market, niche market, mass market, market challenger, market forces, market leadership, market research, market saturation, market share, market supply
4 a saturation; flood b niche; dominate c challenger; leadership d competitive; been forced out of

Grammar

Conditionals (future reference)

1 **Extract 1**
 A d B a A e B h A f B c A b B g
 Extract 2
 A g B c A f B e A b B a A h B d
2 *If*-clause: Present Simple, Past Simple, *can* + infinitive, *going to* + infinitive, Present Continuous
 Main clause: *will* + infinitive, *could* + infinitive, *might* + infinitive, Present Simple, *may* + infinitive, *would* + infinitive, *going to* + infinitive, *can* + infinitive, Present Continuous
 Both: *can* + infinitive, Present Simple, *going to* + infinitive
3 a Supposing they offer you a promotion, what will you do?
 b Provided that the market research is positive, we'll go ahead with the new design.
 c Unless we lower the price, we'll lose the contract.
 d You can go to the conference as long as you give a talk.

Phrase bank: Decision-making
a 5, 9 b 1, 12 c 2, 7 d 4, 10 e 6, 11 f 3, 8

08 Influence

Learning objectives

In this unit, students examine the question of influence in business and how you can get what you want from superiors, peers and subordinates. They begin by discussing who does the decision-making in their own company and whether it is possible to be influential even if you are not in a position of authority. They read and discuss an article on how to be a middle-management leader and then listen to extracts from conversations in which people try to get colleagues to do something for them. Students identify the relative status of the people involved and then do some work on the language used before practising their own influencing skills with a partner.

Digital resources: Unit 8

Online Workbook; Extension worksheets; Glossary; Student's Book answer key; Student's Book listening script; Fast-track map

1:1 The way you handle this unit with a single student will depend on their position in the company. If they are from top management, you may wish to concentrate on discussing how they get their subordinates to do what they want them to do, though it would also be interesting to ask them to reflect on the techniques used by those below them in the hierarchy to try to influence them. Students from lower down the company hierarchy may be more interested in how they can influence those above them.

Warm-up

Focus attention on the photo. Ask the students to explain what they think it represents (perhaps a woman climbing up the company hierarchy). Ask them how easy or difficult they think it is to rise up the ladder in their own company.

1 Focus attention on the cartoon, and elicit or explain that what is shown is not really a 'decision-making process'. Ask whether the students have ever been in a meeting where they felt that all the decisions were made by the most senior person present, with everyone else just agreeing and 'rubber-stamping' his or her decisions.

2 Ask students to say how decisions are made in their company. Focus attention on the cline and point out that *top-down* means all decisions are made by the top management and *inclusive* means that all levels of management are involved in the decision-making process. Ask them to put a mark to show where their own company comes on this cline.

3 Have a class discussion of this question. Encourage students who think it is possible to give examples of strategies and techniques which might work for people lower down the hierarchy who want to be influential.

SUGGESTED ANSWER

Authority is given to you by your employers and is connected to your status in the company hierarchy. Influence is a personal skill which enables you to communicate more persuasively. It has nothing to do with status. Some people naturally have it; others don't. But it can be developed.

4 Ask students to work with a partner to discuss this question, then encourage them to report back to the class on their ideas.

5 Ask students to work in groups of three and divide up the article on page 51 between them so that they each read the introduction and one other paragraph. They then discuss with each other what they have read, and compare it with ideas and responses that have come up so far in the lesson.

SUGGESTED ANSWERS

Subordinates need to be motivated, given a sense of autonomy, praised when they do something well and you need to show a certain amount of empathy with their situation. A bit of personal warmth can also go a long way.
Peers will be more open to your suggestions if they like you, feel they owe you a favour or have helped you out in the past. Flattery can also work well – as long as you sound sincere!
Superiors will be more convinced by your arguments if you address their personal concerns, use the power of consensus or uniqueness and back up your proposals with some hard facts.

1:1 As this is quite a long text, you may want to ask your student to read it at home and come to the next lesson prepared to discuss it.

6 1.42 Go through the instructions with the class and reassure them that all they have to do is identify the topic of each conversation and whether the speaker is managing up (getting a superior to do something), managing down (getting a subordinate to do something) or managing sideways (getting a peer to do something).

ANSWERS

a The speaker wants Édouard to look at a design brief. ↓
b The speaker would like to take some unpaid leave. ↑
c The speaker needs Pam to entertain some Japanese guests. →
d The speaker thinks the company should attend the Moscow trade fair. ↑
e The speaker would like Rafael to run an induction session for him. →
f The speaker would like Heather to lead negotiations with GMK. ↓

08 INFLUENCE 49

PEOPLE SKILLS

1.42

Conversation a

Édouard, could I ask you to take a look at this design brief? I realize you already have a lot of work on this week, but it's absolutely essential that we get back to the client on this by Friday. And I think you may find it an interesting change from what you normally do. Can I leave it with you?

Conversation b

John, about my request to take some unpaid leave – I was wondering if you had a moment to talk about it. Only, I know how you like to encourage your trainers to gain some outside experience and I think this is a really great opportunity to do that. You said yourself we need to make savings and with business a little slow this quarter I thought it might be a good time for me to do something like this.

Conversation c

Pam, could I ask you a favour? We've got the people from Shimamura coming over next week, and I'm supposed to be taking them out to dinner and a show, you know. But something's come up and I was wondering if you could take care of it. I know I already owe you one for standing in for me last time! But, to be honest, you're much better at this sort of thing than me, anyway. Would you mind? All the arrangements are made. It's just a case of turning up.

Conversation d

Simone, thanks for agreeing to see me. I wanted to talk to you about the Moscow trade fair. I really think we should attend this year. I mean, just about everybody who's anybody is going to be there – all our competitors, for sure. Now, I know you're worried about the cost, but have a look at this report I just received. It's completely independent, by the way. And it shows the financial benefits of attending the conference over a 24-month period. Pretty impressive. So, I wondered if you could think about it, please. I'll leave the report with you ...

Conversation e

Er, Rafael? Listen, mate, I've got a bit of a problem and I was hoping you might be able to help me out. You remember a couple of weeks ago I took the Morelli account off your hands because you were busy with the Brazilians? Yeah, well, now it seems they want me to do a full audit of their whole business and it's going to mean an enormous amount of work I wasn't expecting. So I was wondering if you'd run the induction session for me again. You said how much you enjoyed it last time. And it would be a real help to me if you could.

Conversation f

Heather, I've been wanting to have a word with you. I'd like you to lead the negotiations with GMK. I was very pleased with the way you handled the Korean deal and I think you're ready to take on a bit more responsibility. What do you say? Do you think you're up to it?

---

7 **1.42** Go through the instructions with the class and allow them time to read the expressions before you play the recording again. Ask them to say for each expression which tactic is being employed (the words and expressions in bold in the article).

ANSWERS

a understand the pressure: the speaker sympathizes with Édouard's heavy workload.
b mission-critical: the speaker stresses the importance of the task.
c motivate: the speaker stresses the change to Édouard's routine.
d non-job-related work: the speaker refers to John's attitude to managers doing this.
e cost conscious: the speaker refers to John's desire to save money (and also appeals to consistency).
f consistent: the speaker refers to a previous occasion in which Pam helped.
g flattery: the speaker tells Pam that she is better than him at entertaining guests.
h consensus: the speaker emphasizes that the company's competitors all think it's a good idea to attend the Moscow trade fair.
i data from reliable expert sources: the speaker uses an independent report to address Simone's concern about costs.
j good working relationship: the speaker stresses the friendly relationship he has with Rafael.
k owe a favour: the speaker reminds Rafael of a favour he did him recently.
l consistent: the speaker points out that the last time Rafael did him a similar favour, he enjoyed it (also some motivation here).
m praise: the speaker compliments Heather on earlier work.
n motivate: the speaker refers to the greater responsibility Heather is capable of taking on.
o motivate: the speaker challenges Heather and appeals to her sense of self-worth and ambition.

8 Students work with a partner and decide who will be Speaker A and Speaker B. Ask them to turn to their respective pages and read the situations. They each have information about three business situations, but seen from different roles within the company. Their task is to have a conversation and try to influence their partner into seeing things their way and doing what they want them to do. They may need plenty of time (perhaps at home) to prepare for their conversations, but discourage them from reading from a prepared script.

1:1 In each situation, it is Speaker A who initiates the conversation, so you may want to take the role of Speaker B here.

MANAGEMENT SCENARIO B

Meetings on the go

Learning objectives

This scenario is based on asking a colleague for a favour and handling unscheduled meetings – meetings on the go. In this case, Alan asks his colleague Heather to attend a meeting in Paris in his place, which she doesn't really want to do. Various meetings take place in corridors and in the kitchen until the situation is finally resolved.

Digital resources: Management Scenario B

In company in action B1–B3 and worksheet; Extension worksheets; Glossary; Student's Book answer key; Student's Book listening script; Fast-track map

Warm-up

Ask the students to brainstorm reasons why someone might have to cancel a conference presentation at the last minute. Put students' ideas up on the board, and ask them to decide which reasons are acceptable and if there are any that they would consider unacceptable.

1 Give students time to read the email and find the answers to the questions. For question d, have a class discussion about how easy it is to say *No*. Point out that Alan and Heather are peers in the company. Would it be easier to say *No* if Alan was a superior? Or a subordinate?

ANSWERS

a He can't give the presentation he's supposed to give at the Infotech conference in Paris next week because his grandfather is seriously ill back home in the States and he wants to fly out to see him.
b He wants Heather to stand in for him at the conference and give the presentation.
c He sounds fairly desperate! He says Heather's his last hope.
d It's hard to say no to people who ask you favours, especially when they're in an unfortunate situation. However, you do also have to consider your own situation if doing them the favour is going to make life very difficult for you.

2 **B1** Read the instructions with the class and the list of strategies. Before you play the video, ask the students to predict which strategies they think would be most likely to work. Play the video, and ask them to tick the ones Alan uses and say which one seems to be the most successful.

SUGGESTED ANSWERS

Alan uses flattery (telling Heather how brilliant she is at presentations), incentives (mentioning 'it's not every day you get to go to Paris' and how Anton will be impressed by her willingness to step in at the last minute), emotional pressure (he tells her the sad story of his grandfather and implies that, if Heather doesn't help him, he has no further options) and appeals to fairness (pointing out how he did some overtime for Heather when she was doing an evening course). It's hard to say which strategy works best – maybe it's the incentives or the final appeal to fairness.

B1
Part 1
Alan: Hi, Heather! So you're back, then. How did it go in Milan?
Heather: Oh, hello, Alan. Don't even ask! Complete disaster!
Alan: Oh, no – what happened?
Heather: Well, obviously we didn't get the ABI contract.
Alan: Ah.
Heather: Turns out they were just using us to get their existing supplier to lower their prices. It was a complete waste of three days, As if I haven't got enough on my plate as it is! I've just come out of a meeting with Anton and he seems to think it's all my fault!
Alan: Ugh! I'm sorry, Heather. I know how much work you put into that proposal. So, er, I don't suppose you had time to read my email, then?
Heather: Your email? ... Oh, your grandfather. Yes, sorry, Alan ... How is he?
Alan: Getting worse, I'm afraid. I really need to book my flight home today. Did you get a chance to think about standing in for me in Paris?
Heather: Erm, now, look, Alan ...
Alan: I know it's a lot to ask. But you know I wouldn't ask you if there was any other alternative. But please, Heather, I'm desperate! You know, my grandfather practically brought me and my brother up, and I just ...
Heather: Alan, Alan. This really isn't a good time. I've lost the ABI deal. I've just been shot down by Anton. I've got work piled up to the ceiling. And, to crown it all, they've given me this useless assistant to train up.
Alan: Tony?
Heather: Yes, Tony. He can't seem to do anything on his own. I have to babysit him the whole time!
Alan: Look, I could take on some of your workload if you like when I get back from the States. Or I could lend you my assistant. Kim's great.
Heather: Look, I'm sorry, Alan. But I don't think I can help you right now. Why don't you just explain the situation to Anton. I'm sure he'll understand.
Alan: Like the way he understood about your problems with ABI, you mean? Please, Heather. You know you're brilliant at presentations. Much better than I am,

B MEETINGS ON THE GO 51

MANAGEMENT SCENARIO

anyway. And it's not every day you get to go to Paris, is it?

Heather: Alan …

Alan: You know Anton is going to kill me if I cancel my presentation at the last minute. But if you step in you'll be his favourite sales rep again. I did all that overtime for you, remember, when you were on that evening course. Heather, can't you help me out here?

Heather: Okay, let me think about it and I'll get back to you.

Alan: Thanks, Heather! You're a star!

Heather: I'm not promising anything, mind you. But maybe I can offload some paperwork onto Tony. It's about time he did some work!

3 B1 This would be a good opportunity to let the students watch the video with the sound turned down, and ask them to evaluate Heather and Tony's behaviour based on their facial expressions and body language alone. You could also pause the video at strategic points, and ask students to predict what they think Heather and Tony are saying. Then play it with the sound turned up, and ask them to decide where on the scales Heather and Tony's behaviour should be marked.

SUGGESTED ANSWER

Heather is certainly authoritative, bordering on aggressive. Of course, she's under a lot of stress and Tony is not proving to be very helpful. Tony is not very accommodating. He does have a genuine point about his training, but his tone is a little disrespectful at times.

B1
Part 2

Heather: Tony! If you can spare a minute …?

Tony: Oh, Heather, hi. I was just on my way to make some photocopies.

Heather: Yes, well, you can drop whatever you're doing and come with me. There's a whole load of work that's piled up while I've been away and now Alan's dumped a presentation on me in Paris next week. So I've got a long list of things I need you to do before this evening.

Tony: I've got a training session this afternoon. This will be the third one I've had to cancel, Heather. … You know I was promised a hundred hours of training when I took this job and I've hardly had any so far!

Heather: I'm afraid I can't help that. This is more important.

Tony: But Heather!

Heather: Look Tony, I don't have time to discuss the terms of your contract right now, okay? You're my assistant and right now I need you to assist! Go and get your laptop and meet me in my office in five minutes …

4 Ask students to discuss the questions with a partner and then report back to the class on their ideas.

SUGGESTED ANSWER

Heather ends the conversation with Alan by saying she'll think about it and can't make any promises. But it's going to be quite difficult for her to say no now. By using a firm 'No', or even asking for more time to think about it, perhaps Heather wouldn't have raised Alan's hopes. In her conversation with Tony, she could have been more understanding of his training needs so that they could come to a compromise that would suit them both.

5 Give students plenty of time to read the article and decide which of the advice contained in it Alan, Heather and Tony took or failed to take.

SUGGESTED ANSWER

All of the speakers seem to be in a rush and so perhaps they would have done better to fix up meetings with each other when they had a little more time to discuss things. Heather is probably a bit too direct with Tony and Tony seems so determined to refuse more work that he fails to see an opportunity to help Heather out during a very busy week. Given the high-stress environment in which they're all working, getting Heather to appreciate him more may be more useful to Tony in the immediate future than the training he says he needs. Heather does well not to agree to stand in for Alan straightaway, but Alan seems to assume she will now do so. And perhaps she gives too many reasons for why she can't help him – this gives Alan a chance to start negotiating – offering, for example, to take on some of Heather's workload when he gets back from the States.

6 B2 Go through the instructions with the class before you play the video so that the students know that all they have to do is decide how they would rate Anton's leadership skills. Then play the video and ask them to discuss the question.

SUGGESTED ANSWER

Anton's leadership skills seem to be pretty good in the conversation with Tony. At first, he has to struggle to remember Tony's name, but he recovers quickly from that and shows an interest in what Tony's telling him. He's firm about the work ethic at the company and is careful not to undermine Heather's authority, but accepts that Tony has a case about not getting the training he was promised. He's sensitive to the fact that Tony may be worried about what Heather will say when she finds out he's been talking to Anton behind her back and comes up with a sensible plan of action.

B2

Tony: Um, Mr Vega! Mr Vega!

Anton: Tony … You're Heather's new assistant, aren't you? How's it going?

Tony: Well, actually, that was what I wanted to talk to you about. Do you have a moment?

Anton: Well, I'm on my way to talk to Alan about the Paris conference next week. But, sure, what's on your mind?

Tony: Well, as you know, I'm supposed to get a hundred hours training as part of my traineeship.

Anton: Yes?

Tony: But Heather's keeping me so busy, so far I've only had about ten. I've tried talking to her about it, but I'm just working flat out the whole time.

B MEETINGS ON THE GO

MANAGEMENT SCENARIO

Anton: Well, it is a busy office. We all work very hard.
Tony: No, I know that, Mr Vega. It's just that, without the training, I'm finding it really difficult to do some parts of my job …
Anton: Okay, look Tony, why don't I have a word with Heather about this? Don't worry, I won't mention that you've spoken to me. There has been a lot of pressure this month, what with Milan and Paris, so I can understand she needs you to help her out. But, obviously, you must get the training you're entitled to. As you say, you'll be no use to us without it! So leave it with me and we'll work something out, okay?
Tony: Thanks a lot, Mr Vega. Okay, I'd better get these papers to Heather. She's got a big presentation to do in Paris next week.
Anton: Sorry, Heather's got a presentation in Paris, did you say?
Tony: Yeah, that's right. She's standing in for Alan and I'm helping her prepare.
Anton: Right, off you go then …

7 Ask students to discuss the questions with a partner, and report back to the class on their predictions and ideas.

8 B3 Play the video for students to check their predictions in 7.

B3

Alan: That's right, Mom. Hopefully I'll be able to fly out at the weekend. Listen, Mom, I'll have to call you back later, okay? Okay, bye.
Anton: Ah, Alan, just the person I was looking for. Have you got a moment?
Alan: Anton. Yeah, sure. Actually, I was just on my way to speak to you.
Anton: Yes, I expect you were. What's this I hear about Heather doing the Infotech presentation instead of you?
Alan: Ah … she told you!
Anton: No, but word gets around. Alan, you know I specifically asked you to do the Infotech presentation because that conference attracts the kind of organizations you mostly work with. Besides, Heather's incredibly busy at the moment. And, frankly, I don't appreciate people making their own arrangements without consulting me first … Now, why can't you go to Paris?
Alan: Um, it's my grandfather. He's rather seriously ill, and I really need to be with him and my family …
Anton: Your grandfather?
Alan: Yes, I know it sounds like a poor excuse. But we're really close. And … I know you say to keep our personal lives out of our jobs, but I just …
Anton: Why can't you go and see him after the Infotech conference?
Alan: The doctors aren't very optimistic at this stage.
Anton: Oh, I see … Look, Alan, I'm sorry about your grandfather, but I do need you in Paris next week. For a start, you speak French and Heather doesn't.

So I suggest you get yourself on the next plane to wherever it is your parents live in the States, and then get back here for next Thursday so you can go to Paris on Friday.
Alan: Oh, thanks, Anton, that's great! But how will I have time to get everything prepared?
Anton: You'll have to sort something out. I'm staying out of this, Alan. Talk to Heather and see if she can help you. Oh, and while you're at it, you can tell her that I've got another lead for her in Milan, so she may have to fly back out there again before the end of the week …

9 Ask students to work with a partner. Tell them to turn to page 126 and follow the instructions there. Remind them not to change the basic facts of the situation and point out that they will need to complete a feedback form in 10 so they should pay close attention to everything that happens in their conversation. As they perform their conversations, go around offering help and encouragement.

SUGGESTED ANSWER
Alan now has a difficult job trying to persuade Heather to help him prepare for a presentation (which she will not be going to Paris to give) as well as doing all her own work – not to mention the fact that she may have to go back to Milan in the next couple of days as well! To get the outcome he wants, he will probably have to negotiate and offer to share some of Heather's workload when he gets back. Heather can either say she's changed her mind about helping him at this point or perhaps use the situation to her advantage. Maybe she can swap assistants with Alan. Or maybe there are other options.

10 Ask students to complete the feedback form on page 130.

1:1 Once you have had the conversation between Alan and Heather, reverse roles so that your student gets a chance to play the other part. Ask them at the end which one they thought they played most successfully.

B MEETINGS ON THE GO 53

09 Small talk

Learning objectives

Small talk can be a minefield when engaging in international business, because both cultural and personal factors come into play as well as any language difficulties. This unit addresses the issues of what is normal or acceptable in different cultural contexts, and looks at some techniques for making successful small talk before getting down to business.

A game-like exercise gives students a chance to talk about their own experiences – a useful skill as small talk often revolves around personal experiences.

They are then taught some adjectives to use to describe their experiences. Finally, they try out their skills in a conference dinner roleplay.

The grammar focus is on the Past Simple and the Present Perfect, and the lexical focus is on common adjectival collocations, and exaggeration and understatement.

You might like to refer students to the work they did in Unit 1 on taboo subjects and techniques for keeping the conversation going.

Digital resources: Unit 9

Online Workbook; Extension worksheets; Glossary; Phrase bank; Student's Book answer key; Student's Book listening script; Fast-track map

In this first section, students begin by doing a quiz about cultural differences when it comes to small talk.

Warm-up

Focus attention on the quotation from John D Rockefeller, and ask them for their opinions on whether – and if so, how far – friendship and business can be mixed. How many of their closest friends are business colleagues and does this link affect either the friendship or the business in any way? Ask them if they think it is important to build friendships in business.

1 Do this as a whole-class discussion and encourage students to relate their own personal experiences of business small talk.

2 Ask students to work with a partner and turn to their respective pages. When they have discussed each of the dilemmas in turn and made their decisions, ask them to turn to page 140 and read the analysis there. Note that it is dangerous to make any sweeping generalizations about cultures, so be prepared for students to disagree with the analysis of the test or the diagram from *When Cultures Collide* in the next section. Encourage open discussion but be careful not to encourage comments on particular nationalities that may cause offence.

1:1 Be sure to give your own honest reactions to the dilemmas and make sure the student realizes that what you say is not the 'correct answer' but a reflection of the way things are done in your culture.

Getting down to business

This section further discusses the implications of cultural context on business small talk with a diagram. This shows how much small talk different nationalities are likely to engage in before they get down to business. Students then listen to extracts from meetings and match each to one of the countries in the diagram. They then listen again for specific information to answer questions and do some grammar work on some of the things that are said.

1 Students will be guessing or giving a personal opinion when they fill the diagram in for the first time. Allow them to discuss their answers with a partner or in small groups if they wish. Then discuss answers in a class feedback session but don't confirm any answers at this stage.

ANSWERS
a Germany   b Finland   c USA   d UK
e France   f Japan   g Spain and Italy

2 **2.01–2.07** The recordings should give students the answers that Richard D Lewis believes to be correct. Note that the names of the countries are not always given in the extracts. The students must work them out from clues.

ANSWERS
Extract a: Japan (clues: Sakamoto, Mizoguchi Bank, Usami-san, green tea)
Extract b: Germany (clues: Berlin, Wolfgang)
Extract c: Italy (clues: Juventus, Lazio, Italian football, Luigi)
Extract d: UK (clue: cricket)
Extract e: Finland (clue: Finland)
Extract f: USA (clue: New York)
Extract g: France (clue: president of France)

2.01
Extract a
A: Er, how do you do. I'm Tom Pearson, Export Manager, Falcon Petroleum.
B: How do you do, Mr Pearson. I am Sakamoto, Assistant Director of International Investments, Mizoguchi Bank. Please sit here opposite the door. You'll be next to Usami-san.
A: Oh, okay. I sit here, right?
B: That's right. Have you tried green tea before, Mr Pearson?
A: Er, yes, I have. I had it last time I was here. I like it very much.

2.02
Extract b
A: Good morning, everyone. I'd like to introduce you all to Dr Alan Winter, who's come over from the Atlanta

BUSINESS COMMUNICATION

office to spend a few days at our research centre. Welcome to Berlin, Dr Winter.
B: Thank you very much, Wolfgang. It was kind of you to invite me.
A: Okay, let's get down to business, shall we?

2.03
Extract c
A: ... And then Juventus scored the winner. It was an incredible goal! Did you see the Lazio game last night, Miss Sterling?
B: Yes, I did. Wasn't it a great match? One of the best I've ever seen. But then, there's nothing like Italian football.
A: So, you like football, then?
B: Oh, yeah. I love it. In fact, my father was a professional footballer.
A: Really?
B: Yes. He wasn't a superstar or anything, but he, er, played for Leeds.
A: Leeds United?
B: Yes, that's right.
A: They were a great team in the 70s, weren't they?
B: Yeah, that's when he played for them.
A: Amazing. Wait till I tell Luigi. Our new partner's father played for Leeds United, ha!
B: Where is Luigi, by the way?
A: Oh, he'll be here soon. He's never the first to arrive, not Luigi ...

2.04
Extract d
A: Rain stopped play again yesterday, I see.
B: Sorry?
A: The cricket. They cancelled the match.
B: Oh, they didn't! Well, we certainly haven't seen much cricket this summer.
A: No. Chocolate biscuit?
B: Oh, have we got chocolate ones? Business must be good.
C: Right, everyone. Er, I suppose we'd better get started ...

2.05
Extract e
A: Right, shall we start? First of all, this is Catherine Anderson from London. I think this is your first time in Finland, isn't it, Catherine? Or have you been here before?
B: Actually, I came here on holiday once, but that was a long time ago.
A: Well, we hope you enjoy your stay with us. Now there's fresh coffee if you'd like some before we begin ...

2.06
Extract f
A: Okay, you guys. Thanks for coming. Now, to business ... Oh, did you all get coffee?
B: Hey, wait up. I've got a great one here.
C: Oh no, it's one of Marty's jokes.
B: See, there's this guy George goes for a job, right? And it's a really cool job. Right here in New York. Big money. So, anyway, he takes a test, like an aptitude test, you know, him and this woman. There's two of them. And they have to take a test to get the job.

C: Yeah, yeah, so ...?
B: So they both get exactly the same score on the test, George and the woman – 99%.
C: Uh huh.
B: So George goes into the interviewer's office. And the interviewer says, 'Well, you both got one question wrong on the test, but I'm sorry, we're giving the job to the other candidate.' So George says, 'Hey, that's not fair! How come she gets the job?' And the interviewer says, 'Well, on question 27, the question you both got wrong, she wrote "I don't know" and you wrote "Neither do I".'
C: That's a terrible joke, Marty.
B: No, you see, he copied her test, right?
A: Marty, we've heard the joke before. It's ancient. Okay, everybody, time to work.
B: I thought it was funny.

2.07
Extract g
A: As you know, Albert, I'm the last person to talk about other people's private lives. If the president of France himself wants to have an affair, I don't care. I mean, this is not the United States.
B: Yes, quite.
A: What I do worry about is what's going on between our vice-president and our head of finance.
B: They're having an affair?
A: Haven't you heard? I thought everybody knew.
B: No! No one ever tells me anything.
A: I mean, it's not the affair I care about. It's how it affects our meetings. Haven't you noticed?
B: Noticed what?
A: How they always agree on everything.
B: Well, now you mention it ...

3 2.01–2.07 Go through the questions with the class so that students know what information they are listening for. Encourage students to answer the questions from memory before playing the recordings again.

ANSWERS
a Opposite the door, next to Usami-san
b A few days
c Professional footballer
d Chocolate biscuits
e She was on holiday.
f 99%
g The vice-president and the head of finance agree on everything.

4 With multinational groups, encourage students to explain why they have put their nationality in a particular place on the diagram in 1. With single nationality groups, find out how much agreement there is on the position on the diagram their nationality should occupy.

5 2.01–2.07 When students have underlined their chosen forms, ask pairs to stand up and read out the conversations. The rest of the class should stand up, too, if they believe the conversations to be correct and remain seated if they believe there is a mistake. Students who believe that they are correct (or when the class is divided)

09 SMALL TALK   55

BUSINESS COMMUNICATION

can appeal to you to indicate whether there is a mistake or not. Play the recordings again as a final check at the end.

> **ANSWERS**
>
> a Have you tried; have; had; was
> b has come; was
> c scored; was; Did you see; did; Wasn't it; have ever seen
> d stopped; cancelled; didn't; haven't seen
> e have you been; came; was
> f copied; 've heard; thought; was
> g Haven't you heard; thought; knew

> **Language links**
>
> Direct students to the *Language links* section on pages 58–59 for further explanation of the construction and use of the Past Simple and Present Perfect, and exercises to practise these tenses.

Talking about experiences

In this section, students prepare sentences about their own experiences which will be useful when making small talk. They use these in a game before looking at a range of adjectives which can be used to enhance what they say.

1 Give students time to complete the sentences. Be prepared to help with any unknown vocabulary.

It is always helpful and encouraging to the students if you can join in with activities such as these, so complete the sentences for yourself and be prepared to mingle with the students in 2 and talk about your own experiences. The students will appreciate it and you will get a good idea of how well they are coping with the task.

2 Give students plenty of time for this exercise because it is useful language practice in talking about experiences, responding to what is said, asking questions and keeping a conversation going.

3 Ask students to work individually to match the nouns to the adjectives. They can then compare with a partner before you check the answers with the class.

> **ANSWERS**
>
> a city b weather c economy d clothes e people f movie
> g news h job i car j holiday k hotel l book

> **Language links**
>
> Direct students to the *Language links* section on page 58 for more practice of useful language and strategies for making conversation more interesting, using exaggeration and understatement.

At a conference dinner

In this section, students do a roleplay in which they practise small talk at a conference dinner. They put into practice the language and strategies learned in this unit. This roleplay is guided so students don't have to use their imaginations too much. This will ensure they can concentrate on fluency and using the language they have been studying to keep the conversation flowing. However, although it is nice to keep an element of spontaneity in this activity, students should prepare the information they'll need before they start. For example:

Which city are they in? (They should choose one they both know quite well.) Has it been a good or bad conference in general? What talks did they go to? What did they eat? Did they enjoy it? Where are they staying? What's it like? What's the weather been like? How has that affected what they've done?

Go through the instructions with the class, and then give them time to read through their roles and think about what to say. Discourage them from writing their lines down and simply reading them out. Point out that they should respond to what they hear, rather than ignoring it and just going on to the next item on their role card. Remind them to listen carefully to what their partner says so that they can respond appropriately.

> **Language links**
>
> **ANSWERS**
>
> **Vocabulary**
>
> **Exaggeration and understatement**
> 1 a Yes, it was absolutely freezing!
>   b Yes, it's absolutely fascinating!
>   c Yes, it's absolutely enormous!
>   d Yes, it's absolutely tiny!
>   e Yes, it's absolutely gorgeous!
>   f Yes, it's absolutely boiling!
> 2 a Well, it isn't exactly the most interesting I've ever read.
>   b Well, it wasn't exactly the most amazing I've ever had.
>   c Yes, it wasn't exactly the most exciting I've ever been to.
>   d Yes, it hasn't been the most relaxing I've ever had.
>   e Well, it wasn't the funniest I've ever heard.
>   f Yes, it isn't the safest place I've ever been to.
>
> **Grammar**
>
> **Past Simple or Present Perfect**
> 1 a a point in time: 1; a period of time: 3; both: 2
>   b came to America, started a business; Past Simple
>   c have been extremely successful, have been the market leader; Present Perfect
> 2 ago: a week, a couple of days, over an hour, years, a long time
>   for: a week, a couple of days, over an hour, years, a long time
>   since: the 1990s, 2001, Christmas, the day before yesterday, half past four, last month, the oil crisis, Thursday
> 3 a No b No c No d Yes e Yes, Yes f Maybe, No
> 4 a did ... get b was c didn't mean d have noticed
>   e wasn't f hoped g have now decided h Have ... heard
>   i said j wanted k haven't done l didn't ... tell
>   m didn't make up n thought o has already brought
>   p have had q haven't ... shown r have ever asked s was
>
> **Phrase bank: Engaging in small talk**
> a enjoying b staying c staying d giving e going
> f been g been h made i heard j seen k found
> l tried m met n met o had p have q meet
> r come/go s see t read

10 Email

Learning objectives

This unit examines email's impact on people's lives and the style in which email messages are written. Students begin by talking about attitudes to email. They then look at the style of English used for writing emails and identify some of the words that are often missed out. They also look at some rules for email, and complete and improve some examples. Finally, they work in groups to exchange emails.

The grammar focus is on future forms and the lexical focus is on collocations relating to computers.

Digital resources: Unit 10

Online Workbook; Extension worksheets; Glossary; Phrase bank; Student's Book answer key; Student's Book listening script; Fast-track map; Quick progress test 2; Mid-course test

---

In this first section, students explore attitudes to email, and learn different ways of expressing likes and dislikes.

Warm-up

Focus attention on the quotation from Lucy Kellaway and ask for comments. How does carelessness in emails affect the impression the receiver gets of the sender? What problems does it pose if the email is in a foreign language? Ask students to correct the mistakes.

Elicit or explain the meaning of *proofread* (to check a written text for mistakes) and ask students whether they take the time to proofread their emails. Ask whether they would proofread a letter, and see if there is any difference in their attitudes to emails and letters.

1 Students work with a partner to discuss the question. Encourage them to give reasons.

2 Go through the instructions with the class and ask them to label the phrases. Ask some of them to complete the incomplete phrases with ideas of their own.

ANSWERS

L: I'm a big fan of ... It's really cool. The really neat thing is ...
H: I'm not crazy about ... I'm not keen on ... It drives me nuts. That really bugs me. What I can't stand is ... What really annoys me is ...

3 Students work with a partner to try to predict what the interviewees will say and to put their ideas in the table in note form. Have a class feedback session.

4 2.08 Play the recording, and ask the students to tick any of their ideas that are mentioned and to make a note of anything they hadn't thought of.

ANSWERS

Loves: jokes and silly emails; provides a permanent record; people respond to emails more than phone calls
Hates: being cc-ed on emails that are irrelevant to you; junk mail, chain emails and jokes; emoticons; people expect an immediate reply; long emails and big attachments; bosses can read them

2.08

Erm, well, being cc-ed on every little thing drives me nuts. I'd say 60% of the messages I get have nothing to do with me.

What I can't stand is all the junk, the stupid jokes, all the meaning-of-life stuff that seems to fill my inbox. All those things, you know, like, 'Send this to ten more people or a disaster will hit your city.' I mean, come on!

I think all the silly stuff is quite cool, actually. The jokes, the slideshows. I mean, it's just a way of keeping in touch. It's not meant to be taken seriously!

The really neat thing is that you can go back through your emails and see what's been said. You have a permanent record of every discussion. Which is really useful sometimes.

What really annoys me are those little smiley things, emoticons. Just childish.

I'm a big fan of email. You leave a voicemail, nobody gets back to you. You send an email, it always gets through. I think people are better about answering their email than their phone.

People expecting an instant reply – that really bugs me. I mean, okay, so you sent me an email. Like I'm supposed to drop everything and answer it?

Well, I'm not crazy about 15-paragraph emails. Or those 20-megabyte attachments that take an hour to download. When do these people get any work done?

I read somewhere that 20% of email gets read by the boss, which is kind of scary. I'm not keen on the idea that Big Brother is watching me!

5 Ask each student to describe a particular 'pet hate' with regard to email to the class. If no one mentions style or linguistic accuracy, you may need to bring up the subject in preparation for the next section.

BUSINESS COMMUNICATION

Writing emails

In this section, students look at the style of emails and some suggested rules for writing them. They read an extract from a book on how important the ability to write well is in business and they practise changing formal letters into a style more suitable for emails. They then work on making emails clearer and better organized.

1 Do this as a class discussion, making sure that everyone understands the extract from the book. See how many students agree with the writer. Find out how important the ability to write well is in their own language.

2 Focus attention on the part of the extract where the writer talks about 'connecting', and how good business writing establishes a relationship between writer and receiver. Students work with a partner to discuss ways of creating this connection with people they email. In a class feedback session, put the students' ideas on the board.

3 Check the answers by having one student read out the rule and another provide the reason.

ANSWERS
a 4 b 8 c 6 d 3 e 1 f 7 g 2 h 5

4 Ask students to look at the words that have been crossed out in the examples. What types of word are they? Give students time to read through the email and decide what the missing words might be. Tell students that one of the words missing is a preposition.

SUGGESTED ANSWERS
The three types of grammar words are pronouns, verbs and articles.
Hi Rosa – I've been in meetings all day, so I just got your message plus the attachment. It sounds great – I particularly like your suggestion about the discount rates. One or two points are a bit unclear, perhaps, but basically it's good stuff. You could add something about the packaging.
You've done a nice job, anyway.
I'll see you on Friday. Leo

5 Elicit or explain that fixed expressions are sequences of words which often occur together, and that they are particularly common in formal letters, e.g. *Thank you for your letter of ..., I look forward to hearing from you.* Although the language of emails is in many ways simpler than that of formal letters, the lack of formulaic expressions may make email writing more challenging.

Explain to students that with these emails there is a pre-existing relationship between the sender and the receiver. A more formal style would be appropriate if this relationship did not exist.

ANSWERS
A Hi Louisa
Got your message on the 12th September. Sorry, but I can't make the meeting on the 21st. Could you do me a favour and send me a copy of the minutes?
Cheers
Tom Hunt
B Good news: as of 2 Jan we are offering substantial discounts on all orders over €1,000. Shall I send you further details and a copy of our new catalogue?
C Bad news: the board turned down your proposal. Sorry about not getting back to you sooner on this, but I've been in Montreal all week.
D Are we still okay for 3rd May? My flight gets in about 11 am. About my presentation on the 4th, could you make the necessary arrangements? I'm sending you a list of the equipment I'll need as an attachment.
See you next week.
Charlotte De Vere
E Following our telephone conversation this morning, please send me a full description of the problem and I'll pass it on to our technical department.
Thanks. If you have any questions, let me know.
Speak to you soon.

6 Elicit or explain that a new paragraph begins where there is a change of idea. Although emails are less formal than letters, it is still helpful for clarity if they are divided into paragraphs. Discuss with students what makes a good subject line for an email: it's short, creates a context and gives clues about what is in the message.

To practise writing good subject lines, give each student two pieces of paper. On one, they write a short message of one or two lines. On the other, they write the subject line for that message. They then exchange the message only with a partner. They each read the message they have received, write a subject line for it at the top and return it to the sender, who compares it with the original subject line. Pairs can discuss the reasons for any similarities or differences between the two. (With thanks to John Hughes for this idea.)

SAMPLE ANSWER
Subject: Quarterly figures
Otto
How are you doing? Got the joke you sent me – very funny. Spoke to Cheryl in accounts today. She sends her regards.
On the subject of accounts, I don't seem to have your quarterlies. Did you send them in?
I've emailed you those statistics you wanted, by the way. Hope they come in useful for your presentation. Let me know how the presentation goes. And don't forget those figures.

BUSINESS COMMUNICATION

7 Give the students time to read the email through before they start making improvements to it.

SAMPLE ANSWER

Dear Mr Nordqvist,
Thank you for your hospitality during our stay. Karen and I felt that the meeting was a great success and we look forward to discussing our ideas in more detail.
I passed on your comments to Diane Lee and she assures me she will contact you over the next couple of weeks.
It was a pleasure meeting you and exploring the possibilities of a joint venture between us.
Best wishes
Sam White

8 Remind students of the need to build a personal relationship with the person receiving the email and that one way to do this is to include some personal touches.

SAMPLE ANSWER

Dear Mr Nordqvist,
First of all, many congratulations on your recent promotion and also on the birth of your child. Please pass on my very best wishes to your wife.
Thank you for your hospitality during our stay. Karen and I felt …

Language links

Direct students to the *Phrase bank* in the *Language links* section on page 66 for more useful phrases for emails, divided into categories according to their function.

Changing arrangements

1 2.09–2.11 Go through the questions with the class before you play the recordings so that students know what they are listening for.

ANSWERS

Message 1: a On Wednesday.
            b Sarah has to be in Edinburgh on Monday.
Message 2: a It's fully booked.
            b Find another hotel for them.
Message 3: a About 45 minutes.
            b PowerPoint, projector and screen.

2.09
Message 1

Hi Koichi, it's Sarah Greenwood here. There's been a change of plan. Peter and I were hoping to arrive in Nagoya on Monday. That's not going to be possible now, I'm afraid, because I have to be in Edinburgh that day. So, we're aiming to get there by Wednesday, but that should still give us plenty of time to get organized before the presentation.

2.10
Message 2

Hi Koichi, it's Sarah again. Peter and I were planning to stay at the Radisson, because it's near, but apparently there's a conference next week and it's already fully booked. Sorry, I was going to email you about this yesterday. Could you find us somewhere else? Thanks very much.

2.11
Message 3

Hi Koichi, it's me again. Just one more thing, sorry. We're intending to keep the presentation itself quite short – about 45 minutes – to allow plenty of time for questions and we're going to use PowerPoint, so we're going to need a projector and screen, if you can organize that. Thanks, see you on Wednesday.

Language links

Direct students to the *Language links* section on page 65 for more collocations relating to computers.

2 Encourage students to try to remember what Sarah said, but play the recordings again for them if necessary. Check the answers before going on to 3.

ANSWERS

a were hoping to   b 's not going to be   c 're aiming to
d were planning to   e was going to   f 're intending to
g 're going to   h 're going to

3 Do this exercise with the whole class.

ANSWERS

1 b, h   2 c, f, g   3 a, d, e

Language links

Direct students to the *Language links* section on pages 65–66 for further explanation of the use of future forms and exercises to practise these forms.

4 This could be set for homework. Start students off by brainstorming suggestions for Koichi's subject line.

SAMPLE ANSWER

Subject line: Arrangements for Nagoya trip
Hi Sarah
Thanks for letting me know about the change of plan. Have booked rooms for you and Peter at Nagoya Holiday Inn. No problem with equipment – have already arranged projector and screen. Have a good time in Edinburgh. Looking forward to seeing you on Wednesday. Let me know flight details and I'll meet you at the airport.
Koichi

10 EMAIL

BUSINESS COMMUNICATION

You've got mail

Go through the instructions with the class and then ask students to work in groups of three or four. To make this more authentic and fun, prepare a box to put at the front of the class in which completed emails can be posted and from which they can be collected. Reading out the names of students who have incoming mail will keep the activity moving briskly. Use separate boxes for the different groups. Go through the useful introductory phrases in the box at the side of the page with the class and make sure everyone understands them. You might like to ask for a few suggestions for situations in which they might be used.

Students start writing their emails. Ensure that there is enough space on each piece of paper for subsequent responses. Allow plenty of time in class for students to compare their email sequences.

1:1 This exercise could be done by email. Send your student a series of emails over the coming week, and ask them to reply and to bring the complete series of emails to the next lesson.

Language links

ANSWERS

Vocabulary

Computers

1 keyboard; website; search engine; homepage; database; spreadsheet; desktop; help menu; hard disk; banner ad
2 a surf the Internet b enter data into a computer
  c run a program d download files off the Net
  e click on an icon f transmit a virus g crash a computer
  h install software i burn CDs j send an attachment
  k empty the trash l browse the Web
  m upgrade to a better model n cut and paste text
3 1 crashed 2 Net 3 emptied 4 virus 5 emailed
  6 attachment 7 error 8 occurred 9 clicked
  10 download 11 program 12 files 13 data
  14 backups 15 helpline 16 upgrade 17 technician
  18 desktop 19 printer 20 type 21 computer 22 ROM
  23 keyboard 24 spam 25 shut 26 insane
  27 Resources 28 retrain

Grammar

Future forms

1 a 5 b 2 c 4 d 3 e 8 f 1 g 6 h 7
2 a 2 b 8 c 7 d 1 e 3 f 5 g 4 h 6
3 a going to b intending to c planning to
  d aiming to e hoping to
4 a you're giving b I will be c I'll help d isn't e I'll still have
  f are going g you're going to have h I'll give i we're going
  j It'll take k I'm just going to check l I'll be

Phrase bank: Email

a 5 b 8 c 1 d 3 e 7 f 2 g 4 h 6 i 16
j 14 k 15 l 9 m 12 n 13 o 10 p 11

11 Presenting

Learning objectives

This unit is about presenting successfully. Students begin by identifying elements of a good presentation and ranking them in order of importance.

The next section emphasizes the importance of delivery, and teaches students to distinguish between the delivery required for a presentation and that employed in normal conversation. They analyze a short extract from a talk on entrepreneurship by Guy Kawasaki to see the effect of employing correct pausing and emphasis.

The focus on delivery continues in the next section, and students are introduced to devices such as repetition and rhetorical questions, which will enhance their presentation style. The emphasis then moves on to the best way to structure a presentation using discourse markers to help listeners recognize in which direction the presentation is going.

The use of visuals is examined next. Students then listen to a presentation involving visuals, and analyze what the speaker says and how he presents his material.

Finally, they practise making their own presentations with a framework to guide them.

The grammar focus is on past forms, and the lexical focus is on expressions and collocations relating to presentations.

Digital resources: Unit 11

Online Workbook; 📹 *In company* interviews Units 9–11 and worksheet; Extension worksheets; Glossary; Phrase bank; Student's Book answer key; Student's Book listening script; Fast-track map

---

This first section focuses on what makes a good presentation. Students rank qualities in order of importance and discuss good presentations they have been to.

Warm-up

Ask students to identify the photo on page 67 (Dr Martin Luther King giving his famous *I have a dream* speech at the Lincoln Memorial, Washington DC in August 1963) and find out if anyone has ever heard a recording of the speech. Ask why he was such a powerful speaker and if they can name any other impressive public speakers. Focus attention on the quotation from film star John Wayne and ask whether they think this is good advice for people speaking in public. Then ask how often your students give presentations at work and if they enjoy them.

1 Students choose the words to complete the list. Encourage them to talk about successful talks they have been to where these elements were particularly noticeable.

ANSWERS
a talk b knowledge c appearance d humour e contact
f attitude g voice h visuals i language j preparation

2 Students work with a partner to rank the elements in 1 in order of importance. Let them compare and discuss their results with other pairs, then have a class feedback session. Praise any use of the phrases in the box.

3 Elicit suggestions for other elements that make a good presentation. Write them on the board and discuss their ranking in the overall list.

Language links

Direct students to the *Phrase bank* in the *Language links* section on page 73 for more useful language for giving presentations.

Delivery

The focus in this section is on how the way we sound differs when we give a presentation as compared with normal conversation. Students learn to distinguish between the two and focus on aspects of delivery that mark out a presentation. They read and listen to part of a talk by Guy Kawasaki, and focus on where he uses stress and pauses for effect.

Warm-up

Ask students to talk about giving presentations. How do they feel about presenting? Are they nervous? Do they look forward to it or dread it? What are the best and worst aspects of giving presentations?

1 You might like to ask several students to read the text in different ways: one to a neighbour as if it is an interesting piece of gossip; one as if they are a spy passing on secret information to a contact; one as if they are selling a course on presentation to the class, etc. Then have a class discussion on how useful the advice is.

2 🔊 2.12 Go through the instructions. Tell the students in advance that the six extracts are in pairs and that the extracts in each pair are delivered by the same speaker, but in two different ways.

ANSWERS
a C b P c P d C e C f P

> 🔊 **2.12**
> **Extract a**
> They tried it. They liked it. So they bought it.
> **Extract b**
> They tried it. They liked it. So they bought it.

11 PRESENTING   61

BUSINESS COMMUNICATION

> **Extract c**
> We can never be the biggest, but we can be the best.
> **Extract d**
> We can never be the biggest, but we can be the best.
> **Extract e**
> Did you know that the whole thing was absolutely free?
> **Extract f**
> Did you know that the whole thing was absolutely free?

3 Allow pairs to compare their ideas with other pairs before you have a class feedback session.

4 2.13 Go through the instructions with the class and find out if students are familiar with Guy Kawasaki. Elicit what they think is involved in being a 'chief evangelist'. (An evangelist promotes the use of a particular product through presentations, articles, blogging, etc. Guy Kawasaki is considered to be a pioneer of evangelism marketing: developing customers who believe so strongly in a product that they convince other people to buy it.)

Elicit from the class the reasons why we pause when we speak (to take a breath, to allow listeners to digest what has been said, to allow thinking time, for dramatic effect, etc). Encourage students to read the extract aloud in order to get a feel for what sounds right as they mark the pauses. Allow them to work with a partner or in small groups if they wish. Then play the recording for them to check.

> **ANSWERS**
> The <u>first</u> thing I <u>figured out</u> / and <u>learned</u> / sometimes the <u>hard</u> way / about <u>entrepreneurship</u> / is that the <u>core</u> / the <u>essence</u> of <u>entrepreneurship</u> / is about <u>making meaning</u> / many many <u>people</u> / start <u>companies</u> to make <u>money</u> / the <u>quick flip</u> / the <u>dotcom</u> phenomenon / and I have <u>noticed</u> / in <u>both</u> the companies that I have <u>started</u> / and <u>funded</u> / and been <u>associated</u> with / that those <u>companies</u> / that are <u>fundamentally founded</u> to change the <u>world</u> / to make the world a <u>better</u> place / to <u>make meaning</u> / are the <u>companies</u> that make a <u>difference</u> / they are the <u>companies</u> to <u>succeed</u> / my naïve and romantic <u>belief</u> / is that if you <u>make meaning</u> / you'll probably <u>make money</u> / but if you <u>set out</u> / to <u>make money</u> / you will probably <u>not make meaning</u> / <u>and</u> you <u>won't</u> / <u>make</u> / <u>money</u>.

> 2.13
> The first thing I figured out / and learned / sometimes the hard way / about entrepreneurship / is that the core / the essence of entrepreneurship / is about making meaning / many many people / start companies to make money / the quick flip / the dotcom phenomenon / and I have noticed / in both the companies that I have started and funded / and been associated with / that those companies / that are fundamentally founded to change the world / to make the world a better place / to make meaning / are the companies that make a difference / they are the companies to succeed / my naïve and romantic belief / is that if you make meaning / you'll probably make money / but if you set out to make money / you will probably not make meaning / and you won't / make / money.

5 2.13 Play the recording again for students to underline the strongly stressed words. Ask them to discuss the questions with a partner or in small groups, then have a class feedback session.

> **ANSWERS**
> See answers to 4 for the underlined strongly stressed words.
> We tend to pause after stressed words, which are usually the main 'content words', such as nouns and verbs.
> If we pause less often, it sounds more fluent (but not enough pausing can become monotonous and difficult to follow).
> If we pause more often, it can sound powerful and dramatic (but too much pausing can sound pretentious or aggressive).

A team presentation

The focus in this section remains on the delivery of a presentation. Students are given material to present, and have to decide where to pause and which words should be stressed. They are invited to make the presentation in two different ways and decide which way sounds best.

1 The aim of having the students present the material together is to give them the security of a joint presentation before doing any public speaking alone. Before they start, elicit the difference between presenting clearly and professionally, and presenting enthusiastically and dramatically.

With a small class, you could ask each pair to do their presentation in front of the class, perhaps with the others deciding which presentation style they are using each time and commenting on how successful they think it is. With larger classes, give help and encouragement as students practise giving the presentations together.

> **1:1** Ask your student to make the whole presentation, moving from point to point following the arrows on the chart. Be sure to praise the student's performance before looking at how to make improvements.

2 Explain that rhetorical questions are those asked purely for effect; an answer is not expected or required.

> **ANSWERS**
> a A bank which ...
> b Funny kind of bank? Unbelievable? Even a little magical?
> c ... efficient, safe and secure; You can, naturally, choose when, where and how to deal with your money.
> d A bank designed around you, which doesn't expect you to fit round it.

3 Students should have little trouble matching the techniques to the reasons they are effective. Ask if such techniques are common in the students' own languages. Your students may be interested in discussing why grouping points in threes creates a satisfying sense of completeness. For some reason, three items in a row achieve a degree of persuasion that one and two cannot.

> **ANSWERS**
> 1 b   2 c   3 a   4 d

62   11 PRESENTING

BUSINESS COMMUNICATION

Structuring a presentation

In this section, the focus is on the best way to organize material for a presentation. The aim is to teach students techniques for making their presentations clearer and easier for the audience to follow.

1 When the students have completed the expressions with the correct prepositions, you might like to ask them to read each one and complete the sentence in an appropriate way. By doing this, they hear the expressions in action. This could be done after the matching activity in 2.

ANSWERS
a off b on c back d to e about f of g for h up

2 Students identify the functions of the expressions they have just completed.

ANSWERS
1 c 2 h 3 g 4 a 5 e, f 6 b, d

Using visuals

Many successful presentations involve the use of visuals. Correct use of these will enhance a presentation and make the information more accessible to the audience. In this section, students learn techniques for referring to visuals.

> **Language links**
> Direct students to the *Language links* section on pages 72–73 for more practice of expressions students will find useful when making a presentation.

1 The phrases in this exercise help focus the audience's attention on a visual. You might like to ask the students which one is the beginning of a rhetorical question (f).

ANSWERS
a Have b see c point d show e give f mean

2 Graphs are common in business presentations and students will find it useful to learn these basic ways of referring to movements on a graph.

ANSWERS
rise a   level off g   fluctuate c   peak d   recover f
bottom out e   fall b

A technical problem

In this section, students listen to and analyze a presentation given by a stock trading company manager.

1 🔊 **2.14–2.16** Play all three recordings first for the students merely to listen and gain a general understanding of the content of the presentation, its structure and how successful it is. Then go through the instructions in Parts A–C so that students know what information they are listening for. Then play the individual recordings, pausing for students to discuss and decide their answers to each set of questions.

ANSWERS
a 1 and 4
b 1 The number of months since they went online.
  2 The number of hits a day nine months ago.
  3 The number of months Gary Cale has been with the company.
  4 The number of hits a day three months ago.
c Slow access speed, website too complicated, poor search engines.
d To win back customer confidence and to make a profit.
e b
f 1, 2 and 4

🔊 **2.14**
Part A

A: Okay, this brings us on to the next item on our agenda this morning, which is online business. Now, I know some of you are concerned about the recent performance of E-Stock, our online subsidiary. So I've asked Gary Cale, our new head of e-business, to bring us up to date. Over to you, Gary.

B: Thanks, Michelle. To start off, then, I know you have all seen the figures up to the last quarter – disappointing to say the least. Nine months ago, when we first went online, we were getting over 250,000 hits a day. Three months ago, when I joined this company, we were getting just 60,000 and it was obvious we were failing to attract sufficient customers to our website. So, what was going wrong? In a word, technology. The problem was not the service we were offering, but the website itself.

🔊 **2.15**
Part B

B: Now, three things make a good website. First, access to the website must be fast. The slow access speed of our website meant people were getting bored waiting for pages to load and simply going somewhere else. Second, a good website must be easy to use. Ours was so complicated, customers sometimes didn't know if they were buying or selling! And third, a good website must have excellent search engines. Ours didn't. To give you an example of what I mean, a fault we hadn't noticed in the programming caused 1,500 people to invest in a company that didn't even exist. Yes, embarrassing. I'm glad I wasn't here to take the blame for that one! Okay, to move on. Greenbaum-Danson is unquestionably one of the world's leading financial services companies. We're the biggest, oldest and most respected firm in the business. But to succeed in online stock trading, to succeed in any area of e-business, you need a first-class website. So, creating a first-class website was our first priority. The next thing was Internet advertising, winning back the customer confidence we'd lost. That's a longer job, but we're making progress. The final thing, and this always takes time in e-business, will be to actually make a profit. Well, we can dream!

11 PRESENTING   63

BUSINESS COMMUNICATION

2.16
Part C
B: Have a look at this. It's a graph showing the number of trades our customers make per day on our website. As you can see, the figure was fluctuating for the first three months and then fell sharply to bottom out at just 10,000 trades a day. For a company of our size, that wasn't too impressive. But look. We're up to nearly 40,000 trades now, our highest ever, and still rising. Okay, I'm going to break off in a minute and take questions. So, to sum up. One, improvements in our website have led to more hits and increased trading. Two, advertising on the Internet will help us win back customers. Three, profits will follow. E-trading in stocks is the future. In the US alone, it's the way a quarter of the public choose to buy their shares. This is the information age and the Internet is the ultimate information provider. I'm reminded of what banker Walter Wriston once said: 'Information about money is becoming more valuable than money itself.' Thank you.

2 This exercise focuses more closely on the choice of tenses used by the presenter in the recordings in 1.

ANSWERS
at the same time: a, b
one after the other: c, d

Language links

Direct students to the *Language links* section on pages 72–73 for further explanation of the construction and use of the Past Continuous and the Past Perfect, and exercises to practise these tenses.

Giving a short presentation

In this section, students use the skills they have been learning to give their own presentations.

Go through the instructions with the class and make sure they understand that they only have to choose one of the situations. Give students plenty of time to prepare their presentations and allot class time to hearing each of them. You might like to set the preparation for homework to enable students to do some research on the chosen product or person. This would give them more facts to work with and they would, as a result, be able to use more of the expressions in the boxes.

Encourage students to use their own experience and knowledge as the basis of their presentations, but allow them to invent the details if they wish. Reassure them that the language in the boxes is there to help them, but they can make changes to it if they wish.

You will probably have established in earlier discussions that the worst presentations are those in which speakers simply read out written speeches. Remind students that they should not read their presentations but can refer to brief notes from time to time if they find this helpful. Remind them, too, of the skills they have practised in earlier sections of this unit: eye contact and body language, good delivery with correct stress and pauses, a clear structure so the audience can follow what is being said, etc.

Public speaking can be an ordeal, so ensure that other students are quiet and pay attention to each speaker, and that the response to each presentation is positive and encouraging.

1:1 You could make a presentation for the situation which your student has not chosen. This will give the student extra listening practice, and you can provide a good model, demonstrating all the target features: contrasts, rhetorical questions and groups of three. Make sure you retain the guessing element of the exercise by reminding your student not to tell you who or what the subject of their presentation is and not revealing your own.

In company interviews action Units 9–11
Encourage students to watch the interview and complete the worksheet.

Language links

ANSWERS

Vocabulary

Presentations

Communication skills
1 a a point   d a graph
   b figures   e jokes
   c an issue   f questions

Trends and change
2 a [↓][↗] b [∧][↑] c [↗][↓][∨] d [↗][↑][∧]
   e [→][↘] f [∿][↓] g [↗][↘] h [↘][↑]

Grammar

Past Continuous
1 a 2 b 1 c 4 d 3
2 Hello, Inge. Er, sure. I was just going out for lunch, but …
   Well, I saw Dieter the other day …
   Actually, I decided a month ago, but I didn't think anybody knew about it yet.
   The whole department was talking about it when I came in …
   They were still talking about it when I left.

Past Perfect
3 a everyone else's departure
   b forgetting your passport, getting halfway to the airport, realizing your mistake

Past Simple, Past Continuous or Past Perfect
4 a had been   b decided   c was just clearing   d suddenly remembered   e had happened   f was   g had come   h came up   i did   j set   k was   l got back   m was leaving   n thought   o had gone   p had set up   q proceeded   r were enjoying   s heard   t had finally built up   u crashed

Phrase bank: The language of presentations
a okay   b started   c myself   d parts   e overview
f minute   g us   h here   i on   j graph   k themselves
l earlier   m point   n detail   o perspective   p little
q moment   r up   s talk   t questions
The advice is: Keep it short and simple.

12 Impact

Learning objectives

This unit continues the theme of presentations with a look at achieving maximum impact when presenting. Students discuss what creates impact in a presentation and what kills it. They then read a text which offers 'the four Cs of presenting with impact' and listen to eight short extracts from presentations which employ these techniques. They also do some work on stress, rhythm and intonation.

A second listening gives them the opportunity to hear two entrepreneurs making a product pitch to a group of venture capitalists and they then practise presenting their own product with impact.

Digital resources: Unit 12

Online Workbook; Extension worksheets; Glossary; Student's Book answer key; Student's Book listening script; Fast-track map

Warm-up

Elicit or explain the meaning of *impact* in the context of giving presentations (the power of making a strong, immediate impression). Ask students to talk about the presentation they have been to that had the most impact. Can they say why it left such an impression on them?

1:1 YouTube™ clips are ideal for one-to-one teaching. You will find a lot of clips which show both good and bad presentations. Some of the TED talks (TED.com/talks) are also good for demonstrating high-impact presentations.

1 Focus attention on the cartoon and ask students to work in groups to talk about any business presentations like this that they have attended. Encourage them to report back to the class.

2 Have a class discussion of these questions.

SUGGESTED ANSWERS
A lot of presenters overload their visuals with data because they think this will make them look well prepared and help them remember what to say. Unfortunately, this often leads to them reading out their slides. Not only does this create the impression that they don't know their material, it also confuses the audience, who can read a lot faster than the presenter can speak. So they quickly learn to ignore the presenter and read ahead! A much better idea would be to learn the key points by heart, have the details on numbered hand-outs in case you need them and prepare simple, visually powerful slides to remind you of what to say next.

3 Students work with a partner to decide on the factors that create and kill impact, and make two lists. When they have finished, pool ideas as a class and put all suggestions in a table on the board. Make sure the pairs keep their lists as they will need them in 4.

SUGGESTED ANSWERS
BRAVO! a steady pace with some variation in the voice; good use of pauses; a relaxed posture and conversational but professional tone; simple, striking visuals; a few well-chosen key figures and/or pieces of information; short, relevant (perhaps amusing) stories, etc
BORING! a hurried pace or over-hesitation; a forced smile; too many ums and ers; fidgeting; little or no eye contact; overcomplicated visuals; too much jargon; too much data; illogical structure; bad jokes; long pointless stories; no reference to the audience, etc

4 Go through the instructions with the class before asking students to work with a partner (the same one they worked with for 3). Explain, if necessary, that 'the four Cs' will be four words beginning with the letter C that the author considers are the key to presenting with impact. Allow plenty of time for students to make their initial predictions and to read the text. When they have finished, encourage them to report back to the class on their discussions and find out if students came up with any other words beginning with C that are equally valid.

5 2.17–2.24 Go through the instructions and the eight descriptions with the class before you play the recordings, so students know what information they need to listen out for. Play the recordings more than once if necessary, and pause between each extract to give them a little thinking and processing time.

ANSWERS
a 4 b 7 c 1 d 6 e 8 f 2 g 3 h 5

2.17
Speaker 1
Of course, everyone in this room is an experienced IT professional. I myself have been in the personal computer business for about 15 years now. And I was fortunate enough to be part of the team at Apple® that developed the first iPhone and iPad. So I guess you could say I've learned quite a bit about portable and mobile devices.

2.18
Speaker 2
Okay, so much for the product specs. What about the sales prospects? Now, I know what you're thinking. You're thinking how can there be a market for such a niche product? So let me reassure you that we've carried out extensive market research and the figures are very, very promising. You'll find a full breakdown in your product information pack, but let me just share with you some of the most exciting results.

PEOPLE SKILLS

2.19
Speaker 3
So that's the Orion 7. Let me tell you, this revolutionary new product is going to be huge! As we've seen, the technology behind it is absolutely cutting-edge and we've made several radical changes to the functionality and design of the old Orion 6. This is the product that's not only going to destroy the competition – it's going to totally transform the industry!

2.20
Speaker 4
Now, in this country we all tend to think that the unemployment situation has gotten out of control. But here's something that might surprise you. Did you know that right now, right here in the USA, there are three million unfilled jobs? Three million genuine job openings! Those are the latest figures just posted. What's more, those jobs are only being filled half as fast as in previous recessions. We don't have a job shortage, ladies and gentlemen, so much as a skills shortage! And that's where we come in …

2.21
Speaker 5
Talking of the failure rate of start-up companies, that reminds me of the joke about the entrepreneur who goes to his bank manager and asks her: 'How do I start a small business?' 'Simple,' says the bank manager. 'Buy a big one and wait!'

2.22
Speaker 6
Okay, so those are the key product benefits. And that was the first thing I wanted to talk to you about this morning. Now, let's see how we measure up against our main competitors. Well, in terms of overall performance, there really is no comparison. Frankly, the Zamira leaves the competition standing. And when it comes to compatibility – well, as you can see, the figures speak for themselves.

2.23
Speaker 7
Now, the text-flow process itself is quite complex. So we've broken it down into three simpler stages. Have a look at this. This diagram shows you how text and images from the original digital source reconfigure themselves to fit the screen of your tablet or mobile. As you can see, …

2.24
Speaker 8
You ask how Leo and I started our business. And I can tell you exactly how. Seven years ago, I was getting bored at the company I was working for and applied for another job. Now, the firm I was applying to had hired a recruitment agency to do the interviewing and guess who the interviewer was? That's right – Leo! He said: 'If you want my honest opinion, you'll be wasted at this company. Why don't you start your own business?' I said: 'But I don't know anything about starting a business!' He said: 'I do!' And that was how it all began …

6 **2.17–2.24** Ask students to turn to the listening script on pages 152–153 and to follow along as you play the recordings again. Ask them to focus on the stress, rhythm and intonation, and to highlight any useful phrases they would like to remember for use in their own presentations. Have the class talk about what they noticed about the speakers' intonation. Ask them which person they found easiest to listen to and which they think had the most impact.

7 **2.25** Elicit or explain the term *venture capitalist* (someone who invests money in a new enterprise) and make sure students understand the situation before you play the recording. Ask them to listen and decide which of the things in 5 the two presenters do not do.

ANSWER
They don't tell a story.

2.25
A: Good morning. And thanks for taking the time to talk to us. We want to talk to you about cookery. That's right, cookery. … Did you know that cookery books are the second best-selling type of book, outselling romance novels, biographies, self-help, science-fiction …? In fact, apart from murder mysteries, you name it, they outsell it … Frankly, the figures are staggering! Roughly 60 million cookery books are bought a year! … Switch on daytime TV and chances are there'll be cookery programmes on every single channel. In Britain alone, there are around 50 scheduled cookery series! … Why is cookery such a giant industry? … Well, we all eat. And a lot of us, it seems, would like to be able to cook. But, sadly, many of us still can't boil an egg.

B: That's where we come in. TastePal is a mobile phone app that caters for the 28% of us who, according to a recent survey in the States, just can't cook. Now, TastePal doesn't try to teach you how to cook, because we know you probably don't even have the ingredients in your kitchen to make a decent meal! … No, the idea is this … You tell us what you do have in your kitchen cupboards and TastePal comes up with a selection of simple recipes using just those ingredients. We can't guarantee it'll be a culinary masterpiece, but it will be tasty, nutritious and easy to prepare. Plus, if you're going to the supermarket, TastePal will suggest a couple of things you could buy to make it even better!

A: Here's a screenshot of the app. As you can see, the user interface couldn't be simpler – with drag-and-drop touchscreen icons for food categories and animated cartoons for how to prepare the meals. Who's our market? Students, young professionals, single people mostly – frequently male. Exactly the right market for a mobile app.

B: Now, I guess you're thinking: 'But aren't there apps for this already?' And, indeed, there are – a few. But most of them are little more than digital checklists and recipe instructions – tiny text, difficult to follow. None of them uses animation. And none of them has the extra functions of TastePal. TastePal keeps a log of the meals you like and alerts you when you're running low on what you need to make them. TastePal also alerts you when you're not getting a balanced diet. And it will tell you how to estimate measures if you don't have the right equipment – which we're pretty sure you won't.

A: My business partner Jim's a trained chef. And I have six years' experience in designing mobile apps, including two award-winning apps for the iPhone. We're looking for 50,000 euros to cover further development and marketing costs in return for 20% of the business. Thanks a lot.

8 **2.25** Remind students what N.A.B.C. is (see the article about the four Cs: need, approach, benefits, competitors). Then play the recording again and ask them to identify the entrepreneurs' N.A.B.C.

ANSWERS

N = Young people (especially male) who want to be able to cook, but can't.
A = A mobile phone app which tells you how to prepare meals with the ingredients you already have.
B = The customer will be able to cook simple, nutritious meals easily; the app logs your favourite meals, alerts you when you're running out of essential ingredients and also when you're not getting a balanced diet.
C = Other apps are just simple checklists and recipes; none of them is as visual or user-friendly; none of them has the extra functions of TastePal.

9 Ask students to work with a partner and turn to page 129. They will need quite a lot of preparation and research time, particularly if they decide to invent their own, totally new app. Much of this may have to be done for homework, so make sure the pairs are able to work together outside class. Allow plenty of class time for the presentations to be made, and encourage listening students to take notes and ask questions at the end of each pitch. This is the culmination of quite a lot of work on presentations, so it could perhaps be used for assessment, with students incorporating as many of the techniques and as much of the language for presentations that they have learned as possible.

MANAGEMENT SCENARIO C

Morale problems

Learning objectives

This scenario is based on the issue of poor morale in a sales team and how motivation can be improved. Students begin by reading an email from the marketing director to Anton Vega in which she raises the issue of poor performance and low morale. They then watch a video in which Anton talks to his team. They discuss how well he deals with them and how he might improve his motivational skills. After reading an article about how to motivate a team, they watch another video and compare Anton's performance in handling his staff this time. Finally, they work with a partner to practise delivering a motivation session and evaluating their partner's performance.

Digital resources: Management Scenario C

In company in action C1–C2 and worksheet; Extension worksheets; Glossary; Student's Book answer key; Student's Book listening script; Fast-track map

Warm-up

Focus attention on the photo, and ask students to say where they think the people are and what they are doing. Encourage them to speculate on how the people are feeling (look at facial expressions and body language).

Focus attention on the title *Morale problems* and elicit reasons why people working for a company might have low morale. If necessary, start them off with a few ideas: overwork, feeling undervalued, threats of redundancy, etc.

1 Go through the instructions with the class, and give them time to read the email and answer the questions.

ANSWERS
a Six
b The financial climate has affected the performance of all the sales units.
c Anton's unit has been having morale problems.
d One with Gabrielle and another with his sales team.
e She doesn't sound at all happy! She's polite but direct in the first paragraph of her email. And by the second paragraph, she's already become more critical.

2 C1 Go through the instructions with students before playing the video and make sure they understand all the things in the list. As preparation, you could play the video without sound first and ask students just to say if the meeting goes well. Then play the video with sound and ask students to tick what Anton does wrong. Elicit answers from the class.

ANSWERS
He blames people (Alan, in particular). He refuses to listen.
He makes threats (about possible job losses and salary cuts).
He divides the team (by praising some team members and criticizing others).

C1
Anton: So, those are our sales figures for the last quarter. And I don't need to tell you what they were like for Q2 because you already know – they were just as lousy. So that makes six months running we have failed to meet our targets. I just came out of a meeting with Gabrielle this morning and she wants answers. And, frankly, so do I. Yes, Alan?

Alan: It's the leads. They're no good. We can't be …

Anton: Alan, I don't want to hear any more complaints about the leads, okay? Those are quality leads. If you can't close on those leads, if you can't secure the business, that's your fault! Now what's going wrong, people? Because I may as well tell you, if this goes on, all our jobs are on the line.

Heather: I think part of the problem is that we're all so massively overworked, Anton. Since the sales units were downsized, everyone's been under an enormous amount of pressure. Tony here's had almost no training …

Anton: Don't bring me problems, Heather, bring me solutions! All the units were downsized, not just ours! Now, I know you've probably been the best performer these last two quarters. You're mostly meeting your targets, sometimes exceeding them. One or two others, however, are simply not pulling their weight.

Alan: Now wait a minute. You know I had some personal problems …

Anton: Not now, Alan, please. Look, everybody, it's no good making excuses. I know times are tough, but we're slipping badly. Gabrielle thinks, and I'm beginning to agree with her, that increasing basic salaries for all units was a mistake and we should consider going back to a mostly commission based system for underperforming units.

Alan: You mean, other teams are going to be making more than us?

Anton: Those that meet their targets will, yes.

Heather: But that's absolutely ridiculous!

Anton: Now, now, now, look everybody, please can we all just calm down! It's not going to help if we all start losing our tempers …

3 Students work with a partner to discuss the question. Ask them to report back on the advice they would give Anton to improve his motivational skills.

SUGGESTED ANSWER

Anton should not have let his personal stress make him lose control and criticize his team so directly. If this is supposed to be a motivation session, it's a terrible one! He should probably have begun by asking his team to voice their complaints and offer suggestions as to how things could be improved.

68 C MORALE PROBLEMS

MANAGEMENT SCENARIO

4 Students work with a partner to look at the words and phrases in the box, and check which ones they already know. Allow them to help each other with any unknown items, but discourage them from looking them up in a dictionary. Ask them to try to use the context of the article to work out what they mean. Give students plenty of time to read the article, or perhaps set the reading for homework.

5 Ask students to work individually to find points in the article that they agree and disagree with. Let them compare with a partner and then have a class feedback session to find out how much consensus there is.

6 📹 **C2** Go through the instructions with the class and make sure everyone understands the three criteria on which they are to judge Anton's performance in his second team meeting. Ask them to watch and decide on their own rating before comparing with a partner.

📹 **C2**

Anton: Thank you, Alan ... Okay, thanks, everyone, for making the time to come in again this afternoon. Um, I think I'd better start off with an apology. My behaviour at this morning's meeting was totally out of order. As Heather said, we've all been under a lot of pressure. I have my share of that too; senior management's giving me a very hard time, as you can imagine. But, still, that's no excuse for behaving the way I did. I know you all have your problems right now. You're overworked. You have some issues with the leads you're getting from telemarketing. And I haven't been listening to you. Well, I'm listening now. So, what I suggest is that we spend the next hour identifying everything we can think of that is currently preventing us from achieving our targets the way we always have in the past. We'll brainstorm some ideas about what we can do to reverse that situation, from today. I promise I'll do everything I can to make that happen, but I need your input. Let's start with the workload problem. Heather, is there anything we can do to help ease the pressure you're under ...

Anton: Okay, everybody, I think that's been a lot more productive than any of us expected, me included! We obviously need to, er, take this discussion further, but let's wrap things up now and agree to meet in ... how about a week today? Tony, you'll circulate the minutes of this meeting tomorrow morning?

Tony: Yes, Mr Vega. I mean, Anton.

Anton: Okay, great. Now, before everyone goes, there are a couple of things I'd like to say. Yes, you guessed it, it's motivational talk time! As you know, I've been at FIS nearly ten years now. I think that's longer than just about everyone here, except Alan. Well, he didn't get to look that old for nothing! Anyway, those of you who've been around since then will remember we used to be called IT consultants, not sales reps. And that's what we were – consultants. Because it was our expertise that made us the best team at FIS six years in a row. Yeah. Three years ago, Alan was top consultant. And the year before that. He doesn't know it yet, but I'm counting on him to do it for us again.

The rest of you are newer, but you're smart and I know we can help you to do better. As Heather says – and Heather, I'm expecting great things of you – when we were downsized 18 months ago, a lot of things changed. New management, new structure. They don't call us consultants now. They call us sales representatives. Well, that may be what they call us, but this is a team of qualified consultants and from now on that's how we're going to behave. We're here to grow the business of the team. And from now on, we coordinate, we collaborate, we communicate and we show FIS that amongst their sales staff, they still have one unit of IT professionals, of consultants. Okay, that's enough of the speech, let's get back to work.

---

7 Have a class discussion on what Anton did right in his second meeting.

SUGGESTED ANSWER

Anton begins with a sincere apology, but doesn't overdo this. He admits his mistake and moves on. He is, after all, the boss. He uses the difficult situation everyone is in (and the pressure he is also under from senior management) to unite the team and adds a little bit of humour to keep things light. He knows he was very hard on Alan at the previous meeting, so he makes a special effort to praise him now for his past performance and makes it clear the team needs Alan to succeed. He also promises the newer members of the team that he'll work harder to support them. He uses his long experience at the company to make it clear that his team were not so long ago the best at FIS. This makes it more understandable that he should be disappointed with the performance now. And he makes the distinction between a sales rep and a consultant to show that he takes his team's expertise seriously, and wants them to start working together more collaboratively and professionally. He focuses on intrinsic motivators (teamwork, professionalism, matching past performance) rather than extrinsic ones (salaries, bonuses). He also closes on a joke to put everyone at ease.

8 Ask students to turn to page 134 and follow the instructions there. They will need some time to prepare their motivation speeches – this could be done for homework, particularly if they choose to devise their own. Make sure that they understand they can deliver Anton's speech in their own style, make up their own speech based on personal experience or use the team profile given as a basis for their speech. When they are ready, they should perform their motivation speeches to a partner. Point out that in 9 they will be required to evaluate their partner's performance so they will need to listen carefully and perhaps make notes when their partner is speaking.

9 Focus attention on the feedback form on page 136 and ask students to complete it for their partner. Encourage them to discuss their feedback forms and see if each speaker agrees with the assessment.

1:1 If there is time, you could prepare your own motivation speech for your student to listen to and evaluate. This would give them an extra model of a good speech, and would be an opportunity for you to introduce further structures and vocabulary which are relevant and useful for your student.

C MORALE PROBLEMS

13 Being heard

Learning objectives

This unit is about meetings, with particular emphasis on cultural differences in discussion styles and ways of making your voice heard.

Students look first at opinions on the function of meetings and explore differences between cultures, moving on to an exploration of the acceptability of assertiveness in meetings. This provides an opportunity for practising modal verbs which indicate a speaker's attitude to what is being said.

Cultural aspects are then explored further with information from a communications expert on the different discussion styles in different cultures. Students listen to extracts from business meetings and identify the cultural types they represent.

The next section provides students with some useful strategies for interrupting so that they can make their views felt in meetings. They practise using these techniques by taking turns to read a text and interrupt the speaker. The unit ends with four scenarios of a British salesman's experiences in different cultures. Students identify and discuss the different attitudes displayed to such things as relationship-building, time, interruption and delegation.

The grammar focus is on modal verbs, and the lexical focus is on collocations relating to meetings and expressions for stating opinions.

Digital resources: Unit 13

Online Workbook; Extension worksheets; Glossary; Phrase bank; Student's Book answer key; Student's Book listening script; Fast-track map

---

In this first section, students look at different attitudes as to why we hold meetings. They complete sentences giving different points of view and talk about their own opinions. They then listen to some business people from different countries complaining about meetings and discuss what they say. Students then examine the question of how assertive they are in meetings and practise using modal verbs to complete a questionnaire on assertiveness in meetings.

Warm-up

Ask for reactions to the quotation from Michael Eisner. In a multinational class, ask different nationalities to say whether conflict is an acceptable or even desirable element of business meetings for them. You could also ask them what constitutes 'conflict' in their culture(s).

Brainstorm what makes an effective meeting and write students' ideas on the board. Leave them up as you might want to refer to them when completing the sentences in 1.

---

1 Students complete the sentences with the words from the box. Check the answers and ask students to choose which statement most closely describes the type of meetings they normally have.

ANSWERS

a exchange b make c discuss d chat
e find f criticize g waste

2 2.26 Reassure students that the eight extracts are quite short. Make sure they understand that all they have to do is to match the extracts to the correct topics. Go through the topics with the students first so that they know what they are listening for. Pause the recording after each extract to give them time to scan the list and identify the correct topic.

Though the comments in the extracts are likely to be based on personal opinion rather than cultural preference, ask students to speculate on what nationality each of the speakers might be.

ANSWERS

a 5 b 3 c 1 d 6 e 2 f 7 g 8 h 4

2.26

Extract 1
It's a joke, really, this idea that everyone's opinion is valued. I mean, how much can you disagree with the boss? After all, she's the boss!

Extract 2
You often leave a meeting not really knowing what you're supposed to do next, what the action plan is. I usually end up phoning people afterwards to find out what we actually agreed.

Extract 3
Nobody seems to come to the meeting properly prepared. If you want a copy of the report, they don't have it with them. Need to see the figures? They'll get back to you. It's hopeless!

Extract 4
You often get several people all talking at the same time. So no one's really listening to anyone else. They're just planning what they're going to say next. It's survival of the loudest!

Extract 5
They're usually badly organized. Nobody sticks to the point. People get sidetracked all the time. It takes ages to get down to business. As they say: 'If you fail to plan, you plan to fail.'

Extract 6
You know even before you begin who's going to argue with who. The facts don't seem to matter. It's all about scoring points, looking better than your colleagues and impressing the boss.

BUSINESS COMMUNICATION

Extract 7

I try to stop them over-running. We sometimes hold meetings without chairs. That speeds things up a lot! I've even tried showing the red card to people who won't shut up, like in football. Not popular.

Extract 8

Well, to be honest, everybody knows we don't actually decide anything in meetings. The boss already knows what he wants to do anyway!

3 Go through the statements again and ask students which of them apply to the kinds of meetings they have.

4 Establish the meaning of *assertive*. Someone who is assertive is confident and good at making their views known – and often good at getting their own way.

Assertiveness is different from rudeness, though in some cultures it may be interpreted as such. Employees in British and American companies where assertiveness is, on the whole, valued may even be offered assertiveness training if it is felt that they are weak at putting across their point of view.

Where assertiveness ends and rudeness, aggression and bullying begin is something you could discuss with the students. Ask them to tell the class if they have had any experience of being in a meeting in which they were made uncomfortable by someone's assertive behaviour.

5 Students work with a partner to complete the statements in the questionnaire using the words from the box. Check the answers to make sure each pair has a correctly completed questionnaire. They should then discuss each statement, and decide whether they agree or disagree.

Refer the students to page 131 for comments on their answers, which divide them into the types of animals they are in meetings: mice, foxes, horses or bulldogs. Ask students for their reactions to the comments. If they like the animal idea, you could use this as a way of dividing them into groups for later exercises.

ANSWERS

a conflict b rubbish c silences d time
e things f people g conversation h room

> **Language links**
>
> Direct students to the *Language links* section on page 83 for more practice of vocabulary for meetings, and useful language for introducing comments and opinions.

6 When students have matched the modal verbs in 5 to their meanings, ask them to make their own sentences using each of the modal verbs.

ANSWERS

1 c (*should*) 2 a (*shouldn't*) 3 b and d (*have to* and *must*)
4 g (*don't have to*) 5 h (*can*) 6 e and f (*can't* and *mustn't*)

> **Language links**
>
> Direct students to the *Language links* section on pages 83–84 for further explanation of the form of modal verbs and some exercises to practise them. Modal verbs are auxiliary verbs that show the speaker's attitude and express such things as obligation, necessity, permission, probability, ability, etc.

Cultural differences

In this section, students look at three different discussion styles identified by Fons Trompenaars, a communications expert. Students say which group they would place different nationalities in, based on their own experience. They then listen to extracts from three business meetings and match them to the three styles.

1 In all questions of cultural differences, it is important to point out that identifying differences between cultures does not imply that one is better than another. Celebration, rather than criticism, of the differences between cultures should be the aim. It is also very hard to generalize about cultures and students' experiences may be very different from what culture gurus put forward as 'facts'. Those experiences should be valued and students should be encouraged to express them.

2 There are no fixed answers here. Students should decide where to place the different nationalities according to their own experience.

3 2.27–2.29 Remind students of the three cultural types identified in 1. Play each recording more than once if necessary so that students can identify the cultural type.

ANSWERS

Extract 1 = Culture 2   Extract 2 = Culture 1   Extract 3 = Culture 3

2.27

Extract 1

A: Okay. You've all had a chance to look at the quarterly sales figures.

B: Yes. They're terrible.

A: Agreed, but if I could just finish. We're 30% down on projections. The question is why?

C: Can I just come in here? It seems to me that our marketing strategy is all wrong.

B: Now, just a minute. Are you trying to say this is our fault?

C: Well, what else can it be? I mean, we're offering generous discounts …

B: Look, sorry to interrupt again, but …

C: No, hear me out. We're offering very generous discounts to our biggest customers as part of our introductory offer. And sales are still slow. Something's going wrong and I say it's the marketing.

13 BEING HEARD 71

BUSINESS COMMUNICATION

> **B:** Well, if you ask me, the problem is the product itself.
> **C:** And what is wrong with the product? BabySlim is an innovative addition to our product line.
> **B:** Innovative, yes. But there is no market for diet baby food. I said so at the very beginning. Who's going to admit they've got a fat baby?
> **A:** You know, maybe she has a point …
>
> 🔊 **2.28**
> **Extract 2**
> **A:** So, that's the position. The company has been officially declared bankrupt.
> **B:** Yes.
> **A:** And our chief executive officer has been arrested on charges of corruption.
> **B:** Yes.
> **A:** Of course, our company president has been on television to make a public apology.
> **B:** Of course.
> **A:** But there was nothing he could do.
> **B:** Of course not. Gentlemen, it is a black day in our company's proud history.
> **A:** Yes. A very black day. Very, very black.
> **C:** Can I just come in here?
> **B:** Please, do.
> **C:** Well, it's just a suggestion, but shouldn't we all be looking for new jobs?
>
> 🔊 **2.29**
> **Extract 3**
> **A:** Now, just a minute, just a minute!
> **B:** There's no way we're going to accept this!
> **A:** Could I just …?
> **B:** They can't make English the official company language!
> **A:** Could I just …?
> **B:** If head office thinks we're all going to speak English from now on …
> **A:** Could I just finish what I was saying?
> **B:** Frankly, it's bad enough that we have to speak English in these meetings.
> **A:** Please! Let me finish. No one is suggesting we can't speak our own language.
> **B:** But that is exactly what they are suggesting!
> **C:** Can I just say something?
> **B:** Go ahead.
> **C:** Well, as I understand it, this is only a proposal at this stage.
> **A:** That's precisely what I was trying to say – before I was interrupted.
> **B:** Now, hang on a second …
> **C:** If I could just finish … The idea is to introduce English gradually over the next two years …
> **B:** Oh, no! Not while I'm in charge of Human Resources.
> **A:** Yes, well, that brings us on to item two on the agenda: restructuring the Human Resources department.

Interruption strategies

Interrupting someone and dealing with interruptions, especially in a foreign language, can be rather intimidating for students. This section will give them some useful techniques.

1 Establish the meaning of *interrupt* (to stop someone speaking in order to make a point yourself). Go through all the strategies in the list for interrupting and preventing interruption, making sure everyone understands them, and ask students to tick the ones they think are the most effective.

Allow them to compare answers with a partner before checking with the class. If anyone chooses gesturing or glaring as effective techniques for preventing interruption, ask them to demonstrate the gesture or look they would use.

2 Point out that students heard all these expressions in the last listening exercise. They should be able to order them fairly easily, but allow them to work with a partner or in small groups if they wish.

ANSWERS
a just a minute
b let me finish
c no, hear me out
d hang on a second
e sorry to interrupt again
f if I could just finish …
g Can I just come in here?
h Can I just say something?
i Could I just finish what I was saying?

3 Students divide the expressions into the two categories and identify the two that can be in both categories.

Ask students to practise the expressions in 2 by having them prepare a few sentences on how they feel about being interrupted. They then start saying these to a partner who has to interrupt, using one of the expressions from 2. The first student should try to prevent the interruption. Do not let this go on for too long as there is extended practice of these techniques in the next section.

ANSWERS
interrupting: a, d, e, g, h
preventing interruption: a, b, c, d, f, i
both: a, d

> **Language links**
>
> Direct students to the *Phrase bank* in the *Language links* section on page 84 for more on techniques for interrupting and preventing interruption.

Hang on a minute!

This section gives students practice in groups of using the interrupting techniques they have just learned.

1 Ask students to work with a partner and decide who will be Speaker A and Speaker B. Ask them to turn to their respective pages. They will need time to read their articles

72 13 BEING HEARD

and decide where to pause so that they can deliver them confidently enough to try to fend off any interruptions from their partner.

Students then take turns to try to read the text aloud in under a minute. When they do this, make sure they understand that they can't simply ignore the interruptions and carry on reading. They have to deal with them by using phrases such as *No, hear me out*, etc and then continuing.

This could also be done in groups of three, with the third person each time acting as time-keeper and awarding the speaker a grade on the *Interruptometer*, according to the length of time it takes them to complete the text. Each group could then put forward a champion reader for a play-off with other groups to find the person in the class who displays the most determination and assertiveness in getting to the end of the text within the time limit.

2 Repeat the activity without the time limit. The student doing the reading should deal briefly with any questions before continuing to read.

> **1:1** Allow your student to practise trying to interrupt you first so that they can glean some good techniques for keeping going from you, which they can use when it is their turn.

Meeting across culture

In this section, students each read one of four scenarios about the experience of a British businessman doing business abroad. Students then answer questions on their scenarios and discuss the different attitudes displayed in each with students who have read a different scenario.

1 Divide the class into four groups. Each group should read a different scenario and answer the questions on it. You could go around and check the groups' answers individually or bring the class together at the end to go over the questions.

ANSWERS

a stick to an agenda; hold up the conversation; negotiate terms; make concessions
b get underway; is in progress; haggling; rhetoric
c raise objections; allocate time; exchange emails; reach agreement
d set up; gets going; back up; goes through
e talk business; schedule a meeting; work as a team; press for a decision
f cuts in; win over; overrun; work something out
g be granted a meeting; follow protocol; clear up a misunderstanding; quote figures
h mystified; chit-chat; courtesy; premature

2 The new groups can be any size you like, but should be made up of at least one member of each of the original groups. They discuss the different attitudes displayed in the scenarios to the topics in the box.

Have a class feedback session with groups reporting on what they discussed. Ask them to say in which of the four countries they would feel most at home when doing business. If any of the students come from the countries featured in the extracts, ask them to say how accurate they think the descriptions are.

> **1:1** As four texts in one go is rather a lot for one student, you might like to ask your student to read one or two of them at home and bring the answers to the questions to your next lesson.

Language links

ANSWERS

Vocabulary

Meetings
a the agenda
b ideas
c an opinion
d a point
e agreement
f comments
g an action plan
h details
i a decision

Comments and opinions
a If you ask me
b Frankly
c On the other hand
d Incidentally
e As a matter of fact
f Clearly
g Luckily
h Overall
i Strangely enough
j In short
k Essentially
l In theory

Grammar

Modal verbs
1 a 5 b 6 c 2 d 3 e 4 f 1
  g 11 h 9 i 7 j 12 k 10 l 8
2 a Yes
  b No
  c 1 I couldn't talk to you then. 2 I hoped we'd meet again.
    3 I had to fly to Geneva.
  d That must be right.
  e 3
  f 4
  g Yes
  h Yes or No
  i Yes
  j Only 2 is possible

Phrase bank: Interrupting and preventing interruption
1 Interrupting: a, b, k
  Preventing interruption: c, g, i, j
  Both: d, e, f, h, l
2 a 1 b 2
  ↘↗ : b
  ↗↘ : a
3 1 f 2 a 3 d 4 c 5 g 6 e 7 b

13 BEING HEARD

14 Snail mail

Learning objectives

This unit is about office paperwork, particularly letters. Students begin by thinking about the kinds of documents they see in a day and attitudes to paperwork. They then discuss means of communication they would consider first in a number of situations.

Business letters and common mistakes made in them are examined next, and students practise correcting letters. Finally, they work in groups to write and answer letters on a range of business topics.

The grammar focus is on multi-verb expressions and the lexical focus is on prepositions.

Digital resources: Unit 14

Online Workbook; Extension worksheets; Glossary; Phrase bank; Student's Book answer key; Student's Book listening script; Fast-track map

---

In this first section, the focus is on attitudes to paperwork. The aim is to get students thinking about the kinds of documents they see every day and the best ways to deal with paperwork.

Warm-up

Ask students what they think *snail mail* is and how it got its name. (*Snail mail* is a relatively recent term for mail sent through the postal system rather than by email. A snail is a small animal known for the very slow speed at which it moves. The advent of email has made ordinary mail seem very slow by comparison.)

Focus attention on the quotation from Arnold Glasow and ask students if they think that careless or thoughtless writing is a problem in business today. They may raise the question of email, where standards of accuracy seem to be notoriously poor. Ask them how often they write letters and whether they still consider it to be a good method of communication.

1 Students work individually to list the documents they see in a typical day. They should list document types like emails, faxes, memos, etc without going into the specific contents. Allow them to compare lists with a partner and in small groups. See how many different types the class has come up with by making a class list on the board. This will give students access to more office vocabulary.

Ask students to put a tick next to the items in their lists which they look forward to receiving and a cross next to those which they dread.

2 Students work individually or with a partner to complete the sentences. When they have finished, check the answers, go over any difficult vocabulary and find out which of the sentences reflect the students' own attitudes.

ANSWERS

a mail   b letters   c forms   d trade journals   e contracts
f copies; diagrams   g record; receipts   h invoices; figures
i memos; Post-it®   j questionnaires; report

Communication channels

In this section, students look at all the different modes of communication available to them and decide which they would choose in a variety of situations. This provides an opportunity for practising using prepositions.

1 Ask students to work individually to read the situations and choose the correct prepositions. Check answers with the class before moving on to 2.

ANSWERS

a to   b about   c on   d for   e up   f with
g on   h of   i for   j for   k off   l with

> **Language links**
>
> Direct students to the *Language links* section on page 89 for more practice of prepositions, together with some advice on learning them.

2 Students work with a partner to discuss the situations and choose from the list the mode of communication they would use first in each one. Have a class feedback session, and find out how much consensus there is and what the preferred method of communication is.

In a rush

In this section, students look at a hurriedly written business letter and identify the mistakes in it. They correct the letter and then check by listening to the writer's colleague talking to him about it.

1 Establish that *in a rush* means the same as *in a hurry*. Students work with a partner to read the letter and find the mistakes. Ask them to make a note of their corrections but do not check answers at this stage.

BUSINESS COMMUNICATION

> **ANSWERS**
>
> The letter should have Ms Ramalho's address at the top left-hand side.
> 22nd February
> Dear Ms Ramalho,
> Thank you for your letter of 9th February and for your interest in the new Xenod digital communication system.
> I'm sorry you were unable to attend our presentation in São Paulo last month, but I am delighted to tell you we are planning another one in Brasilia on 30th April.
> In the meantime, I enclose a copy of our latest catalogue and current price list.
> If you have any questions or would like further information concerning our company and its products, please don't hesitate to contact me again.
> I look forward to hearing from you.
> Yours sincerely [or Best wishes]

2 🔘 **2.30** Play the recording for students to listen and check the corrections they made to the letter in 1.

🔘 **2.30**

1
Erm, well, where's the address? You've completely missed the address out. And what's the 'twenty-twost' of February, Rudi? You mean twenty-second. That should be 'nd', right?

2
'My dear Ms Ramalho' is a bit old-fashioned, don't you think? Sounds like a 19th-century love letter, eh? I don't think you need the 'my'. 'Dear Ms Ramalho' will do. And it's a capital 'T' for 'Thank you'. I know it's after a comma, but it's a capital.

3
So that should be: 'Thank you for your letter of ninth February.' Oh, and 'communication' has got a double 'm', Rudi! Try using the spell check.

4
What's this? 'I am such sorry'? That's 'so sorry', isn't it? Actually, I don't think you need the 'so'. Just 'I'm sorry' sounds better ... Okay ... 'I'm sorry you were disabled to attend our presentation'? I don't think that's right! 'Unable', I think you mean.

5
'In the mean time ...' Oh, I think 'meantime' is one word, not two. Yeah, one word. Oh, what's gone wrong here? 'I enclose a copy of our last catalogue'? That should be 'latest'. The last one's the old one, not the new one.

6
Erm, 'current' is with an 'e', not an 'a' – c-u-double r-e-n-t. And it's a price list, Rudi, not a prize list. With a 'c' not a 'z'. We're not running a lottery!

7
'Information' is singular. You don't need the 's'. So, 'If you would like further information' ... uh-huh ... 'please don't hesitate but contact me again.' That should be 'don't hesitate to contact me again'.

8
Right, nearly finished. 'I look forwards to hearing from you.' That doesn't sound right to me. Wait a minute, it's 'I look forward' not 'forwards'. Yeah. And, err, 'Yours fatefully'. That's 'faithfully' not 'fatefully' – f-a-i-t-h, faithfully ... Actually, it isn't, is it? It's 'Yours sincerely' because you've written the woman's name. I'd just put 'Best wishes' if I were you. It's simpler. Er, Rudi, maybe you'd better leave the letter writing to me in future.

Could I see you a moment?

This is both a roleplay and an exercise in correcting mistakes in business letters. Ask students to work with a partner. Tell both students to turn to page 131 and follow the instructions. Focus attention on the useful language in the box, which will help them with ways to describe the mistakes in the letters.

ANSWERS

December 3rd
Dear Mr Barghiel,
I am/'m writing to confirm our appointment on 7 December. Of course, I have your address, but I wonder if you could send me instructions on how to get to your office because I will be coming by car.
Many thanks. I am very much looking forward to meeting you.
Yours sincerely,

7th May
Dear Dr Garland,
With reference to your order (ref No. 606-1), I regret to inform you that the DCS1 is currently out of stock. May I suggest you consider upgrading to the DCS2? If you are interested, I would be happy to send you details.
Let me know if I can be of any further help.
Yours sincerely,

What's missing?

In this section, students practise completing some common expressions from business letters, decide what part of the letter they usually come in, and whether they are formal or informal.

1 Students work individually to complete the expressions, but allow them to compare notes with a partner before checking with the class.

14 SNAIL MAIL 75

BUSINESS COMMUNICATION

ANSWERS
a How are things *with* you?
b I apologize *for* not replying sooner.
c Further *to* our telephone conversation yesterday, …
d See you *at* the weekend. Best wishes, Jim.
e I thought I'd send you a copy *of* this article.
f Sorry I wasn't there *to* meet you when you called.
g *Yours* sincerely, Brian Green
h It was *a* great pleasure meeting you last week.
i Take care *of* yourself.
j How's *it* going?
k Thank you *for* your letter *of* 6 May.
l Get back to me *as* soon *as* you can.
m I look forward *to* hearing *from* you.
n With reference to your fax *of/dated* 3 June, …
o I am writing *with* regard *to* your recent advertisement.
p I'll be *in* touch *in* the next couple of weeks or so.
q *If* I can be *of* any further assistance, do please contact me again.
r Let *me* know when you're next *in* Zagreb.
s It was nice talking *to* you *the* other day.
t Please pass *on* my regards *to* your sales manager, Ms Fontaine.

2 Students decide where in a letter the expressions are likely to come and categorize them according to whether they are formal or informal.

You might like to focus attention on the verb forms in sentences b and m.

ANSWERS
Beginning Formal: b, c, h, k, n, o; Informal: a, e, f, j, s
End Formal: g, m, q, t; Informal: d, i, l, p, r

Language links

Direct students to the *Language links* section on pages 89–90 for further explanation of the construction and use of multi-verb expressions, and exercises to practise these expressions.

Crossed in the post

In this section, students put into practice what they have learned in this unit to exchange a series of letters.

Students work in groups. Go through the instructions with them carefully and ensure that everyone knows what they have to do. Allow plenty of time for the preparation stage, but once the activity has started, keep a strict eye on the time limit and ask the students to 'mail' their letters as soon as each ten minutes is up.

The activity can be extended by employing the option of phoning the other group to confirm or alter the arrangements.

1:1 Completing the entire exercise would mean rather a lot of letter writing for one student, so perhaps choose only one thread to follow. This could also be done outside class using email to exchange letters over the period between one lesson and the next.

Language links

ANSWERS
Vocabulary
Prepositional phrases

1 Dear Mr Savage,
Thank you *for* your letter *of* 12th April. I'm very sorry *about* the difficulties you've had *in* getting one *of* our engineers *to* come and repair the alarm system we installed *in* January. Please accept my apologies. I am as concerned *about* the delay as you are.
The manager who is responsible *for* our after-sales service is new *to* the department and not yet familiar *with* all our procedures, but this is no excuse *for* such a long delay. Rest assured, he is now aware *of* the problem and will arrange *for* an engineer *to* call *at* whatever time is most convenient *for* you. Obviously, this will be free *of* charge. I have also authorized a 10% refund *of* the purchase price.
If you are still not fully satisfied *with* the system, please contact me personally and I shall be happy *to* supply you *with* a replacement.
My apologies once again *for* the inconvenience this has caused you.

Preposition + noun + preposition

2 a regard b agreement c touch d addition e favour
  f case g effect h account i view j pressure k terms
  l accordance m behalf

Grammar
Multi-verb expressions

a put off writing back b remember to open c forget to include
d Forget about spending e recommend using
f suggest you use g should aim to sound h should try to keep
i advise you not to exceed j avoid using k consider enclosing
l can't trust it to pick up m regret relying n can manage to get
o Imagine receiving p Think about redrafting

Phrase bank: Letter-writing expressions

a I hope you are well.
b Thank you for your letter of 12 January.
c My apologies for not replying sooner.
d Further to our conversation last Friday …
e It was a pleasure meeting you last week.
f I am writing with regard to our contract renewal.
g Unfortunately, I am unable to increase the discount.
h What we can do is to offer you a higher credit limit.
i Perhaps we could meet to discuss this.
j I'll be in touch sometime next week.
k I am enclosing a copy of our new catalogue.
l If you require any further assistance, please do contact me.
m I look forward to meeting you again at the conference.
n I look forward to hearing from you soon.
o Yours sincerely, …

15 Solving problems

Learning objectives

In this unit, students look at ways of solving problems. They begin by identifying the time and place where they generally get their best ideas. They listen to a recording about a company that encourages employees to make suggestions and rewards the ones which are adopted. Students then practise making their own suggestions to solve specific problems.

In the next section, they listen to a problem-solving meeting, and learn a systematic way to identify a problem, the objectives and the possible courses of action. They then learn some techniques and a procedure for holding a problem-solving meeting.

They practise giving each other advice on real-life problems and then read about some more creative suggestions for tackling problems.

Finally, they work in groups to roleplay a problem-solving meeting, using the techniques and procedures they have learned and based on actual case studies of problems that major companies have faced.

The grammar focus is on conditionals with past reference, and the lexical focus is on collocations relating to people and products.

Digital resources: Unit 15

Online Workbook; In company interviews Units 13–15 and worksheet; Extension worksheets; Glossary; Phrase bank; Student's Book answer key; Student's Book listening script; Fast-track map; Quick progress test 3

Warm-up

The warm-up question (*What's your 'top tip' for problem-solving?*) could be set for homework at the end of the previous lesson so that students come to class prepared with ideas that they can share.

In this first section, students decide how good they are at problem-solving, and where and when they get their best ideas. They learn about a company that rewards its employees' good ideas, and think up solutions to three real-life business problems and compare their solutions to the ones the companies actually used.

1 Students complete the phrases and tick which ones are true for them.

ANSWERS
a morning   b night   c work   d holiday   e desk   f bath
g shower   h music   i course   j court   k sleep   l book
m meetings   n daydreaming

2 Students compare the phrases they ticked with a partner. Have a class feedback session with a show of hands for each situation ticked.

3 Ask students to try to explain the implications of the Japanese expression in their own words (it is vital for everyone in a company to contribute ideas because if all the ideas are coming from just one person, the wealth of talent possessed by the rest of the staff is wasted). Focus attention on the bulletin board notice. Emphasize that a company is looking for both big and small ways of saving money. Students work with a partner to brainstorm ideas. They then compare their suggestions with others.

4 2.31 Play the recording and ask someone to explain what the idea was.

ANSWER
That the company could save money by reducing the bonus to $50.

> **2.31**
> The first suggestion the company got was a joke really, but it won the $100 bonus. The suggestion was that the bonus should be reduced to $50.

5 Students work in groups of three and decide who will be Speaker A, Speaker B and Speaker C. Tell them to turn to their respective pages and follow the instructions there. Allow plenty of time for students to read their business problems and discuss their ideas for solving them. Encourage them to think of more than one solution to each and allow them to compare with other groups.

> **1:1** The business dilemmas are quite short, so a single student could read them all and suggest ideas for solving them.

6 2.32–2.34 Play the recordings for students to listen and compare their ideas with the companies' solutions. Then invite students to comment on the real solutions.

> **2.32**
> **Problem 1**
> After many expensive and unsuccessful attempts to promote the restaurant with posters and T-shirts, the owner, Martha Sanchez, finally came up with a winner. She offered free lunches for life to anyone who agreed to have the name and logo of the restaurant tattooed on a visible part of their body. To date, 50 people have become walking advertisements.

> **2.33**
> **Problem 2**
> A lot of time was wasted on electronic devices that could authenticate signatures and on educating customers of the bank to look after their cheque books. Someone suggested using passwords, but people always forgot them. Finally, the bank manager had a different idea – why not simply put a photograph of the account holder on each cheque?

2.34
Problem 3

The company quickly realized that there is no way of making industrial cleaners exciting. Special offers and competitions had limited success. So they tried something silly instead. The company's name was changed to the New Cow Corporation. All products were labelled with the New Cow logo, the hotline was changed to 800-BURGERS and its company address to 1 Beef Avenue. Did it work? Well, growing at a rate of 10% a year, New Cow currently employs more than 300 people and enjoys sales of over $80 million.

Suggestions

This section looks at the structure and purpose of problem-solving meetings, and teaches students language for making suggestions.

1 The table divides the process of solving a problem into identification of the problem, assessment of the objective and suggestions for action. Students complete column 3 with the phrases given. Do not check answers at this stage.

2 2.35–2.39 Play the recordings for students to check their answers to 1.

ANSWERS

1 What if we offered it on a sale or return basis? (d)
   Another option would be to sell it direct online. (b)
2 Supposing we bought the company out? (i)
   Alternatively, we could just manufacture our own components. (j)
3 How about raising prices? (g)
   The answer could be to shift production to somewhere like South-East Asia. (a)
4 Why don't we delay the new product launch? (c)
   Couldn't we just sell it off at a discount? (f)
5 What about encrypting our most confidential information? (e)
   Maybe it's time we involved the police. (h)

2.35
Extract 1

A: Okay, we both know the problem. Basically, we can't get retail stores to stock our new product. They say it's too expensive. So the question is: how do we get access to the customer?
B: What if we offered it on a sale or return basis?
A: No, I don't think so. If we did that, we'd just create cash flow problems for ourselves.
B: Hmm. Well, another option would be to sell it direct online.
A: It's a possibility, but I really don't think we know enough about e-commerce to take the chance. And if we start bringing in Internet specialists, we could end up spending a fortune.
B: Of course, we wouldn't have this problem if we'd priced the product more sensibly in the first place.

2.36
Extract 2

A: Right, our objective for this meeting is to think of ways we can get the supplies we need. As I'm sure you've all heard, our sole supplier is about to go bankrupt!
B: Hopefully, it won't come to that, but if it does, we'll certainly have to act fast. Suppose we bought the company out?
A: What, and took on all their debts? I don't think so!
C: Alternatively, we could just manufacture our own components. I've spoken to our technical department. They say they can do it.
A: Yes, but do you have any idea how long it would take to get an in-house production facility operational?
C: Well, what choice do we have? Unless we do something, we'll be out of business within six months!
B: What I want to know is why our suppliers didn't tell us they were in trouble. If we'd known this was going to happen, we could have had our own production plant up and running by now.

2.37
Extract 3

A: What I want to know is: how do we maintain our profit margins with labour costs rising the way they are?
B: Well, it seems obvious, but how about raising prices? I mean, even with a 2% price rise, we'd still be very competitive.
C: No, I'm afraid that's not an option. This is an extremely price-sensitive market.
B: I know that, but what else do you suggest? If we don't cover our costs, we'll soon be running at a loss.
A: Now, let's not panic. The answer could be to shift production to somewhere like South-East Asia. We've talked about it before.
C: And close down our plants here? Wouldn't it be easier if we just tried to renegotiate with the unions – get them to accept a lower pay offer?
A: If we'd been able to get the unions to accept a lower pay offer, John, we wouldn't be considering outsourcing to Asia.

2.38
Extract 4

A: Now, what on earth are we going to do about all this unsold stock piling up in the warehouses? If we don't move it pretty soon, there'll be no space for new product. And we'll be left with a lot of old product nobody wants! So, ideas? Anybody?
B: Well, in my opinion, our product development cycle is way too short. Why don't we delay the new product launch to give us time to sell existing stock?
A: This is a technology-driven business, Robert. If we don't continually upgrade our product, the competition will.

BUSINESS COMMUNICATION

B: And if we didn't all keep upgrading every three months, we wouldn't have this problem!

C: Wait a minute, wait a minute! This old stock, couldn't we just sell it off at a discount to create space for the new stuff? Say, 15%?

A: I'd rather not start talking about a 15% discount at this stage, if you don't mind.

C: Well, if we'd discounted it sooner, we wouldn't have had to be so generous now.

🔘 2.39
Extract 5

A: Now, I've brought you all here to discuss a very serious matter. Someone in the company – we don't know who – is passing on information to the competition. I'm sure I don't need to tell you that in a business like ours it is essential we protect our competitive advantage. So, ... what do we do?

B: Are you telling us we have a spy amongst us?

A: If I wasn't, Simon, we wouldn't be here now.

C: Well, let's think. We already restrict access to important files, but what about encrypting our most confidential information as well? It's common practice in most companies these days. I'm surprised we don't do it already.

A: I'm afraid it's more serious than just downloading data off the company server. This person seems to be recording meetings and private conversations as well.

B: You're joking! ... Erm, sorry, it's just that I can hardly believe this.

C: Well, maybe it's time we involved the police. Clearly a crime is being committed here.

A: It most certainly is. And I would have called the police in already if I'd thought it would do any good. But, I don't want our spy, whoever it is, to know we know. So, unless we have to, I'd rather see if we can deal with this ourselves first. And who knows? Perhaps we can even turn the situation to our advantage ...

3 🔘 **2.35–2.39** Go through the questions with the class so that students know what information to listen out for. Students should take notes on their answers to the questions. Pause the recordings between extracts to allow them time to do this. Check the answers with the class.

ANSWERS
Extract 1: To sell it direct online.
Extract 2: They will go out of business.
Extract 3: It's a very price-sensitive market.
Extract 4: The product development cycle is short so old stock piles up.
Extract 5: They may be able to use the spy to feed false information to the competition.

4 Encourage students to compare the collocations they have underlined with a partner and discuss the equivalent expressions in their own language(s).

Language links
Direct students to the *Language links* section on page 96 for more practice of useful collocations for talking about people and products.

5 Students should be able to complete the sentences without listening to the recordings again, but be prepared to play them if necessary. Then ask them to identify which sentences refer to the past and present, and which only to the past. Allow them to discuss this with a partner before checking with the class.

ANSWERS
a wouldn't have; 'd priced   b 'd known; could have
c 'd been; wouldn't be   d 'd discounted; wouldn't have
e would have; 'd thought
1 a, b and c   2 d and e

Language links
Direct students to the *Language links* section on page 97 for further explanation of the construction and use of conditionals with past reference, and exercises to practise them.

Problem-solving techniques

1 Allow students to work with a partner or in small groups to complete the checklist. Ask them to comment on how useful they think this checklist is.

ANSWERS
a define   b brainstorm   c review   d select   e break
f restate   g invite   h criticize   i explore   j eliminate
k draw up   l assign

2 With the same partner or groups, students match the sentences to the steps in the problem-solving process. Check the answers and any difficult vocabulary with the class.

ANSWERS
1 b   2 i   3 d   4 f   5 g   6 a   7 c   8 j
9 k   10 h   11 l   12 e

Language links
Direct students to the *Phrase bank* in the *Language links* section on page 97 for more on the language used in problem-solving and brainstorming.

Everyday problems

This section gives students practice in taking real-life problems and making suggestions for ways of solving them. Because the problems come from the students themselves, this will seem more authentic and they should be motivated to try to solve the problems.

1 Make sure the problems that groups write down are clearly explained, particularly if they deal with industries which students in other groups may be unfamiliar with.

15 SOLVING PROBLEMS   79

BUSINESS COMMUNICATION

2 When students are writing advice, remind them of the structures in column 3 in the table on page 92 which they might find useful for making suggestions and giving advice.

3 Have a class feedback session and find out if students thought any of the advice was useful.

Creativity

In this section, students read about creative ways of solving problems. They summarize what they have read and discuss if the advice is likely to be successful.

1 Establish that creative problem-solving involves thinking of a problem in a different way in order to come up with a new solution. Divide the class into groups and make sure that each group reads a different paragraph of the text, and that every section of text is read by at least one group.

2 Each new group should have at least one member who read each paragraph of the text. They give the other members of the group a summary of their paragraph. They then discuss which they think is the best advice and whether they can give any examples of companies who have successfully used these methods.

> **1:1** You could ask your student to do the reading at home and come to class ready to discuss the different ideas.

A problem-solving meeting

Working in groups, students choose one of two situations and hold a problem-solving meeting following the procedure they have already looked at. They then listen to a recording of what the companies involved actually did.

1 Remind students of the four-step procedure they studied on page 93. Divide them into groups of four to six people and allow them to make their choice between the two situations. Try to ensure that at least one group chooses each situation, though this is not essential. Students work through the steps, conduct their problem-solving meeting, and then summarize the problem and their proposed solutions for other groups. This will take quite a lot of time, so you might want to set some of the preparation for homework.

> **1:1** Choose one of the situations and work through it together with your student. When you hold your problem-solving meeting, try to get the student to lead the meeting.

2 🔘 **2.40–2.41** Play the recording for students to listen and compare their solutions with what the companies actually did. Ask them to say if anything is relevant to their own lines of business and to explain in what way.

🔘 **2.40**

Sony® Ericsson

Whilst on a business trip to New York back in 2001, you find yourself walking down the famous Fifth Avenue when you are approached by an attractive young woman. 'Excuse me,' she says. 'Would you mind taking a picture of me and my boyfriend?' 'Sure,' you reply. 'Thanks a lot!' she smiles and hands you what looks like an ordinary mobile phone, although you notice the screen is full colour. 'But this is a phone, isn't it?' you ask. 'Yeah,' she laughs, 'and a camera! You just press this key here. See? Simple.' You take a couple of shots and remark that it's the first camera-phone you've ever seen. 'Cool, isn't it?' says the boyfriend. 'Latest Sony Ericsson.' You're impressed and decide to check it out next time you're passing a mobile phone store. The rest, of course, is history and today cameras come as standard on every single smartphone.

But what you didn't know at the time is that those two young tourists were actually actors and were being paid to approach passers-by like yourself. They were part of a special campaign by Sony Ericsson. Called 'buzz marketing', the idea was to create publicity for the phone by introducing people to the product and, basically, getting them to want it! In fact, for this particular campaign Sony Ericsson hired 60 actors to do this every day in ten different cities all over the United States.

Buzz, or word of mouth, has now been proven to be the most effective form of marketing in an age when there's so much conventional advertising we've largely learned to ignore it. And, while some say buzz marketing raises ethical questions, the companies who use it stress that the strategy is not to sell but simply to inform. Ethical or not, it's a technique now employed by many of the world's most famous brands. Where product placement places products in movies, buzz marketing places products in your life! And if you think you yourself have never met a buzz marketer – in the street, on the train, at the coffee bar – well, that's the whole point!

🔘 **2.41**

Tata Steel

Tata Steel's managing director, Dr Irani, quickly realized that, whereas in the West there is more provision for those who are made redundant in the form of social security, he had a special responsibility to his own employees. So, he first spent almost a year convincing his people of the need for rightsizing the company.

Then, working in partnership with the workers' union, he developed what he called 'the early separation scheme' or ESS. Within the terms of the ESS, those under 40 years of age who took voluntary early retirement would get their full salary for the rest of their working lives. And older workers would get 20–50% more than their full salary! Furthermore, if they died before reaching retirement age, their families would be paid their salaries for the remaining years. Irani's generosity to his employees looked like madness. And when an Indian industrialist heard about the scheme, he sent him a note saying: 'You either have too much money or not enough brains!'

But Irani knew exactly what he was doing. For the amount the workers who voluntarily left the company got paid remained constant. Had they stayed, it would have gone up annually. And by saving on the extra payroll tax and pension plan contributions, Tata Steel's labour costs declined immediately. Tata ran 40 ESS schemes over the next decade. As a result, by 2004 the workforce had been reduced by 30,000.

But Irani went even further. Instead of offering guaranteed jobs to the children of loyal employees, he began to offer them training at the newly set-up RD Tata Technical Institution. If he could not offer the next generation employment, he could at least increase their employability. And for those who left the company, there was free financial advice and career counselling. Tata is now a textbook case of humane human resource management and a model corporate culture. And this, together with a one billion dollar investment, has made Tata Steel the highly efficient, globally competitive firm it is today.

In company interviews Units 13–15
Encourage students to watch the interview and complete the worksheet.

Language links

ANSWERS

Vocabulary

People and products
1 a products   b both   c products   d staff   e products
   f staff   g products   h products   i staff   j staff
   k staff   l both

The workforce
2 a recruit   b take on   c relocate   d transfer   e lay off
   f dismiss   g down tools   h take industrial action   i instruct
   j teach   k quit   l resign   m motivate   n inspire
3 a unreliable   b inflexible   c disorganized   d impatient
   e irresponsible   f uncreative   g inconsistent   h uninspiring
   i uncommitted   j impractical   k inarticulate   l dishonest
   m irrational   n indecisive   o unsupportive   p incompetent
   q unassertive   r unsociable   s inconsiderate
   t uncompetitive
4 a creative   b inflexible   c supportive   d incompetent
   e inconsiderate   f disorganized   g committed   h indecisive
   i inspiring   j unreliable   k consistent   l uncommitted
   m competitive   n unsociable

The production line
5 a go out of   b halt   c scale down   d withdraw
   e reintroduce   f reduce
6 a launch   b step up   c boost   d halt
   e withdraw; reintroduce

Grammar

Conditionals (past reference)
1 a Past Perfect   b would, could, might   c Present Perfect
   d 3 and 6   e 1, 2, 4 and 5
2 a done; have   b would; could   c could; tried
   d promised; would   e have; known   f hadn't; wouldn't
   Example b does not contain the Past Perfect.

Phrase bank: Problem-solving
a 3, 7   b 5, 8   c 1, 6   d 2, 4

Brainstorming
a sell it online; sold it online
b to sell it online/selling it online
c sell it online; sold it online
d sell it online
e selling it online
f to sell it online
g sell it online
h sell it online
i selling it online
j to sell it online
In both cases, *sold* makes the suggestion more tentative/hypothetical.

16 Collaboration

Learning objectives

This unit is about the importance of teamwork. It begins by asking students to say how much of their own job involves teamwork and what qualities are needed to be a productive team-player. They read and discuss an article about creating team spirit in meetings, and then listen to a project team talking about a problem they are having. Finally, they work in teams to roleplay a project meeting in which they brainstorm solutions to business problems.

Digital resources: Unit 16

Online Workbook; Extension worksheets; Glossary; Student's Book answer key; Student's Book listening script; Fast-track map

This first section explores what makes a good team-player.

Warm-up

Focus attention on the title and ask students what they understand by the word *collaboration*. Ask them to suggest business situations where collaboration is important and those where they think it is better for individuals to work on their own.

1 Give students time to think about their jobs and decide what percentage involves teamwork. Ask them to put a mark on the scale and compare with other students. Encourage them to say what aspects of their work involve teamwork and how they feel about it.

2 Focus attention on the cartoon and explain or elicit that the point is that true collaboration means listening to everyone's ideas, and if one person – usually the most senior person – is making all the decisions and ignoring everyone else's ideas, this is not a collaborative situation at all. Make sure students understand the useful idiom *to keep something to yourself*. Here it refers to not putting your ideas forward in a meeting.

3 Read the instructions with the class and emphasize that all the candidates are equally professionally qualified to take part in the project, so what you are looking for now is personal skills that will make a good team-player. Ask students to work individually or with a partner to brainstorm the personal qualities that an ideal team-player would have. Then have a class feedback session.

4 Ask students to work individually to complete the sentences, then discuss as a class whether these cover the same ideas they came up with in 3. Ask them to say whether they know anyone with the qualities listed.

ANSWERS

a reliable   b constructive   c committed   d supportive
e flexible   f engaged   g co-operative

5 Give students plenty of time to read the article and answer the questions. When checking answers, encourage a class discussion of the last three questions.

SUGGESTED ANSWERS

a T.E.A.M. = together everyone achieves more; P.P.R. = positives, possibilities, reservations
b Teams obviously don't always function better than individuals. Pros: you can draw on a wider pool of talent; you can be more innovative; you can delegate more; you can work faster and accomplish more within a timeframe – as the Japanese say, 'none of us is as smart as all of us'! Cons: there can be personality clashes; some team members may not do their share of the work; some may not buy into the project as much as others; if the team is multicultural and/or virtual, there can be communication problems; some members may not have as much support from their line managers as others.
c In a good team, synergy is created when people combine their efforts to be more effective than they are as individuals – 'the whole is greater than the sum of the parts'
d People used to working on their own may find it hard to adjust to teamwork. This is especially true if they have a lot of personal ambition and a drive to compete rather than collaborate. Put two or more such people together and you have a battle of egos! And one way for them to do battle is to try to win arguments with each other and score points with the boss. Claiming group ideas as your own and saying 'I told you so' when things go wrong are common ways of scoring points.
e Cultures which are described as collectivist (Geert Hofstede) or communitarian (Fons Trompenaars) tend to be more accustomed to working in groups and putting group needs first. This needn't just be a question of national culture, however. Many Asian cultures are quite strongly collectivist, but their corporate culture may also be rather hierarchical, with the boss very much in charge. On the other hand, corporate cultures where the hierarchy is flatter may be better suited to self-managed teams (SMTs).
f P.P.R. is a good example of a communication technique that encourages collaboration even when there are disagreements and that values contributions from all team members.

6 2.42 Go through the instructions and the options with the class before you play the recording, so that students have some idea of what they are going to hear and what information they need to listen out for.

ANSWER

c

2.42

A: Okay, look, the problem is this: we simply can't move forward on this project because we never get any answers from the client! I mean, whenever we ask KNP for their input on anything, they just sit on it for weeks without getting back to us. So we fall further and further behind schedule. Frankly, Rolf, it's driving me mad!

82   16 COLLABORATION

B: Hmm. Okay, well, thanks, Richard. It sounds like we have a pretty serious communication problem here. Does anyone have any suggestions? Yes, Elaine?

C: Erm, it's just a thought, Richard, but maybe you're trying to involve KNP too much.

A: How do you mean?

C: Well, I mean, you're agreeing objectives with them at the planning meetings, right?

A: Yes, of course.

C: And then you're asking them for further input between meetings as well?

A: Erm, well, it's a complicated project, Elaine. And new issues keep coming up.

C: I understand that. But here's an idea. Instead of waiting for them to get back to you on every issue, why not simply go ahead with what you think is best based on what you agreed with them at the meeting and then just ask them to confirm that decision?

A: Well, it's an idea. But I still think we need to keep them closely involved in the decision-making process at every stage.

B: Richard, I think we've already established that trying to keep the client involved is not working too well. Elaine, I really like your idea of just asking for the final go-ahead on each decision. What I especially like about it is that instead of having to come up with fresh ideas of their own, KNP just has to say yes or no. That's going to make things a whole lot easier! And it would certainly solve the problem of getting them to respond more quickly too.

A: What makes you think that?

B: Well, they'll know that there's a time constraint on their reply because we're already going ahead with whatever it is. If they still like what we're doing, no problem. But if they don't, well, they'd better get back to us *right away* or we'll be heading in the wrong direction.

A: Hmm, I'm not so sure.

B: Well, I like this idea of just asking for the green light at each stage. And if we did that, we could also give them more progress reports: as agreed at our last meeting, we've done this and this; and now we're going to do this – is that still okay with you? From what you say, Richard, it sounds like KNP are not as engaged in this project as we are. Maybe we need to keep them in the picture more. Perhaps another thing we could do is give the decisions we want them to approve a priority rating, so they pay attention to the really important ones. And, Elaine, if we combined your idea with Kevin's idea of setting up a client extranet, there'd be a single website they could always go to to find out what's been done, what's next and what they need to okay. And they could do that with the click of a button.

C: Good idea.

B: Now, the only thing is: I'm not sure if we could ask for approval on every decision we take. As Richard says, some of these decisions do require client involvement before we take action. If we go ahead and they're not happy, it could waste a lot of time … and resources. And I'm also a bit worried about KNP feeling we're taking control away from them. Elaine, how do you think we could manage that?

7 2.42 Go through the things students need to identify before you play the recording again. Make sure they can identify Elaine (the woman) and Rolf (the second man who speaks). Check answers with the class.

> **ANSWERS**

a Go ahead with what's best, based on what's been agreed at the planning meetings with KNP, and just ask them to confirm those decisions.
b He likes the fact that KNP simply has to say yes or no to each decision because this will make replying easier for them. He likes the fact that knowing that the project team is going ahead as agreed will make them respond faster if they've changed their minds.
c KNP could be given more progress reports to involve them more in the project. Decisions KNP needs to approve could be given a priority-rating to make sure they notice the important ones. Elaine's idea could be combined with Kevin's idea of setting up a client extranet where KNP can check on progress at any time and approve actions simply by clicking on a button.
d Some decisions require such an investment of time and resources that they may need more client involvement before action is taken. KNP may sometimes feel that control is being taken away from them.

8 Allow plenty of time for this activity. Go through the instructions and the problems with the class, then ask students to work in teams. Make sure they choose someone to be the facilitator and that they swap roles for each problem. They may need time outside of class to think of solutions to the problems which they can put forward in the meeting and to prepare what they are going to say. When they hold their meetings, go around giving help and encouragement.

> **SUGGESTED ANSWERS**

a Perhaps you could electronically tag the shopping carts so that they set off an alarm or lock the wheels when removed from the supermarket car park; provide a free service for those (such as the elderly or disabled) who are unable to carry their groceries home; hire contractors to hunt down abandoned shopping carts; produce a series of posters ridiculing cart-thieves; petition the government to increase fines for the offence of stealing shopping carts.
b Perhaps you could make it possible for customers to upload their photo to your website and superimpose the jewellery onto their picture; produce high-definition videos of all your products, so that customers get a more three-dimensional feel for what they are buying; set up customer feedback blogs for each product, so people can share views on products they've bought; pre-pay for return of goods and not invoice customers until their product orders have arrived and been tried on.
c Perhaps you could increase staff salaries in quarterly increments to reward loyalty; rotate staff so that they deal with different kinds of enquiry to prevent the boredom of routine; provide regular (and fun) training events; offer fringe benefits to long-term employees (health or social club membership, subsidized mobile phone accounts, a loyalty-points-based gift programme); give more experienced staff responsibility for training more junior members; give staff with the best customer feedback each year the opportunity to receive a management education and become a manager.

MANAGEMENT SCENARIO D

Tricky conversations

Learning objectives
This scenario is based on handling difficult conversations in the workplace. Students read some emails Heather Sherwood has sent, each of which outlines a problem she has with one of her colleagues and which she wants to meet them face to face to discuss – leading to some tricky conversations. Students say how they think Heather should deal with each person and then watch the video to see what happens. They evaluate Heather's success, read an article giving advice on dealing with difficult conversations and then watch Heather's follow-up conversations with her colleagues. Finally, students practise having their own tricky conversations with a partner and evaluate their performance.

Digital resources: Management Scenario D
In company in action D1–D2 and worksheet; Extension worksheets; Glossary; Student's Book answer key; Student's Book recording script; Fast-track map

Warm-up
Ask the students to brainstorm reasons why a conversation at work might be 'tricky' or difficult. What kinds of things do people find it difficult to talk about?

1 Focus attention on the photo and ask students to say what they think is happening and how the people are feeling. Give students time to read the emails and decide what they think the answers to the questions might be.

SUGGESTED ANSWERS

a It seems as if Heather agreed with Alan that they would both make the case for an increased budget in their meeting with Gabrielle.
b Alan obviously didn't support Heather when she raised the issue with Gabrielle.
c The email looks like a thank-you note, but, in fact, it appears that Anton may be trying to take all the credit for an idea which was, at least partly, Heather's.
d We can't really be sure. But the fact that he says he had to revise the figures a bit suggests that maybe he claimed all the work was his.
e It's a week overdue and she says it would have helped her make a case for a bigger budget in her meeting with Gabrielle.
f It seems as if Tony has done a lot of work on the report and may see it as his project. So bringing someone else in to help him finish and perhaps take some of the credit won't make him happy.

2 Have a class discussion, brainstorming ways of dealing with each person. Point out that Alan is a peer, Anton a superior and Tony a subordinate.

3 D1 Play the video and ask them to match the conversations to the descriptions.

ANSWERS

Conversation 1 c   Conversation 2 a   Conversation 3 b

D1

Alan: Hi, Heather! You wanted a chat?
Heather: No, I don't want a chat, Alan. I want to know what on earth you think you were doing in the meeting this morning?
Alan: Excuse me?
Heather: What do you mean, excuse me? You know exactly what I'm talking about!
Alan: Oh, you mean the budget thing?
Heather: Yes, the budget thing, Alan! You agreed to back me up when I talked to Gabrielle about the increase. You do agree we need the budget increase, don't you, Alan?
Alan: Yes, of course.
Heather: So, what happened? You completely ruined everything! If you'd supported me the way we'd agreed, we could have got it. But you just sat there! Never said a word. You made me look foolish, Alan. And what's worse, now we won't get that increase and it's all your fault!

Anton: Come in.
Heather: Right, what's this about the client website idea?
Anton: Well, I told you in my email. Gabrielle loves it. We're going ahead with it.
Heather: Are we, now? But without me?
Anton: Er, I'm not sure what you mean, Heather.
Heather: Oh, I think you are, Anton. Whose idea was this in the first place?
Anton: Well, it was ours, but …
Heather: It was my idea, Anton. I came to you with it. You told me to go away and produce some figures. I did that. And now you've taken it to Gabrielle as if it was all your idea. Do you know how much effort I've put into this? On top of all the other work I have to do. It's taken me hours and hours …
Anton: And that's why I said I'd handle it from here on, Heather. You're busy …
Heather: Oh, don't give me that! This is my initiative, Anton, not yours. And you're trying to take all the credit because you want to impress Gabrielle after our disastrous performance last quarter!
Anton: Now, just a minute! I am not trying to take all the credit. I made it very clear to Gabrielle what your contribution has been …
Heather: Really? Well, she certainly didn't mention that at our budget meeting this morning, which I notice you skipped.
Anton: Ah, yes, well. How did it go?
Heather: Don't try to change the subject, Anton. This website idea is my baby and I want full involvement!

84   D TRICKY CONVERSATIONS

MANAGEMENT SCENARIO

> **Heather:** Okay. So, Tony, how's that report coming along? You know it was supposed to be finished by last week?
> **Tony:** Yes, I know, I'm sorry about that. Frankly, it was just a lot more work than anyone expected …
> **Heather:** Look, Tony, I just want to know, is it going to be finished this week, or not?
> **Tony:** Well, I'm going as fast as I can, I just need a bit more time. I haven't been able to access all the files …
> **Heather:** I see. So you haven't even gone through those yet. Right, then, I'll have to borrow Kelly from Nigel for a few days to help you get this thing finished by Friday. Gabrielle wants to see a copy and we're never going to get that budget increase authorized if I don't have that report. Do you know Kelly?
> **Tony:** Yes, but I don't need any help. I've got this covered, okay? I just need a few more days …
> **Heather:** I'm afraid we don't have a few more days. I'll call Nigel and see if he can spare Kelly as soon as possible. Okay, thanks, Tony …

4 Give students plenty of time to read the article and decide which of the advice contained in it might have helped Heather in each situation. Discuss as a class.

5 Ask students to discuss the questions with a partner, and then to report back on what she should do in each situation and how she could have been more diplomatic.

6 🎥 **D2** Ask students to watch the three conversations and see how far Heather's behaviour matches what they suggested in 5.

> 💿 🎥 **D2**
> **Alan:** Listen, Heather, about this morning. I'm really sorry I didn't back you up in the meeting as we agreed. It's just that I could see there was no point. Gabrielle was very clear about our financial situation. There's just no room in the budget for an increase for anybody right now. You know that.
> **Heather:** Yes, I know, Alan. Look, I'm sorry too, I shouldn't have exploded like that. But we did agree to support each other. I just wish you'd warned me you weren't going to say anything about it.
> **Alan:** Well, it was a bit difficult to do that in the meeting, wasn't it? To be honest, once you saw how things were, I was surprised you raised the matter at all. Everybody's budget's going to be frozen next year, by the look of it.
> **Heather:** Yes, but we are a special case, Alan. We do have the company's two main clients to look after and we need that increase.
> **Alan:** I agree. Do you think it would help if we arranged a private meeting with Gabrielle and Anton to discuss things further? Maybe without involving the other units?
> **Heather:** It's worth a try, I suppose.
> **Alan:** Okay, I'll speak to Anton about it first thing in the morning.
> **Anton:** Ah, Heather, I'm glad I bumped into you. Listen, I've had a chat with Gabrielle and she's happy to let you lead the client website initiative, since it was mostly your idea – provided, that is, you don't mind doing some overtime to get it done?
> **Heather:** Oh, I see.
> **Anton:** I said I'd ask if you were okay with that because I know how busy you are.
> **Heather:** No, no, that's fine. I don't mind working overtime to get it completed.
> **Anton:** Great. And, look, I'm sorry if it looked like I was trying to take all the credit for this. Well, maybe I was just a bit. It hasn't been an easy year.
> **Heather:** Yes, I know, Anton. It's been tough for all of us. And thanks for speaking to Gabrielle. I'm sorry; I shouldn't have accused you like that. It's probably because I'd just come out of that disastrous meeting with her about the budgets for next year.
> **Anton:** Ah, yes. Alan spoke to me about that just this morning. He says you and he would like to arrange a meeting with me and Gabrielle to see if we can sort something out.
> **Heather:** Do you think she'll agree? That would be fantastic.
> **Anton:** I don't see why not, we'll talk to her about it in the morning …
>
> **Heather:** Hi, Tony. Got a minute?
> **Tony:** Yeah, sure, Heather. What is it?
> **Heather:** I had another look at it last night and you're right, we didn't allocate enough time to it.
> **Tony:** Oh, right.
> **Heather:** But, I do have to get a copy on Gabrielle's desk by Friday because Alan and I have another meeting with her on Monday. So I'm afraid I can't see any alternative to bringing in Kelly to help you.
> **Tony:** Oh, right.
> **Heather:** But, look, it's you who's done all the hard work, so I don't see any reason for Kelly to do anything but the routine stuff to help you out – like checking those files, for instance.
> **Tony:** Yeah, sure.
> **Heather:** And there's no way Gabrielle's going to read the whole thing over the weekend, so just get me an executive summary by Friday, will you? I'll give that to Gabrielle and then you and Kelly can get the rest done next week. But don't worry; I'll make sure you get all the credit. I know what it's like not to be appreciated.
> **Tony:** Thanks, I'll get right on to it …

7 Ask students to work with a partner and decide who will be Speaker A and Speaker B. Ask them to turn to their respective pages and follow the instructions there. They each have one difficult conversation they have to initiate. Point out that they will need to fill out a feedback form in 8, so they should pay close attention to what happens in their conversation. As they perform their conversations, go around offering help and encouragement.

8 Ask students to complete the feedback form on page 128.

> **1:1** Try to find time for both conversations so that your student has a chance to be both the initiator of the 'tricky conversation' and the person on the receiving end.

D TRICKY CONVERSATIONS

17 Eating out

Learning objectives

This unit is about eating out with business colleagues and clients. The aim is to give students some useful language to use when they are either the hosts or the guests at a business meal, and to encourage discussion of cultural differences in expectations and manners when it comes to food. In the final section, they roleplay a business lunch, using the language and skills they have studied in the earlier sections.

The grammar focus is on the passive, and the lexical focus is on collocations relating to food and drink.

Digital resources: Unit 17

Online Workbook; Extension worksheets; Glossary; Phrase bank; Student's Book answer key; Student's Book listening script; Fast-track map

---

In this first section, students discuss their experiences of business lunches and talk about the kinds of restaurants they like. They also try to identify food from a photo.

Warm-up

Ask students to tell you about the last business meal they had, describing the food, the place and the people present. Focus attention on the quotation from Alfred Hitchcock and ask them to explain what it means (if people talk during a meal, they don't notice the quality of the wine and the food, so it is wasted). Brainstorm reasons why business lunches are so popular. These might include the fact that the company pays, that it is a chance to eat in classier restaurants than you might usually go to, that it is a pleasant way to build up a relationship with a client, that getting clients to do a deal with you can be easier if you give them a good lunch, etc.

1 Students work with a partner to discuss the questions. Point out that using *I thought* makes a suggestion less direct. It gives the other person space to decline the offer or make another suggestion, so it is more polite.

2 When students have completed the diagram, they will have 12 useful expressions for talking about their favourite restaurants. If you have time, you could ask students to practise them with a partner, taking turns to invite the other out for a business lunch and using one of the expressions to describe where they are going.

You could use the stimulus of the photo to start a discussion of the role of café life in the students' countries. Are cafés useful as informal places for a business discussion? Where do short, informal discussions normally take place? This can then naturally lead into 3.

ANSWERS

a, b, c down the road, round the corner, five minutes from here
d, e, f specializes in fish, does an excellent lasagne, you might like
g, h, i you can get fresh oysters, they know me, I sometimes go
j, k, l a fantastic view of the city, a superb menu, a very pleasant atmosphere

> **Language links**
>
> Direct students to the *Phrase bank* in the *Language links* section on page 107 for more on useful phrases for eating out.

3 Students discuss their favourite places with a partner and then report back to the class.

Ask what catering facilities students' companies provide for business meetings. Is it acceptable to invite a client to eat in their company canteen or to provide a sandwich for lunch to be eaten in the meeting room?

4 Demonstrate the activity by focusing attention on the photo and questioning them about some of the items, using the expressions from the speech bubbles. Then ask them to work with a partner to continue the discussion. Go around offering help and encouragement, and explain any unknown expressions.

Ask students if there are any foods that they would avoid suggesting or serving to clients. Elicit the sorts of food that might cause offence and the reasons why they are best avoided.

> **Language links**
>
> Direct students to the *Language links* section on page 106 for more practice of vocabulary for food and drink.

Who said it?

In this section, students learn useful expressions for having a business lunch with a client or colleague.

Warm-up

Brainstorm some of the expressions students think they are likely to say or hear during a business lunch.

1 Go through the instructions with the class. Point out that some of the things could be said by either the host or the guest, depending on the circumstances, but are most likely to be said by one rather than the other.

To make checking the answers more interesting and lively, read out the utterances and ask the students to point left (host), right (guest) or both ways at once (either) to indicate who they think probably said each one.

BUSINESS COMMUNICATION

> **ANSWERS**
> a G b H c H d H e E (G more likely) f H g H h G
> i H j H k E (G more likely) l H m E (G more likely) n E
> (H more likely) o G p E q H r E s E (H more likely) t H

2 🔊 **2.43** Play the recording for students to listen and compare with their own answers. Make sure they realize that the man is the host.

> 🔊 **2.43**
>
> **A:** So, here we are. Hmm, it's a bit more crowded than usual.
> **B:** Nice place. Do you come here often?
> **A:** Mm, yes. It's very convenient and the food is excellent, but it looks like we may have to wait for a table today. This place is getting more and more popular. …
>
> **A:** Our table's going to be a couple of minutes, I'm afraid, but we can sit at the bar if you like.
> **B:** Oh, okay. I see what you mean about this place being popular.
> **A:** Well, we shouldn't have to wait too long. Now, what would you like to drink?
> **B:** Oh, just a fruit juice or something for me.
> **A:** Okay … er, excuse me.
>
> **B:** … So, I'm not really sure how I ended up in financial services.
> **A:** Me neither. I studied law at university, but I never wanted to work for a bank. Right. I'll just see if our table's ready.
>
> **A:** Okay, this is their standard menu …
> **B:** Mm. It all looks very good.
> **A:** … and those are the specials. Let me know if you want me to explain anything.
> **B:** Thanks. I may need some help. So, what do you recommend?
> **A:** Well, they do a great lasagne. But perhaps you'd like something more typically English.
> **B:** Mm, yes. And perhaps something a bit lighter.
> **A:** Is there anything you don't eat?
> **B:** No, not really. I'm allergic to mussels, that's all.
> **A:** Oh, that's a pity. The mussels are a speciality. But, erm, you could try the lamb. That's very good here. It comes with potatoes and a salad.
> **B:** Mm. That sounds nice. But isn't it a little too heavy?
> **A:** Well, you could have it without the potatoes. Or perhaps you'd prefer the cod …
>
> **A:** Shall we order a bottle of the house red?
> **B:** Well, maybe just a glass for me. Could we order some mineral water, too?
> **A:** Sure. Sparkling or still?
>
> **B:** This is absolutely delicious. How's yours?
> **A:** Not bad at all. More to drink?
> **B:** Not for me, thanks. So, how do you think the meeting went this morning?
>
> **A:** Quite well, I think. Of course, we still have a lot of things to discuss …
>
> **A:** Now, how about a dessert?
> **B:** Oh, better not. I'm on a diet.
> **A:** Me too. But it doesn't stop me. How about poached peaches? That's not too fattening.
>
> **B:** Right. I'll get this.
> **A:** Oh, no, you don't. I'm paying.
> **B:** But you paid yesterday, James. It's my turn.
> **A:** No, no, I insist. You're my guest.

Table manners

This section introduces some cultural differences related to eating out.

> **Warm-up**
> Ask students what they understand by the expression *table manners*, and to give examples of good and bad table manners in their country. Start them off with a few examples, e.g. in Britain it is bad manners to put your elbows on the table; it is good manners to wait until everyone is served before you start eating.

1 Allow students to discuss their answers to the quiz with a partner or in small groups, but discourage them from looking at the answers on page 134 until they have finished. Find out if anyone knew any of the information already or if they just guessed.

Ask them to tell the class about any other customs they are aware of that are different in different cultures.

2 Elicit the meaning of *passive* and an example of it. If students need more work on this, you might like to go through the form of the passive in the *Language links* section on pages 106–107 and do some of the practice exercises before asking them to identify the passives in the quiz. Students might find it helpful if you identify (or ask them to identify) the types of passives used here. These are given in brackets after the answers.

> **ANSWERS**
> the soup is often eaten (Present Simple passive)
> cheese is normally served (Present Simple passive)
> you may be asked (modal passive)
> they can be seen (modal passive)
> need to be offered (infinitive passive)
> like to be invited (infinitive passive)
> is usually eaten (Present Simple passive)

17 EATING OUT 87

BUSINESS COMMUNICATION

Sticky situations

This section is about how to deal with food that, for one reason or another, you can't or don't want to eat. Students learn some polite ways to decline food and ways to offer certain dishes or discourage people from choosing them.

Warm-up
Ask students to work with a partner to create the most disgusting combinations of food that they can imagine. These should be real foods but combined in very unappetising ways, e.g. chocolate-covered oysters in curry sauce. Perhaps ask them for a complete menu with starter, main course and dessert. Then have a class vote on which meal they would least like to eat.

2.44–2.46 Encourage students to read through the questions first so they have some idea of what each conversation is about and what questions they will have to answer. Play the recordings. Pause after each recording to give students a chance to note down their answers to the questions. Allow them to discuss their answers with a partner or in small groups before checking as a class. Ask students to practise the language for offering and declining food by offering each other some of the disgusting dishes they produced in the *Warm-up* activity.

ANSWERS
Conversation 1
a Fugu can be poisonous.
b 1 unusual 2 exotic 3 not like it 4 prefer something else
  5 try something else
c Maybe I'll have the tempura instead.

Conversation 2
a He doesn't want to try squid.
b 1 like to try the local speciality 2 love it 3 enjoy this
  4 really special 5 very good
c Actually, I hope you don't mind, but could I just have something a bit simpler?

Conversation 3
a She's on a special diet.
b 1 fried 2 boiled 3 roast 4 grilled 5 baked
c 1 of 2 in 3 with

2.44
Conversation 1

A: … So, Hiro. What's this fugu? It's a kind of fish, isn't it?
B: Ah, yes. Er, it's rather unusual, er …
A: Traditional Japanese dish, eh?
B: Yes, but, er, it's a little exotic. You may not like it.
A: No, no, I like trying new things. Fugu sounds good to me.
B: I think you'd prefer something else. Fugu can be … a little dangerous.
A: A bit spicy, you mean? Don't worry about that. I love spicy food.
B: No, not spicy. It's, er … It's poisonous.
A: It's what?
B: Poisonous.
A: Poisonous?
B: If it isn't cooked the right way, yes.
A: Well, I …
B: Some people love it. And this is a very good restaurant, but 30 people die every year from bad fugu. Really, I think you should try something else.
A: Yeah, well, sure. I think you're probably right. Maybe I'll have the tempura instead.
B: Yes, tempura. Much better idea, David.

2.45
Conversation 2

A: Now, Hans, we thought you might like to try the local speciality.
B: Ah, yes?
C: Yes, it looks a little strange at first. But you'll love it. You like shellfish, don't you?
B: Well, I like prawns. And the mussels we had the other day were excellent.
C: Then you'll really enjoy this. It's squid.
B: Squid?
C: Yes, like octopus, you know?
B: Yes, I know what squid is.
C: Ah, but this is not just squid.
B: No?
A: No, this is something really special. It's served in its own ink – as a sauce.
B: It's served in ink?
A: Yes, you know, the black liquid that squid make.
B: Erm, yes. It sounds a bit … Actually, I hope you don't mind, but could I just have something a bit simpler?
C: Well, if you're sure you don't want to try it. It's really very good.
B: Yes, I'm sure it is, but, erm …

2.46
Conversation 3

A: Now, is there anything you don't eat, Louise?
B: Well, I am on a special diet at the moment, Jean-Claude. I hope that's not a problem.
A: No, of course not. This is a very good menu. I am sure we can find something you'll like. What can't you eat?
B: Well, I can't eat anything fried. In fact, no fat at all. Nothing made of pastry or cooked in oil. No red meat, of course. Not too much sugar. I can eat white fish but only boiled.
A: What about the chicken here? That's very plain and simple.
B: Is there a sauce on it?
A: Yes, it's a delicious cream and wine sauce.
B: No cream, I'm afraid.
A: No cream?
B: Or wine. I'm not allowed any alcohol at all. Not that I drink much anyway.
A: I see. Well, I'm sure they'll serve it without the sauce.

B: Hmm. How's the chicken cooked?
A: Er, it's roast chicken, I imagine.
B: I can only have grilled.
A: I'll ask them to grill it.
B: Hmm. I'd prefer fish really.
A: Well, how about the trout?
B: Is it boiled?
A: No, baked in the oven.
B: Hmm. I may not like it. What does it come with?
A: It comes with potatoes and fresh vegetables.
B: Oh, I can't eat potatoes. All that carbohydrate! Vegetables are okay. But no beans and …

The business lunch

In this final section, students put together everything they have learned in this unit to roleplay a business lunch. Go through the instructions carefully and make sure that both partners prepare adequately. Focus attention on the useful phrases in the box on the left of the instructions. Give assistance where required for drawing up the details of the business plan and the menu. If possible, have pairs made up of students of different nationalities so that Speaker B is genuinely not familiar with the dishes they are being offered. Ask some pairs to perform their roleplays for the class.

1:1 Allow the student to choose whether they want to be Student A or Student B. You might like to change roles and do it again later in the course. With a single student, you could actually go out to a restaurant to do the roleplay.

Language links

ANSWERS

Vocabulary

Food and drink

What's it like?

1 a lunch   b steak   c salad   d fish   e meat   f vegetables
   g dish   h food   i fruit   j bread   k cheese   l dessert
   m water   n coffee

2 heavy (note: this adjective is the only one in this list not formed from a noun), juicy, spicy, crusty, chocolatey

3 oily, fruity, tasty, fatty, peppery, nutty

What would you like to order?

4 a sauce   b bottle   c fish   d tart

5 Suggested answers:
   Does this dish contain nuts?
   Could I have a glass of water, please?
   Is the quiche hot or cold?
   What is the house special?
   What would you recommend?
   Are there any side dishes?
   Could we have the bill, please?
   Could I look at the menu, please?

Grammar

The passive

1 a email   b the fax machine   c by   d the passive sentence

2 a can be insured   b has been asked   c to be insured
   d was covered   e were written   f might be injured
   g were insured   h is believed   i would have been destroyed
   j was taken out   k could be heard   l was estimated
   m was captured   n was dragged   o being rescued
   p has not been claimed

Phrase bank: Eating out

a Complimenting your host   b Describing dishes
c Recommending dishes   d Avoiding disasters
e Being a good host   f Ordering the meal   g Talking shop
h Fighting over the bill

18 Telecommunications

Learning objectives

This unit is about communication by teleconference and by email and voicemail.

Students first discuss their experiences of video- and audio-conferences, and talk about the advantages of web conferencing. They examine adverts for web conferencing companies, and read reports with statistics about the effects that travel and teleconferencing can have on people, business and the environment.

In the second section, students look at the language of teleconferencing and listen to a conversation between participants in a teleconference about a delayed project.

They then read an exchange of emails, put them in the right order and examine some of the language used in them. Next, they prepare their own email and voicemail messages, and practise dealing with them.

The grammar focus is on reporting and the lexical focus is on managing a project.

Digital resources: Unit 18

Online Workbook; Extension worksheets; Glossary; Phrase bank; Student's Book answer key; Student's Book listening script; Fast-track map

---

In this first section, students talk about the differences between face-to-face meetings and video- and audio-conferences. They look at advertisements for companies which offer web conferencing, and read some reports about business travel and teleconferencing and the advantages of each. They then talk about the future of teleconferencing and discuss what types of meetings are best held face to face.

Warm-up

Brainstorm all the possible ways of communicating with business colleagues and clients in the office, in your own country and overseas. Write the students' suggestions on the board. If no one suggests terms such as **teleconference** or **videoconference**, introduce them yourself. You might like to point out that the *tele* in *teleconference*, just like the *tele* in *television*, refers to distance.

Find out how often the students hold 'virtual meetings' and whether they prefer them to face-to-face meetings.

1 Find out how many students have taken part in a video- or audio-conference. Encourage them to discuss their experiences and say how they are different from face-to-face meetings. Focus attention on the quotation from Kate Harper. Establish that virtual meetings are those held by phone, video-link, web conferencing, etc, as opposed to those that take place with all the participants in the same room, and find out if the students' experience of such meetings matches Kate Harper's.

2 Give students time to study the advertisements and then ask them to list the advantages of web conferencing which they portray. Explain *work–life balance* and *carbon footprint*, if necessary.

ANSWERS
reducing pollution, lowering travel budgets, travelling less, spending more time with family

3 Give students time to read the reports. Ask them to discuss with a partner how they support or contradict the messages in the advertisements.

SUGGESTED ANSWERS
The first report supports the messages because it suggests that operating on the Internet (telecommuting) will reduce carbon emissions and improve workers' quality of life. The second report contradicts the messages because it suggests 80% of business travellers enjoy spending time away from home on business trips.

4 Find out if students were surprised by any of the statistics and why.

5 Go through the types of meetings in the box with the class and make sure that they understand them all. Then ask them to discuss with a partner whether teleconferencing is the future, i.e. it will replace all other sorts of meetings. Then ask them to decide if there are any meetings which they think absolutely have to be done face to face. Ask them to report back to the class on their decisions.

Teleconference: a project meeting

In this section, students study a meeting concerning the construction of a marina complex in Dubai. The company involved is German, and has a multinational team from Germany, Poland and Pakistan working on the project. The project has been delayed and the Dubai client is unhappy. Students initially read emails sent to set up a teleconference and then listen to the meeting itself. They examine some of the language used in the meeting and then put one of the participant's notes in order. Finally, they roleplay their own teleconference.

1 2.47–2.48 Go through the background information with the class and make sure that everyone understands the situation. Give students time to read the email, and ask them to say who will be participating in the meeting and what the main agenda items are.

BUSINESS COMMUNICATION

Go through the questions with the class before you play the recordings so that they know what information to listen out for. You will need to pause between the two extracts and you may need to play the recordings several times to enable students to answer the questions.

ANSWERS

Extract 1
a Port Rashid.
b Peter Kessler wants his input on how to handle the changes to the specifications.
c He is prepared to give them another few weeks to sort out the problems.

Extract 2
a Some workers speak German and some English.
b Two seaports have been closed due to bad weather.
c He is causing some of the problems by changing his mind frequently.
d He needs to bring the changes to the client's attention. They need to take a fresh look at the plan and may have to renegotiate the contract.

2.47
Extract 1

A: Excuse me, Mr Kessler. Mr Gorsky has joined you.
B: Ah, thank you. Hello, Jarek.
C: Hello, Peter. Sorry, I had a bit of a problem getting through.
B: That's okay. We're just waiting for Sulaiman. He's emailed to say he's gone down to Port Rashid to see what's happening with our deliveries and he'll phone in on his mobile from there. So, let's go ahead and start. Welcome to the meeting, everyone. Did you all get a copy of the agenda?
Good ... Okay, before we start, let me introduce Jarek Gorsky. Jarek is the new chief engineer at our sister company in Warsaw. I've asked him to join us today because I'd like his input on how we handle some of these changes to specifications the client is asking for.
C: Hello, gentlemen.
B: All right, then, let's get started. As you can see, we have several objectives today. The main one, of course, is to agree an action plan that will get us back on schedule within the next three months. I spoke to Mr Al-Fulani yesterday and explained the situation. He's prepared to give us another few weeks to sort out our present difficulties and I have assured him that that is what we will do. I'm sure I don't need to remind you what's at stake here. Now, I'd like to be finished by 10.30, if that's okay, so can we keep our inputs quite short? And let's also try to keep interruptions to a minimum ...
D: Er, Peter. Sorry to interrupt, but I suggest we skip item one on our agenda until we hear from Sulaiman.
B: Yes, I think that would be best. Let's move straight on to item two ...

2.48
Extract 2

D: So just to recap on what we've said. There are some problems we did not foresee between our two main work teams. There's been a language barrier. Our German engineers and Polish workers are speaking mostly German. The Pakistanis are more comfortable in English and are also having some difficulty with our work patterns, which are different from what they are used to in Dubai.
B: Thanks, Ernst ... Okay, so, are we all agreed that we need some onsite training to resolve this problem? Can I hear your views, please?
D: I agree.
E: Agreed.
F: Yes, I agree.
C: Yeah, I think so.
B: Fine.
A: Excuse me, Mr Al-Fahim has joined you.
B: Ah, thank you. Hello, Sulaiman. How are things at the port?
G: Hello, Peter. Not good, I'm afraid. The bad weather here has completely closed the seaports at Jebel Ali and Port Rashid. Nothing is either going in or coming out at the moment. I have my Pakistani team standing doing nothing while we wait for 800 window units and until those are fitted, we can't complete the wiring and plumbing in the hotel complexes.
B: Don't we have backup supplies in place for a situation like this, Sulaiman?
G: I'm sorry, Peter. This weather is really most unseasonal and we simply could not be fully prepared for it.
B: Sorry, Sulaiman, I can't hear you very well.
G: Oh, ... Is that better?
B: Much better, thanks.
E: Er, could I just come in here?
B: Karim?
E: Yes, it's just that I want to say this is not only a cultural and supply problem. We have had so many changes to specifications – changes almost every week now. The client just keeps changing his mind. And this is making life very difficult for us all.
F: Karim's right. We've had to keep revising our work schemes to cope with all the changes.
B: Yes, it's a good point. I'll certainly bring all these changes to the attention of Mr Al-Fulani when I next speak to him. They're not in our original contract ... Right, we're running short of time. I think what's needed here with all these delays and changes of plan is a fresh look at this entire project on a logistical level. Ernst, Jarek, can I leave that with you?
C: Okay, Peter.
D: Yes, sure.
B: And keep me posted. I'm beginning to think we may even need to renegotiate our contract with Mr Al-Fulani. Okay, I think we've covered everything for now. Let's schedule another meeting for next week. I'll email you the details. We'll have to finish there. Thanks everybody.

18 TELECOMMUNICATIONS   91

BUSINESS COMMUNICATION

2 Go through the words in the box with the class and then ask them to complete the expressions. Allow them to compare their answers with a partner before checking with the class.

ANSWERS
a getting   b waiting   c meeting   d agenda   e introduce
f join   g started   h objectives   i finished   j inputs
k minimum   l interrupt   m skip   n item   o recap
p agreed   q hear   r come   s time   t leave
u covered   v finish

3 Ask students to work individually to number the notes in order. Then allow them to compare with a partner before checking with the class. Point out the use of reported speech and reporting verbs such as *informed, agreed, explained, suggested, emphasized, reminded,* etc in the notes.

ANSWERS
1 Peter Kessler opened the meeting and informed us that
2 Sulaiman had gone to Port Rashid to check on deliveries and would
3 join us later. He then introduced
4 Jarek Gorsky, Ritterman's new chief engineer in Warsaw, and emphasized
5 that the main objective of the meeting was to get the Dubai Project back
6 on schedule. Ernst suggested that
7 we skip item one on the agenda until Sulaiman could join us and went on
8 to outline the communication problems the two work teams had
9 been having. Peter recommended onsite training as a possible solution. Sulaiman
10 joined the meeting at this point and described
11 the situation at the ports as serious. He explained that
12 nothing was moving and that our backup supplies were insufficient to cope with
13 the present situation. Karim reminded us that
14 constant changes to the building plan were also a major problem. Peter promised
15 to bring this to the client's attention and that the contract with Al-Fulani
16 might have to be renegotiated. Ernst and Jarek agreed to
17 have another look at overall logistics and to report back to Peter. Another teleconference
18 was scheduled for next week.

Language links

Direct students to the *Language links* section on pages 113–114 for further explanation of the construction and use of reported speech, and exercises to practise it.

4 Ask students to work in groups and turn to page 133. Go through the instructions with them and give them time to prepare what they want to say. Allow them to make notes, but discourage them from reading from a script. Make it clear that the teleconference cannot last longer than 20 minutes and that everyone must participate. Make sure that every group has chosen a chairperson and that the chairperson is able to run the teleconference efficiently.

Language links

Direct students to the *Phrase bank* in the *Language links* section on page 114 for more useful teleconferencing expressions, grouped according to their function.

1:1 To make this more of a conference, you could play several roles and ask your student to chair the meeting.

An urgent matter

In this section, students read an exchange of emails between two colleagues in a management consultancy. They have to read them and number them in the correct order. They then examine some of the language used in these emails.

1 When checking answers, have two different students read the emails out (one as Jonathan and the other as Sam) so that they can hear the flow of the communication.

You might like to focus attention on the effect of the capital letters in email F. Jonathan's previous two emails have not been responded to and he is getting desperate. The capital letters make words stand out and are the email equivalent of shouting.

Also check that students understand the symbol at the end of email H. This is an emoticon, a symbol made up of items from the keyboard which gives the receiver an indication of the sender's mood. This one is a smiley face (when turned round) to show that the sender is happy. Ask what other emoticons students are familiar with. You could extend the discussion to text-message abbreviations.

ANSWERS
1 A   2 G   3 F   4 E   5 C   6 B   7 D   8 H

2 Before they look at the answer, see how many ideas students can come up with for punch lines to Sam's joke. (The beginning of the joke is the last paragraph in email H on page 111.)

A lot of jokes are sent around the world by email. Ask students if they have received any good ones and, if so, to tell them to the rest of the class.

3 This exercise focuses on some common expressions found in emails. Encourage students to do the matching without looking back at the emails in 1, but allow them to do this if they need to.

Point out that this is a useful bank of language that they can use later on in the unit when they write their own emails.

92   18 TELECOMMUNICATIONS

BUSINESS COMMUNICATION

ANSWERS
a this is just a quick reminder
b the report was due yesterday
c email me if you're having problems
d room to negotiate on fees
e fully itemized costs
f quote precise figures
g give a rough estimate
h set and stick to a budget
i sorry for the delay in getting back to you
j send a first draft of the report as an attachment
k a detailed breakdown of costs for the project
l be under pressure from head office
m get a proposal in on schedule
n let me know what the position is asap

Dealing with messages

This section widens the subject of telecommunication to include voicemail. Students put together everything they have learned in this unit to practise sending and responding to emails and voicemail messages.

1 You will need to allow plenty of time for the activities in this section, but they are worth doing as they practise a range of skills and language that students have learned. Remind students that they can make up all the information for their profiles or use real names if they prefer.

2 Point out that there are some suggested ideas for messages, but the students are free to use their own topics if they wish.

3 If you don't have facilities for students to record voicemail messages, they could write these on paper and mark them 'voicemail'. However, providing facilities for them to record their voicemail messages and print out their emails will pay dividends. The activity will seem much more real, and so students will participate more enthusiastically.

4 Groups swap profiles, emails and messages.

5 The groups read, listen to and discuss the messages they receive. They then work together to decide how they are going to respond to each. You may need to explain that *bin* is often used as a verb, meaning to throw something away or put it in the waste bin.

6 Allow plenty of time for students to prepare their replies and for the original group to read them.

7 In a class feedback session, find out how successfully the messages were dealt with.

1:1 Swap emails and voicemail messages with your student. One-to-one teaching is ideal for teaching communication skills because it is practical to use real email and voicemail. Get into the habit of sending emails and leaving voicemail messages for your student, and encouraging them to respond. You can make arrangements for future lessons, enquire about progress on homework, or anything else that requires a written or spoken response.

Language links

ANSWERS

Vocabulary
Managing a project
a, i   b, f   c, e   d, k   g, j   h, l

Grammar
Reporting
1 a 1   b 3   c 4   d 2
2 a Fritz said he was ready.
  b Akio said he was going to wait and see.
  c Claire said she had had enough.
  d Philippe said he had to be going.
  e Maria said she would be in touch.
  f Sergio said he just couldn't face it.
3 a 5   b 9   c 7   d 8   e 1   f 10   g 6   h 3   i 2   j 4
4 Suggested answers:
a He said his name was Bond, James Bond.
b He asked Sam to play it.
c He asked me if I was talking to him.
d He informed her that he didn't give a damn.
e She invited me to go up and see her some time.
f He told us to hang on because he'd got a great idea.
g He wanted to know what the Romans had ever done for us.
h He invited him to make his day.
5 a raised   b invited   c insisted   d doubted   e pointed out
  f agreed   g wondered   h suggested   i came in
  j reminded   k explained   l added   m warned   n assured
  o recommended

Phrase bank: Teleconferencing
a opening   b managing the agenda   c interrupting
d handling the technology   e managing the discussion
f time-keeping   g closing

18 TELECOMMUNICATIONS 93

19 Negotiating

Learning objectives

This unit begins by reminding students that negotiating is something we do all the time with people we meet and know – it isn't confined to business boardrooms.

Students discuss what makes a good negotiator and listen to three business people sharing their views on the subject.

The focus then changes to negotiation language. Students identify and use softening techniques to make statements less direct and more diplomatic.

The next section also focuses on language and students listen to extracts from different negotiations.

In the final section, they read a text about the business side of football. They then use all the skills and language they have learned in the unit to prepare and perform a guided roleplay negotiation of a football transfer.

The grammar focus is on the language of diplomacy and the lexical focus is on collocations and expressions relating to negotiating.

Digital resources: Unit 19

Online Workbook; 📹 In company interviews Units 17–19 and worksheet; Extension worksheets; Glossary; Phrase bank; Student's Book answer key; Student's Book listening script; Fast-track map

In this first section, students read an extract from one of William Ury's books on negotiating and discuss the situations described in it. They formulate some advice for the people described and decide what they think a good negotiator is. They then listen to business people talking about how to negotiate and answer questions analyzing what was said. Finally, they examine some common collocations concerned with negotiation.

Warm-up

Ask students to list the situations in the past week in which they have had to negotiate. Tell them to include situations with family members and colleagues on everyday matters as well as any actual business negotiations they have been involved in. Ask them to tell the class about any of these situations and how well they think they succeeded in negotiating. Then ask them to brainstorm the skills that a good negotiator needs.

1 Read the instructions with the class and find out if any of the students have read either of the books mentioned. Then ask them to read the extract and say if any of the situations described are familiar.

Students work individually to decide what they would say in response to each of the people in the text. They compare their ideas with a partner.

Have a class feedback session and find out how much consensus there is about the best way to deal with each situation.

2 Ask students to work with a partner and tell them to choose one of the situations. Ask them to decide who will be Speaker A and Speaker B. Give them three minutes to negotiate a deal and then have a class feedback session to compare the solutions reached.

3 Students work alone to complete the sentence and then compare their ideas around the class.

4 🔊 2.49–2.51 Allow students time to look at questions a–d so they know what they are listening for. Check that they know what an *acronym* is. Pause after each recording to allow students time to write down their answers. You may need to play the recordings several times. Allow students to compare notes with a partner or in small groups before checking the answers with the class.

ANSWERS

a 1 create rapport   2 agree on a procedure
   3 set out proposals   4 listen and take notes
   5 have lunch   6 make counter-proposals   7 bargain
   8 agree terms   9 close   10 celebrate
b opening position, target position, walk-away position, fallback position, best alternative to a negotiated agreement
c Most people have an 'I win – you lose' mentality.
d 1 Don't get personal.   2 Don't agree to anything until you've discussed everything.   3 Don't make any concessions without asking for something in return.   4 Ask lots of questions.   5 Don't give in to pressure.

🔊 **2.49**

Speaker 1
Spend as much time as possible at the outset getting to know exactly who you're dealing with. Inexperienced negotiators tend to go straight in there and start bargaining. That may be okay for a small, one-off deal, but it's no way to build a long-term business relationship. So create rapport first. This could take several hours or several months! When you're ready to start negotiations, make sure you agree on a procedure before you begin. And while they're setting out their proposals, don't interrupt. Listen. And take notes. Then have lunch! Don't be tempted to make your counter-proposals and enter the bargaining phase until after a good, long break. You'd be surprised how much you can find out over a decent meal. Bargaining, of course, is the critical phase, but it can be surprisingly quick. If it isn't, break off and fix another meeting. Don't try to run marathons. When you do finally get to the agreement stage, agree the general terms, but leave the details to the lawyers – that's what they're there for. Close on a high note and remember to celebrate!

🔊 **2.50**
Speaker 2

Prepare thoroughly. If you don't, you won't know whether to accept an offer and may end up actually arguing with your own side, which is suicide in a negotiation. So, make sure you establish all the points you're going to negotiate and have a clear idea of your opening, target and walk-away position on each. Your opening position, or OP, is your initial offer – on price or whatever. Your TP, your target position, is what you're realistically aiming for. And your WAP, or walk-away position, is the point at which you walk away from the negotiating table. Always be prepared to do that. Know what your fallback position, or FBP, is – what you'll do if you don't reach an agreement. Some people call this your BATNA, your best alternative to a negotiated agreement. You nearly always have a BATNA, however undesirable. But if you really haven't got one, you'd better be good at bluffing or you're going to lose big time!

🔊 **2.51**
Speaker 3

Ideally, a successful negotiation is a kind of joint problem-solving meeting, where we identify each other's interests, wants and needs, and then explore the different ways we could satisfy those. I say 'ideally', because it hardly ever is like that. Win–win negotiation is a great idea, but most people have a simple 'I win – you lose' mentality. So what do you do with the person who simply won't listen, who keeps interrupting, who becomes aggressive, who makes last-minute demands, who won't make a decision? I must have read dozens of books on negotiation tactics. The problem is, so has everybody else. So they don't really work. My only advice is: don't get personal – ever; don't agree to anything until you've discussed everything; don't make any concessions without asking for something in return; ask lots and lots of questions; and don't give in to pressure. Remember, if the answer must be now, the answer must be 'No'.

Directness

This section looks at the issue of how direct you should be when negotiating. Cultural differences are examined, and ways of making statements more diplomatic are identified and practised.

1 Allow students time to read the joke and discuss it amongst themselves.

Then ask if they think there is a lesson to be learned from it: perhaps, how we word our requests to other people has a great effect on what their response will be.

2 Students work individually to decide where on the line they would put themselves and most people from their own culture.

3 Students work with people who put themselves on the other side of the line. When they try to persuade each other, remind them of the language they have learned in earlier units for expressing your point of view. In classes where students all place themselves on the same side of the line, suggest that they work with a partner and deliberately decide to take opposing views, thinking of reasons for the approach they are representing.

4 Make sure students understand that the first statement in each case is what the negotiators actually thought. However, what we think is not always what we say. Elicit that what we say is usually softer, politer and more diplomatic than what we think.

The students' task is to write what the negotiators actually said using the prompts.

ANSWERS

a Unfortunately, that would not be possible.
b We would find it quite difficult to go higher than seven per cent.
c I'm afraid we're not in a position to accept less than $5 a unit at this stage.
d You may have to pay slightly more if you want that.
e We would need some kind of commitment from you now.
f Shouldn't we spend a little more time looking for a compromise here?
g Wouldn't it be better to agree on a price before we go any further?
h We were hoping you'd be able to pay a deposit today.
i It might not be very easy to get my boss to agree to this.
j I think that's about as far as we can go at the moment.

> **Language links**
>
> Direct students to the *Language links* section on pages 120–121 for further explanation of the language of diplomacy and exercises to practise these structures.

5 Ask students to consider the role of adverbials, verbs, tenses, modals and adjectives in tempering the direct approach. How does a question alter the tone? Ask individual students to give their opinions or have a show of hands from the whole class on which versions they prefer.

ANSWERS

They use less direct language.

The language of negotiations

This section provides students with more language which they can use in negotiations. They listen to extracts from negotiations and complete notes on the positions of two companies involved in a negotiation. For one of them, they try to continue the negotiation; for the other, they analyze the success of the negotiation. They then complete a crossword with some of the expressions they heard in the extracts.

1 🔊 **2.52** Give students a chance to read through the notes headed *Mammoth Construction plc* before you play the recording. Tell them that they can complete these notes as they listen. Check answers before moving on to 2 so that everyone is working from a correct set of notes.

19 NEGOTIATING   95

BUSINESS COMMUNICATION

ANSWERS

Client counter-offer: 7 million euros
Project to be completed within 18 months
Plant to be operational by next September
Our revised bid:
2 million euros in advance
2 million euros mid-contract
3.2 million euros on completion
Total: 7.2 million euros
Schedule overrun penalty: 25,000 euros per week

2.52
Extract 1

A: Now, the next thing is: we'd like to see some movement on price. We had a rather lower figure in mind than the one you've quoted us.
B: Okay. What sort of figure are we talking about?
A: Well, something nearer to seven million euros.
B: Now, let me just check I understand you correctly. You're offering us seven million for the whole construction contract?
A: That's right.
B: And what sort of timescale are we looking at?
A: We would expect you to complete the project within 18 months.
B: How flexible can you be on that?
A: Not very. We were hoping to have the plant fully operational by next September.
B: I see … Can I make a suggestion?
A: Go ahead.
B: Well, would you be willing to accept a compromise?
A: That depends on what kind of compromise you had in mind.
B: Well, what if we offered you an alternative? What if you paid us two million in advance, two million mid-contract and another 3.2 million on completion?
A: On schedule?
B: On schedule. Eighteen months … Or thereabouts.
A: Hmm. So that's 7.2 million euros in all.
B: Correct.
A: And what if you run over schedule?
B: Then there would be a penalty. Let's say 25 thousand euros for each week we ran over schedule.
A: Hmm. I'm afraid this doesn't really solve our problem. What we need from you is a guarantee that the project will be finished on time.
B: And, as you know, I can only give you that guarantee by bringing in more outside contractors.
A: Which ups the price to your original bid of 7.8 million euros?
B: Yes.
A: At the moment, we do not see this as a viable option.
B: Seven point eight million really is my best price on that.
A: Well, in that case, I think that's about as far as we can go at this stage.
B: Now, wait a minute. We're not going to lose this deal for 600,000 euros, surely … How about this …?

2 Ask students to work with a partner and decide who will take each role in the negotiation. Ask them to try to continue the discussion and reach agreement. Go around offering help and encouragement, and ask any particularly successful pairs to perform their negotiations for the class.

3 2.53 Give students a chance to read through the notes headed *Smart Move plc* before you play the recording. Tell them to complete these notes as they listen. Check answers before moving on to 4 so that everyone has a correct set of notes to refer to.

ANSWERS

No. seminars: 8 over 6-month period
No. trainers: 3
Materials to be approved
Max. no. participants per seminar: 16
Full fee: £24,000
Discount: 15% = £3,600
Final fee: £20,400
25% non-refundable deposit = £5,100

2.53
Extract 2

A: Right. We seem to be nearing agreement. But, erm, before we finalize things, can we just run through the main points once more?
B: Sure.
A: Now, you'll provide a series of eight two-day in-company seminars for our telesales team over the next six months. You yourself will be conducting most of the sessions with two other trainers, using materials especially designed to meet our specific needs and approved by us four weeks prior to the first seminar?
B: That's correct.
A: And, er, let me get this quite clear, each seminar is to have no more than 16 participants, is that right?
B: Yes. We find the seminars are much more effective with smaller groups.
A: Hmm, I suppose you're right. It does also mean running more courses, but okay. Now, since we are booking eight seminars, we'll obviously expect a reasonable discount on your usual fee.
B: Erm, yes. Could you give us an idea of what you're looking for? Because with this particular course …
A: I would have thought a 15% discount was fair. So that's eight times £3,000 is £24,000 minus 15%, which is, erm, £3,600. And that would come to a total fee of £20,400. And you'd invoice us on completion of the whole series of seminars. Are these terms broadly acceptable?
B: Er, well, just a moment. We haven't actually agreed on the discount yet. As I was about to say, with this particular course there wouldn't normally be such a large discount. We offer 10% on five or more of our standard seminars, but this is a specially designed course for your personnel only. Obviously, we have to cover our development costs.

96 19 NEGOTIATING

BUSINESS COMMUNICATION

A: I should think you could cover them quite easily on just over £20,000, Mr Smart. No, my mind's made up. Fifteen per cent – take it or leave it.
B: Well, now, I'm afraid we could only accept this on one condition.
A: Which is?
B: Erm, we'd want a 25% non-refundable deposit in advance …
A: Done.
B: You see, … erm, sorry?
A: Twenty-five per cent deposit – no problem. I'll get accounts to make you out a cheque for, let me see, £5,100 … Well, that's it. I think we've earned ourselves a drink!
B: Erm, well, yes. Nice doing business with you.

4 Ask students to discuss with a partner whether or not it was a win–win negotiation.

ANSWERS
Yes, it is a win–win negotiation. Both sides make concessions but both gain something in return and they end up happy.

5 Remind the students that they heard most of the expressions in the negotiations in the previous exercises. When they have completed their crosswords, check the answers and ask for the good advice spelled out in the middle: never lose your temper.

ANSWERS
a position b suggestion c alternative d clear
e compromise f problem g offer h stage i acceptable
j correctly k condition l about m for n at o price
p more q option r agreement s drink

Language links
Direct students to the *Language links* section on page 120 for more practice of useful phrases and collocations for negotiations.

The transfer

This section leads up to a guided roleplay of a negotiation about a football transfer deal. It begins with a text about Manchester United which demonstrates that football is big business and the football transfer system allows players to be traded for millions of pounds.

Students then divide into teams to negotiate the transfer of a football player from his present club to Manchester United. They use the language and skills they have practised in this unit to carry out the negotiation.

Warm-up
Find out what sports the students are interested in and whether the players command large salaries. Encourage discussion of sports other than football as this will be covered in later exercises. Find out what the students' views on sports sponsorship are and, for example, whether they think cigarette companies should be allowed to sponsor sporting events and advertise their products at them.

1 Elicit or explain that *footballers are today's rock stars* means that footballers are known for getting high salaries just as rock stars were in the past. Students may know similar journalistic expressions such as *grey is the new black* (grey is the colour in fashion now to replace black which used to be in fashion). Check the collocations before students go on to read the article.

If you have time and wish to exploit the text further, you could put the following figures on the board, and ask students to find them in the text and explain their significance: 1990, 1991, 1993, 2000, 1,500, £36 million.

ANSWERS
a current market value b corporate image
c money-making industry d stock market flotation
e media coverage f merchandising outlets g blue-chip company
h sponsorship deal i strong brand

2 Students work in pairs to discuss suitable words or phrases to use as paragraph headings.

SUGGESTED ANSWERS
1 Lost tribe
2 Multinational corporation
3 Money-making industry
4 A strong brand
5 Sponsorship deals

3 Invite some pairs to perform their conversations for the class. If all your students are interested in football (or if none of them are), allow them to persuade each other to go to other sporting events.

> **1:1** Get your student to invite you to go and watch their favourite sport. Pretend lack of interest in order to give them practice in persuasion.

4 2.54 This roleplay will take some time to set up and perform, so allow enough time. Go through the instructions with the class. Listening to the details of a football transfer and taking notes will be quite challenging for weaker students. In order to give students a structure for their notes, put the following guidance framework on the board or have it ready on an overhead transparency. Ask them to fill it in as they listen.

Points to be negotiated
What the team gets

Transfer fee: money one team pays to another for a player

Young player: £……………

International star: £……………

What the player gets

(represented by FIFA™ agent who negotiates)

Weekly wage

Average basic weekly wage: £……………

(more for internationals and ……………… players)

19 NEGOTIATING 97

BUSINESS COMMUNICATION

Details of contracts

Usually for two, ... or .... years

Penalty of around £............. for leaving before end of contract

Merchandising percentage of profits from sales of things with the .... on them

Extras for foreign players ....

Students then divide into two teams and turn to their respective pages to find the instructions for their side of the negotiation.

Go around as students prepare, ensuring that they have understood what they have to do.

Allow students to read the listening script describing how football transfer deals are put together and refer to it as they prepare for their negotiation.

2.54

Right, well, when a team wants to sell a player, they agree a transfer fee. That's the price other clubs have to pay them if they want to buy that player. These vary a lot. For a young, talented player with lots of potential, the transfer fee could be around five to ten million pounds. Obviously, for a real international star, it could be, say, 20 or 30 million. Real Madrid paid Manchester United 80 million for Cristiano Ronaldo, but he's an exception! Now, for a team like Manchester United, that 20 million equals a fifth of the club's annual profit. So buying a player is a big decision.

Okay, so, that's what the player's club gets, but what about the player? Well, every professional player has a FIFA™ agent. FIFA's the governing body for world football. And the agent's job is to negotiate terms with clubs who want to buy the player. The average weekly wage at Manchester United is about £50,000, or two and a half million a year. Wayne Rooney gets £250,000 a week, but, again, he's an exception!

Okay, contracts. Players' contracts can be for two, three or five years, and if a player wants to leave before his contract expires, he has to pay a penalty. But they usually work something out. There's no point having players who don't want to play for you anymore.

So, those are the main points to negotiate in a transfer. Other things might include a percentage of merchandising profits – from sales of shirts, caps, boots with the player's name on them. And foreign players will often want a house and car provided as well, since they may only stay a few years. Some ask for free flights home to visit family. Oh, by the way, all those figures I've mentioned are net, not gross. Footballers don't like to worry about how much tax they're going to have to pay!

In company interviews Units 17–19
Encourage students to watch the interview and complete the worksheet.

Language links

ANSWERS

Vocabulary

Negotiations

Conducting negotiations
1 a a deadlock
  b a breakthrough
  c time out
  d terms
  e pressure
  f options

Sales negotiations
2 a B b S c B d S e B f S g S h B i E j E
  k B l S m S n B o B p E q E
3 a order b immediate c a discount d give e times
  f meet g price h hidden i payment j sort out
  k price l trial

Grammar

Language of diplomacy
Suggested answers:
a Unfortunately we would need something cheaper.
b We would be less interested in your economy model.
c Unfortunately, it may not be very easy to sell the idea to my boss.
d Shouldn't we be a bit nearer a decision by now?
e I'm afraid we might not be able to pay straight away.
f I'm not in a position to make any promises at this stage.
g We would find this a little difficult to accept at the moment.
h I understood that you wanted immediate delivery.
i To be honest, we were hoping you would provide after-sales service.
j Our discussions haven't been very productive so far.
k Wouldn't a fixed interest rate be better?
l We were aiming to get slightly further than this this morning.

Phrase bank: Negotiating
a create rapport 2, 11
b agree a procedure 6, 9
c put forward proposals 8, 10
d check the facts 1, 12
e enter the bargaining phase 3, 5
f work out the details 4, 7

98   19 NEGOTIATING

20 Assertiveness

Learning objectives

This unit is about how to be assertive. It begins by asking students to discuss why some people always seem to get their own way and others seem to get walked over. They read and discuss an article about the link between assertiveness and culture, and then match character traits to four basic communication styles. After discussing the pros and cons of each communication style, they listen to and analyze three different versions of the same conversation. They use what they have learned to make lists of dos and don'ts, and finally, they work with a partner to practise being assertive in different situations.

Digital resources: Unit 20

Online Workbook; Extension worksheets; Glossary; Student's Book answer key; Student's Book listening script; Fast-track map; Quick progress test 4

This first section explores the idea of assertiveness by looking at a range of office situations where people might be ignored or taken advantage of by their colleagues.

Warm-up

Focus attention on the title and ask students what they understand by the word *assertiveness*. Ask them to suggest business situations where assertiveness is important and if there are any where they think it is better to let other people have their own way.

1 Focus attention on the cartoon and ask why the man has footprints all over him (someone has walked on him). Elicit or explain the meaning of the two idioms *to get walked all over* (to have other people ignore or discount your opinions and do what they want to do) and *to get your own way* (to have other people allow you to do and have what you want). Ask who they think the other man is and what the situation is (possibly a psychiatrist with the man lying on the psychiatrist's couch seeking help for his lack of assertiveness; perhaps even the psychiatrist has walked all over the man in order to get to his chair).

2 Ask students to work individually to complete the situations with the correct prepositions. Check answers with the class, then ask students to work with a partner to discuss whether they have ever been in similar situations and how they reacted. Encourage them to report back to the class. Be aware that some students may be reluctant to describe situations where they might appear to be weak. Be sensitive if they are reluctant to talk about their own experiences.

ANSWERS
a down; on   b Under; down   c in; in   d on; off

3 Give students time to read the article, and then have a class discussion of what the author says about assertiveness and culture.

SUGGESTED ANSWER
The author says that both corporate and national cultures can affect how assertive employees feel they can be. But the two cultures can also be different, especially in multinational companies, where the corporate culture often reflects the cultural attitudes of the parent company rather than those of the country where the offices and plants are located.

4 Ask students to work individually to complete the diagram, then discuss it as a class. Answers will be very subjective and dependent on both the culture the students themselves come from and those they have come into contact with. Note that the answers on page 127 are simply where Hofstede places these countries.

ANSWERS
Austria (11)   New Zealand (22)   Germany (35)   USA (40)   Argentina (49)   Japan (54)   France (68)   UAE (80)   Malaysia (104)

5 Focus attention on the four communication styles represented by the photos on page 123. Make sure students understand the names given to the styles and ask them to match the character traits to them.

ANSWERS
is open and honest 4   stands firm 4   uses sarcasm 1
avoids conflict at all costs 2   gives in too easily 2
hides their true feelings 2   uses emotional blackmail 3
plays the victim 3   disregards your feelings 1   loses their cool 1
pulls rank 1   tries to get you on their side 3   keeps their cool 4
is respectful 4   shows empathy 4

6 Have a class discussion of this and see if students feel that their own natural communication style changes when they speak English.

ANSWERS
The Bulldozer
Pros: You may get what you want from more passive communicators in the short-term.
Cons: You'll get into a lot of fights with other aggressive communicators; very few people will want to deal with you in the future as you'll get a reputation for being selfish and inflexible.
The Doormat
Pros: If it's a quiet life you want, you'll avoid quite a lot of conflict at work this way.
Cons: You'll be pushed around and overloaded with work, which may create conflict at home; you'll never be a leader if you can't stand up for yourself.
The Prima Donna
Pros: Depending on how good you are at being manipulative, you may get your own way for a while.
Cons: If other people think they are being manipulated, they will begin to feel used and this may cause them to become aggressive; once you have a reputation as a prima donna, your emotional outbursts and flattery will never work again.
The Rock
Pros: You will generally get what you want without damaging your relationship with those you work with; you'll get a reputation for being strong but reasonable – just the sort of person to get promoted!

20 ASSERTIVENESS   99

PEOPLE SKILLS

Cons: There are no real cons as long as you never let your assertiveness degenerate into aggression in difficult conversations.

7 🔊 **2.55–2.57** Go through the instructions and the questions with the class, so that students have some idea of what information they need to listen out for. Be prepared to pause the recording and repeat each conversation several times to allow the students to analyze what they hear and answer the questions. You may also need to repeat them all together so that students can compare them.

ANSWERS

Version 1

a Carmen is rather aggressive and bulldozes through Lars's weak objections. Lars is fairly passive throughout their conversation. He does try to make his excuses, but is mostly ineffectual.

b At first, Carmen doesn't really listen to Lars at all. When she finally realizes he has a social engagement, she's unsympathetic and ridicules the local custom of eating dinner earlier than she's used to. Culturally, she doesn't seem to be very sensitive!

c The apologies and the constant *buts* make Lars sound too defensive. He's the one doing Carmen a favour. He shouldn't need to defend himself.

d Carmen doesn't seem to see the favour she's asking for as a favour at all. She sees it more as an obligation. This is reflected in the language she uses: 'You should put your job before partying with your friends', 'You have to help me with this presentation'. The effect is quite threatening. It works this time because Lars is behaving so passively. But it wouldn't be surprising if he eventually starts looking for another job!

Version 2

a This time Carmen's style is mostly manipulative. Her strategy seems to be to present herself as the overworked victim, whom only Lars can help. For his part, Lars is much too aggressive in his response to her – at times almost insubordinate!

b Carmen doesn't directly bully Lars, but she does use a combination of flattery (telling him he's the best in the office) and blackmail (suggesting that he might be replaced at the Rio conference by a junior member of staff with a better attitude).

c Sarcasm is rarely an effective tactic in a conversation as it makes the other person look stupid – not a great idea when the other person is the boss! Sweeping generalizations ('You're always doing this to me', 'Why don't you ever give me any notice?') are also ineffective as it's easy to contradict them by giving an example of when the thing you're being accused of didn't happen. To be assertive you need to be specific not vague.

d Considering all the emotions flying around, the outcome of the conversation is at least partly successful. But it's really just a compromise where neither person gets exactly what they want. And how likely is it that Carmen's presentation will be finished in an hour?

Version 3

a This time both Carmen and Lars are assertive. Both stand their ground, but there's no bullying or emotional blackmail, no sarcasm or sweeping generalizations. And both clearly express how they feel.

b Both speakers use expressions to show they are listening and understand the other's position: 'I realize it's rather short notice', 'Normally, I'd be happy to help out', 'I appreciate that you've got plans', 'I understand that, yes', 'It's sounds like you have a busy evening ahead', 'I understand this is very inconvenient for you'. This keeps the tone neutral and avoids self-justifications.

c Both techniques work well. Clearly stating how you feel using I-statements is very effective because how you feel can't be questioned. Only facts can be questioned. If I say 'You're pressuring me', you can say 'No, I'm not!' But if say 'I feel like you're pressuring me', you can only say 'Well, that's not my intention'. Repeating your assertion ('I can't this evening') if said non-aggressively and without apology is also difficult to argue against. Some people call this technique the 'Broken Record' because you keep saying the same thing.

d The conversation ends quite well. Lars doesn't give in to pressure and ruin his social plans, but he does offer to help Carmen in three other ways – by asking Joanna to assist her instead, by looking at some of her slides before going to bed and by coming in early in the morning to start work on her presentation. Carmen closes by validating their working relationship – 'I'm glad we managed to sort this out' – and saying she hopes he enjoys his party. She hasn't got exactly what she wanted, but things might even work out better this way overall.

🔊 **2.55**
Version 1

A: Oh, Lars, there you are! Do you have a minute?
B: Er, sure.
A: Only, I need you to work a little late tonight. I have to get this presentation finished and I need you to help me with some of the slides. Shouldn't take more than a couple of hours. Three at the most.
B: Oh, I, er …
A: Problem?
B: Er, no. It's just that I was planning …
A: Great. Well, I'll show you what I've done so far. I've indicated where I need you to drop in some graphics …
B: Actually, Carmen, sorry, but would it be okay if we did this tomorrow instead?
A: What? But I need it for tomorrow afternoon! I don't want to leave everything till the last minute!
B: It's kind of 'last minute' already!
A: What's that?
B: Oh, nothing. But, erm, the thing is, I'd invited a few friends over this evening – sort of a house-warming party for my new flat, you know. They're coming at seven, and I have to prepare the food and everything.
A: At seven! You eat so early in this country! Well, look, Lars, don't you think you should put your job before partying with your friends? You know how it is here. We work to a tight schedule. And it's not like you aren't getting paid overtime for this. Call your friends and tell them to come later. Right now, you have to help me with this presentation! Okay?
B: Erm, yes, I know, but, look, sorry, but some of my friends have kids. And it's a workday tomorrow. They can't really stay that late …
A: Lars, hold it right there! Look, I told you when you took this job there'd be a lot of extra work. You said you could handle that. So handle it! Now, come on! I have to get this done by eight. I've got plans myself.
B: But …
A: No buts, Lars. Now, call your friends and let's get on.
B: Okay, Carmen. Anything you say.

🔊 **2.56**
Version 2

A: Oh, hi Lars. Listen, could I ask you a favour?
B: Uh-oh, I don't like the sound of this! Let me guess. You want me to work late again?
A: Would you? The thing is, I have this presentation to finish for tomorrow and I need someone who's good at producing

PEOPLE SKILLS

graphics to help me out with some of the slides. Frankly, you're so much better at this than anyone else in the office, I'd really like it to be you. It shouldn't take more than two or three hours. What do you say? Will you do it?

B: Look, Carmen, you're always doing this to me!
A: Always doing what?
B: Dumping extra work on me at the last minute! Why don't you ever give me any notice when you want me to do overtime?
A: Lars, I do usually give you notice. But this presentation just came up. I'm covering for someone who's away on sick leave. And I really need your help.
B: Oh, well, that's different then! No problem!
A: So you'll do it?
B: No, Carmen, I can't. I've got some people coming round this evening. It's my house-warming party, as a matter of fact.
A: Oh, really? And you didn't invite me?
B: You mean you would have come?
A: Of course not. I'm far too busy, Lars – battling on here on my own! It would have been nice to be invited, though.
B: Okay, you're invited!
A: Sorry, I can't come. I've got this presentation to get ready. And now my top team member's decided to put his social life first, it's going to take all night!
B: Look …
A: Oh, don't worry about it, Lars. I'll ask Joanna instead.
B: The new kid?
A: The new kid, yes. She's very competent, actually. And very keen to help out. The way you used to be, Lars! In fact, I'm thinking of sending her to the Rio conference with Angelique.
B: Hey, I thought I was supposed to be going to Rio with Angelique!
A: Well, that was before you lost your can-do attitude, Lars. I need someone in Rio who'll be an asset not a liability!
B: Okay, okay. I'll give you an hour, all right? Let's see how much of your presentation we can get done by seven. Then I have to go!
A: Thanks a million, Lars! I owe you one!

🔊 **2.57**
Version 3

A: Ah, Lars. Can you spare me a moment? I've got a favour to ask you.
B: Sure.
A: It's about this presentation I have to get ready for tomorrow's meeting.
B: Oh, yes?
A: Yes, I realize it's rather short notice, but could you possibly stay on for a couple of hours to help me out with some of the slides? I'd really appreciate it. It's just the graphics I need help with, actually, I've got the rest of it pretty much covered.
B: Ah, now that could be a bit difficult, Carmen. You see I have some friends coming round this evening.
A: Oh, really?
B: Yes, it's my house-warming party, actually. Got a few friends coming over to celebrate, you know. Normally, I'd be happy to help out, but tonight I can't.
A: Of course, your new flat! I forgot. Congratulations!
B: Thanks. It's nice to have my own place at last!

A: Of course. Well, now, I appreciate that you've got plans. And I didn't know until today I was even doing this presentation. But there we are. So Lars, I'd really like you to help me out – even if it's just for an hour. You know how important this presentation is.
B: I understand that, yes. But I have these guests coming at seven. Before that I have to cook and get things ready. So you see I just can't help you this evening.
A: It sounds like you have a busy evening ahead! Okay, I understand this is very inconvenient for you. I'm not happy about it myself, to be honest. It's my evening gone too. And I would prefer it if you were able to help me out. You're a lot better at designing graphics than I am, so that would save a lot of time.
B: I really can't help you this evening, Carmen. It would be unfair to cancel my party now at the last minute with some of my guests probably already on their way over.
A: This is a problem, isn't it? Naturally, I'm disappointed that you can't at least postpone your party for an hour or two. I don't often ask you to do overtime. And I'd really like your input on this slideshow.
B: I could look at it first thing in the morning if that's any help. But tonight I can't.
A: Okay, Lars, well, I'd better find someone else to give me a hand this time, then. Maybe Joanna can spare me some time.
B: Yes, Joanna's really good with graphics. I'll ask her if you like. And, look, my party shouldn't go on too late. A lot of my guests have kids and it's a workday tomorrow. If you email some of the data over to me, I'll take a look at it before I go to bed. Then we should be able to finish it off really quickly in the morning. How about that?
A: Yes, that would certainly be some help. I'll do that.
B: And I guess we could both come in half an hour early in the morning to give ourselves a bit more time.
A: Good idea. Thanks, Lars. I'm glad we managed to sort this out. Enjoy your party! See you in the morning.

8 Give students time to decide which items should go in the dos and don'ts lists. Check answers with the class.

> **ANSWERS**
> a Don't b Do c Do d Don't e Don't f Do g Do h Do
> i Don't j Do k Do l Do

9 Allow plenty of time for this activity. Ask students to work with a partner and turn to their respective pages. They each have a different role in the same three situations. They may need time outside of class to prepare what they are going to say. When they hold their meetings, go around giving help and encouragement.

1:1 Without taking on the role of a doormat yourself, allow your student to experience some success in the course of these roleplays! Your superior command of English would make it very easy to win each argument, so be sensitive to the fact that your student is not only struggling with the skill of being assertive, but also with the language. Respond positively to successful moves they make to exhibit assertive but non-aggressive behaviour. On the other hand, make sure that there is sufficient challenge for them to feel that they have earned their success.

20 ASSERTIVENESS

MANAGEMENT SCENARIO E

The difficult customer

Learning objectives

This scenario is based on handling difficult customers in negotiations. Students read an email Heather has received from Anton, telling her that a customer she has had problems with in the past wants their company to bid for a new management information system. Students watch the video to see how Heather deals with the customer and evaluate her success. They then read an article giving advice on uncovering the interests of different sides in a negotiation. They summarize this and say how Heather could have dealt differently with her customer. They then watch the video to see how Heather's negotiation might have gone had she followed this advice. Finally, students practise dealing with difficult demands in a negotiation with a partner and evaluate their own performance.

Digital resources: Management Scenario E

In company in action E1–E2 and worksheet; Extension worksheets; Glossary; Student's Book answer key; Student's Book listening script; Fast-track map; End of course test

Warm-up

Ask the students to brainstorm reasons why particular customers might be considered difficult. What kinds of demands do people make during negotiations with another company?

1 Focus attention on the photo, and ask students to say what they think is happening and how the people are feeling. Give students time to read Anton's email and decide what they think the answers to the questions might be.

ANSWERS

a Definitely not! Anton is presumably trying to be funny. It seems that Heather has had experience of dealing with Lagrange before and he has a reputation for being a tough negotiator who pushes for fast delivery.
b The KKM bid is for a new management information system. Winning the KKM order would help FIS out of its current cash flow difficulties.
c Heather knows more about KKM's business than anyone else at FIS.
d He gave her the authority to be flexible on price to win the order, but to insist on at least 6–8 weeks' lead time to design and set up the system for KKM.
e Anton thought Heather might like some support from Alan at the meeting with Lagrange. As the KKM order is so important to FIS, perhaps he also wants someone to keep an eye on things and make sure Heather doesn't have any personal issues with Lagrange.

2 This writing task could be set for homework.

MODEL ANSWER

Hi, Anton
It's good news about the KKM bid! As you say, winning this order would help us out of our current cash flow difficulties. I'll study the list of KKM basic requirements you sent me and start drafting a preliminary proposal right away.

Thanks for the offer of taking Alan along to the meeting, but I think I can handle Lagrange myself. He is quite a tough negotiator, but I'm very familiar with his business needs and having some room to be flexible on price should make things easier. And don't worry, I won't let him push me around on delivery times!

I'll email you a copy of the proposal for approval before I meet Lagrange next week. If there's anything you'd like me to change or add to it, just let me know.
Heather

3 E1 Read the instructions with the class and the comments. Play the video and ask students to discuss with a partner which comments they agree with, if any.

SUGGESTED ANSWERS

a If FIS's competitors have genuinely said they can deliver in three weeks, then Lagrange's demand that FIS match that is reasonable enough. But Heather is under strict instructions from Anton not to promise delivery in less than six weeks, so she cannot be flexible there.
b Lagrange certainly has an aggressive negotiation style which is unhelpful. It is perhaps unlikely that all (if any) of FIS's competitors claimed they could deliver in three weeks when Anton has emphasized the impossibility of this. Lagrange may well be bluffing to put pressure on FIS to speed up delivery. However, calling his bluff and breaking off the negotiation is unlikely to be effective.
c If Heather had compromised with Lagrange and agreed to deliver the system in less time, she would have made herself very unpopular with Anton and the technical department at FIS. Lagrange seems determined to get delivery in three weeks, so a compromise wouldn't have satisfied him either.
d At first glance, it seems like no deal could be done here as Lagrange's demand (delivery in three weeks) and Heather's offer (delivery in six weeks) are so far apart. But perhaps Heather has not really explored the reasons for Lagrange's demand enough.

MANAGEMENT SCENARIO

🎥 E1

Louis: Heather, lovely to see you again!

Heather: Louis.

Louis: Please, take a seat. Coffee?

Heather: No, thank you. I just had one.

Louis: Now, to business …

Heather: Yes, of course. Did you have a chance to look at the proposal I emailed you a couple of days ago?

Louis: Ah! I didn't.

Heather: Oh, no problem. I brought a copy with me. You might want to spend a few minutes …

Louis: Thanks, perhaps we can look at that later. Heather. I'll get straight to the point, okay? I've already had three of your competitors in my office this morning.

Heather: Oh, I see.

Louis: I really just have one question. As you know, KKM is in the market for a new management information system, and we need it up and running in three weeks. Can you do it?

Heather: You need it in three weeks?

Louis: That's right. Is that a problem?

Heather: Well, now, Louis, you know as well as I do that a system as sophisticated as the one you described in your brief simply can't be designed and delivered in three weeks!

Louis: Can't it? I may as well tell you that all three of your competitors so far have said that it can.

Heather: Really? That surprises me.

Louis: Look, Heather, we've done business before, okay? FIS is a good, reliable company. But if you can't manage to deliver in three weeks, I'm sorry but we're going to have to go to another supplier. So perhaps you'd like to reconsider.

Heather: Louis, I don't care what our competitors have told you. Three weeks delivery just can't be done – by us or by them.

Louis: Are you saying they're lying?

Heather: I'm saying that they'll promise anything to get your business. But just give them the contract and see what happens.

Louis: Okay, well, I guess I'll have to just do that. You see, the lead time on this, Heather, is completely non-negotiable. I'm disappointed you can't be more flexible, but there you go. Perhaps we can do business some other time.

Heather: But, just wait a minute! We haven't even begun to discuss this.

Louis: Well, there's no point is there, Heather, if you can't meet our deadline?

Heather: But, Louis, you're being totally unreasonable.

Louis: I'm sorry, Heather; it's you who's being unreasonable. I've told you what the other suppliers are offering. Now it's up to you to better their offer …

4 Give students plenty of time to read the article and complete the summary. Check answers with the class.

ANSWERS

a In a negotiation, positions are what you want, whereas interests are why you want them.
b Taking up positions often leads to a compromise, which satisfies nobody.
c Uncovering interests, on the other hand, can lead to finding a solution which satisfies both parties.
d The best way to uncover interests is to ask a lot of questions – good negotiators ask twice as many as average ones.
e On hearing your counterpart's position in a negotiation, the most important question to ask is: why?

5 Ask students to discuss this question in pairs and then to report back to the class on how they think she might have handled the negotiation differently.

SUGGESTED ANSWER

She might have asked more questions to find out the real reason why Lagrange was so insistent that delivery must be in three weeks. There may have been another way she could satisfy his interest.

6 🎥 **E2** Ask students to watch another version of the negotiation. Go through the questions before they watch so they know what to look out for. Check answers with the class.

ANSWERS

a No, he's as aggressive and inflexible as he was the first time.
b Heather makes a little more effort to build some rapport at the beginning (e.g. by accepting a coffee she doesn't really want and making a positive comment about Lagrange's office). She also stresses that KKM is a valued client and that she might be able to reduce the lead time from eight to six weeks (of course, she already knew she could manage six weeks!). But, more importantly, she resists the temptation to react negatively to the news that her competitors are apparently offering to deliver KKM's system in three weeks and concentrates instead on trying to find out why Lagrange is in such a hurry.
c By separating Lagrange's need to quickly implement his board's decision from his need to have a top quality management information system, she is able to get round the problem of the three week delivery time.
d Being a good negotiator, Lagrange remembers not to agree to anything without asking for a concession in return – he asks for the same 5% discount he received last time he did business with FIS. Heather, also a good negotiator, suggests that for such a rush job a 3.5% discount would be more appropriate, but she indicates that this is negotiable.

🎥 E2

Louis: Heather, lovely to see you again!

Heather: Louis.

Louis: Please, take a seat. Er, coffee?

Heather: Thank you, I'd love one. Black, please. You've got a new office, I see. Business must be good! Did you get a copy of our proposal?

Louis: I did, thanks. I'll get straight to the point, Heather. I've already talked to three of your competitors this morning.

Heather: Really?

E THE DIFFICULT CUSTOMER 103

MANAGEMENT SCENARIO

> **Louis:** Yes. I just have one question. As you know, KKM is in the market for a new management information system, and we need it up and running in three weeks' time. Can you do it?
>
> **Heather:** Well, I must admit you've caught me by surprise, Louis.
>
> **Louis:** Have I?
>
> **Heather:** Yes, we both know the system you need to the standards you require would take at least eight weeks.
>
> **Louis:** Eight weeks!
>
> **Heather:** Louis, you're a valued customer. So I might be able to shorten the lead time a little. Let's say six weeks. But that would be the best we could manage. Otherwise, we'd be compromising on quality. And I'm sure you wouldn't want that.
>
> **Louis:** I'm sorry, I'm afraid that's not good enough, Heather. Every one of your competitors so far have said they can deliver in three weeks. Frankly, I'm disappointed you can't match them.
>
> **Heather:** Hmm, well, I'd be very surprised if any one of our competitors can match us, Louis, either on quality or lead time. But let's set that aside for a moment. May I ask why you're in such a hurry to set up such a complex system that's so central to your core business?
>
> **Louis:** I fail to see why that's relevant. All you need to know is that that is what we need, and if you can't do it, then …
>
> **Heather:** Well, I mean, presumably you've been planning this for months. If you'd notified us sooner …
>
> **Louis:** Look, Heather all I can tell you is that the board is insisting that we have a new system in operation by the time of the next board meeting and I intend to find a supplier who can deliver.
>
> **Heather:** And the board meeting is … let me guess … in three weeks' time?
>
> **Louis:** Well, yes it is, as a matter of fact, but that's …
>
> **Heather:** Louis, let me make a suggestion.
>
> **Louis:** Go ahead.
>
> **Heather:** Well, I appreciate that you've got the board on your back to get this thing done, but you and I both know better. For the quality and reliability you want, and which FIS insists on providing, we do need at least six weeks.
>
> **Louis:** Heather, I feel like you haven't been listening to what I've been saying.
>
> **Heather:** No, I have been listening, Louis. How about this? I go back to my people and we get the basic infrastructure of your system working in three weeks.
>
> **Louis:** A working prototype, you mean?
>
> **Heather:** A working prototype – exactly. I say three weeks. Maybe, with a little push, we can get you a prototype in two.
>
> **Louis:** Two weeks?
>
> **Heather:** Yes, I think so. Then you've got something to show the directors at the board meeting. And while you're doing that, we'll be working on the fully operational system which will come on stream four weeks later. Quality and reliability guaranteed, as usual.
>
> **Louis:** Okay, I'll admit that's more the sort of offer I was hoping for.
>
> **Heather:** Good. We seem to be making progress.
>
> **Louis:** Of course, we do have the other suppliers to consider. And naturally we'd want the same 5% discount you offered us last time.
>
> **Heather:** I was thinking 3.5% as it's such a rush job. But we can discuss that.
>
> **Louis:** Hmm. Well, you've certainly given me something to think about. A prototype in two weeks, you say?
>
> **Heather:** Yes, you have my word on that, Louis.
>
> **Louis:** Okay, then, let's take a look at the rest of this proposal, shall we?
>
> **Heather:** Yes, let's do that.

7 Ask students to work with a partner and decide who will be Speaker A and Speaker B. Ask them to turn to their respective pages and follow the instructions there. They each have quite a lot of information to take in, so they may need time outside class to prepare. As they perform their conversations, go around offering help and encouragement. Both students may contact you (as CEO) to ask for authorization for a concession, so make sure you have read both sets of notes thoroughly and are up to speed with the content of the negotiation so that you can respond appropriately!

8 Ask students to complete the feedback form on page 138 for themselves. They should then compare with the partner they did the roleplay with to see if they are in agreement.

> **1:1** Allow your student to choose which role they want to play.